Dorothy McRae-McMahon is a retired minister of the Uniting Church in Australia. She has held many local and international positions in the Uniting Church and has been an activist in community affairs for almost 50 years. She is the recipient of a Jubilee Medal from the Queen for work with women in NSW, an Australian Government Peace Award and the Australian Human Rights Medal.

Also by Dorothy McRae-McMahon

*Being Clergy, Staying Human*
*Echoes of Our Journey: Liturgies of the people*
*The Glory of Blood, Sweat and Tears: Liturgies for living and dying*
*Liturgies for the Journey of Life*
*Prayers for Life's Particular Moments*
*Everyday Passions: A conversation on living*
*Daring Leadership in the 21st Century*
*In this Hour: Liturgies for pausing*
*Rituals for Life, Love and Loss*

# Memoirs of
# Moving On

A life of faith, passion and resilience

Dorothy McRae-McMahon

Jane Curry Publishing

First published by Jane Curry Publishing Pty Ltd 2004
220a Glenmore Road, Paddington, NSW 2021

National Library of Australia
Cataloguing-in-publication data:

McRae-McMahon, Dorothy, 1934- .
Memoirs of moving on : a life of faith, passion and resilience.

ISBN 1 920727 09 4.

1. McRae-McMahon, Dorothy, 1934- . 2. McRae-McMahon,
Dorothy, 1934- – Religion. 3. Uniting Church in Australia –
Clergy – Biography. 4. Women clergy – Australia –
Biography. 5. Women in the Uniting Church in Australia.
I. Title.

287.93092

Cover and internal design by Cheryl Collins Design
Cover photo: Dorothy and Carmyl on Kingston Beach, Tasmania, 1939
Typeset in 11.5/16 pt Minion by Midland Typesetters, Maryborough, Victoria
Printed in Australia by McPherson's Printing Group

*This book is dedicated to all those who have moved me on, opening my life to grander possibilities—beginning with my parents, Colin and Beth McRae, and my siblings, Carmyl, Thaïs, John and David; to Barrie McMahon and our children, Christopher, Robert, Lindy and Melissa; my grandchildren, Brook, Xander, Grania and Jessica; to Jenny Chambers; and to the thousands of people who have connected with me in life-enhancing ways in Australia, New Zealand, Asia, the Middle East, Africa, Europe and the United States; and finally, to my partner Ali, without whom this book would never have been written.*

# Acknowledgements

I wish to thank Jane Curry who invited me to write this book and who has been my most encouraging publisher, Elspeth Menzies my truly inspired editor, Andy Palmer my innovative and tireless publicist, and Fiona Inglis of Curtis Brown, the very best agent.

I thank my sister Carmyl who went through the childhood period of this book with me, and who warmly encouraged me and remembered things better than I did.

I thank all those who have put up with the vagaries of my odd life, including my companions in the church and the various movements for change in which I have participated.

Finally, my heartfelt thanks go to my partner Ali who is always my first editor and wise counsellor.

*We never know what lies just beyond the horizons of life.*

*The wonder of the human journey can take us high into the heavens,*

*or into the deeps of the seas and the dryness of the desert.*

*As the great cities rise from the earth,*

*with their true and false aspirations towards grandeur,*

*even there can be found love and justice,*

*amidst the laughter and tears of grief or joy.*

*The human journey is about the connections we create,*

*the mystery of things greater and kinder than we have ever understood,*

*the bridging between people and the universe itself.*

Dorothy McRae-McMahon

# Contents

# Preamble

This is not an autobiography—deliberately not that. My life has been too long to remember in all its detail. I also choose not to involve everybody who has been connected with my journey as though I have the right to engage them in a public story. And I will confess some of my sins, but not all of them by any means!

The major focus of these memoirs is my memories of the events, the people, the places and the experiences which have 'moved me on'—which changed my perceptions of myself, my faith and the world around me. Because I have always been a person of faith, some of this lies within a religious setting, but I hope not in a way which alienates those whose lives are set in another place. Much of my life has been lived in relation to the church, but I hope and believe that this part of my journey is of interest to people of faith or no faith. My faith has simply been part of me from the moment I was born and it has moved and evolved in response to the experiences and events of my life. I hope it has matured and become more open to others and their unique journeys. In fact, there is a sense in which I invite the critique of non-religious people by, if you like, baring my religious soul for their scrutiny!

These memoirs give an account of what it means to move in a variety of ways through many towns and cities as a child, engaging with their different cultures and relationships, and learning to live through moving on in a direct sense. They also give glimpses of places and people in Africa, Asia and the Middle East who changed my life and perceptions of reality as I met and worked with them in their own contexts.

Perhaps, above all, I write to give an account of being one person in the last 50 years of the twentieth century who chose to connect with many movements for change—the anti-white Australia movement, the movement for nuclear disarmament, the anti-Vietnam War movement, the movement against the Marcos regime in the Philippines, the anti-apartheid movement, the women's movement, the movement for lesbian and gay rights and the republican movement.

I give this account in themes, as with my international experiences, because it is really impossible to introduce them in a congruent, concurrent way into my more personal story. My own life journey has been affected by and blended with these 'outer' engagements with causes and a wider world, but the more personal development of my life as it runs alongside my parents, siblings and immediate family is in chapters of its own.

My memories are mostly affectionate ones, often from behind the scenes. After 70 years of life, you never really know whether what you recollect is precisely true. I know that, in some ways, we gather up various experiences and make up our own truths as we go. Others may remember events differently, possibly more accurately. Anyone who has siblings knows that we tell our stories of the past and experience our relationships with considerable variety. However, I guess that what we carry with us in moving on is our own truth, whatever its origins, and that truth is what affects our growing up and the very fabric of our life.

Dorothy McRae-McMahon, April 2004

Part *1*

# Childhood

# 1  Foundations

The anxious faces as they discuss the endless dry, flat, dusty land and the determined faith in the possibility of survival for one day more . . . 'She bit the nose off my best new Christmas doll!' . . . And, 'I think I will go out to my tree and live with Christopher Robin and his friends for a while—especially Piglet, because I really like Piglet.'

If you begin to think back to your earliest memories, it sometimes becomes clear that your way of seeing life and dealing with it may well have been set in your first years. These three sentences capture the moments which I suspect set the scene and express something significant about the ongoing patterns of my life.

But let me go back one step. My father, Colin Farquhar McRae, was born in Gippsland, Victoria, the third of six children. He spent his younger days on the subsistence-level family farm just outside Echuca on the Murray River. He began some engineering training at the technical college, but before completing that, decided to enter the Methodist ministry. In order to do this, he left Echuca for Queen's College at Melbourne University where he studied for his Bachelor of Arts, a Licentiate in Theology and a Master of Arts majoring in philosophy. The last degree was never recognised because he could not afford the money required to graduate.

Before going to Melbourne, my father had already fallen in love with Florence Elizabeth Wenn (whom he always called Beth as she didn't like her name) back in Echuca. They couldn't marry because that was forbidden for Methodist ordinands until they finished their training. Beth was the daughter of a local hardware merchant and city councillor. Her mother died when she was quite young and after remarrying, her father died at the age of 43, leaving my mother, her brother, two sisters and a stepbrother and sister in the care of her stepmother. She was an intelligent young woman but was required to leave school at 14 to work as a milliner in Echuca. She always gave the impression of having a hard early life and an ambiguous relationship with her stepmother.

After my father graduated, they were finally able to marry and travelled to Zeehan in Tasmania where my father had been appointed to his first parish. It was called a circuit in those Methodist days as the minister was expected to make a circuit of a number of congregations as part of his work. This meant that my father, and his enthusiastic wife in the parsonage, moved around the Zeehan–Strahan area in what they always saw as a joint ministry. The expected role of the minister's wife was to support her husband in his ministry and to work with the women in the parish—usually as the chair of their guilds and other groups. My mother fulfilled all these expectations with enthusiasm.

On April 7, 1934, I was born in Zeehan. My mother, so she told me, had passionately longed for a child for all the years in which my father was doing his ministerial training. She loved being pregnant. She spoke of my birth as a wonderful experience and she breastfed me, as she did all her children, with joy. Watching her over the years, it always seemed to me that the best times in her life were related to having babies and little children to care for. I have never really understood why my earliest memories are of trying to keep a small distance between her and myself. Maybe she so wanted a child that she leapt upon me in smothering love as soon as I emerged from her womb? I guess I will never know. Any reflection on this has ended up with a question rather than an answer.

From my very early days, I assumed some sort of anxious care for her emotional wellbeing. Given what a tough survivor she was, this seems strange, but little children only pick up some signals from their parents. The one I received most clearly was that I had a terrible capacity to wound my mother if I was disobedient. Later on I longed for her to smack me or shout with anger—anything but seeing her eyes fill with tears. My father felt much safer to be with as, although I knew he loved me dearly, he was emotionally very restrained—in good Scottish style as trained by his Glasgow-born mother and a father who also probably related to people as his Scottish forebears had done.

My mother always talked about Zeehan as a very tough place to live, in amongst people who were struggling copper miners, and far from her home in Echuca on the Murray. They had no car so travelled everywhere by train. My father rode around the area on his pushbike, as he did for many years to come in other places. At some stage, he had a motorbike but nearly died in an accident when he was riding it and my mother refused to ever let him ride one again.

They lived one week in every month in the vestry of one of the little churches. Mother told of having an aching body there and being asked by the older women whether she stripped the bed every day to dry all the bedding by the fire. She hadn't known to do that, but when she did, steam filled the room which explained her aching body. In that part of the world it rained incessantly.

My parents had to be ready to leave for the Mallee in Victoria three weeks after my birth. They had no money for a cot or pram for me so my mother found an old wooden vegetable box and lovingly lined and padded it with cloth. I travelled in this box across Bass Strait on the *Taroona* ferry. My parents sat up all the way and cared for me. We kept the cot as a toy box for many years and I can still see its carefully pleated covering, faded from the original pink.

We arrived in the Mallee when the wheat farmers there were suffering from a seven-year drought. The town where we lived was called Beulah and my mother used to sing a song about Beulah as some sort of Biblical paradise. It probably was a nice little country town and my parents felt more at home there as they were not far from the Murray River. There was a vacant block next to the parsonage and my father kept chooks there and a black and white cow which he milked each day. I used to watch his big red farmer hands milking and working enthusiastically in the earth. Although this was the last time he had a chance to keep a cow, the first

Carmyl, Dad and me with our cow, Daisy, 1937

thing my father did everywhere we went was to build his chookhouse and
set up a vegetable garden with compost bins.

My mother learned to scald the milk, separate the cream and make
butter. I enjoyed watching her churn the milk and get out her pats to shape
the butter into blocks and squeeze out the buttermilk, and I used to have a
try myself. She must have continued to make butter for quite a while
because I remember as an older child preferring to have bought butter
rather than homemade. I suspect this was partly because commercial
butter had extra salt in it.

My earliest memories include the fear of preparing for dreadful dust
storms when we tried to stuff things into every crack in the house as the
sky became a forbidding dark reddish colour and we waited anxiously for
the storm. When the storms hit, everything went dark, the wind would
howl in relentless fury and the dust defied all our efforts to keep it out of
the house. I also remember being a small, silent child listening to the
farmers tell of their hard lives, anxiously asking their minister what it
could mean and then firmly deciding that if they were to survive they

needed to share all that they had. I would stand near my parents and watch everyone's face, trying to understand what was happening, seeing their tears and their determination. I saw people passing around spare eggs or milk and sharing precious vegetables from their parched gardens. They always seemed to be knitting and patching and altering things to fit others as they stretched what clothing they had to meet needs. This experience of human hardship and survival is part of the foundations of my life.

I have no memory of ever playing with other children. My mother told me that she helped set up the baby health centre in the town, but I suspect my own life was fairly solitary. The exception to this was the arrival of my energetic and now much-loved sister Carmyl. She was born two years and four months after me and was a quite different personality—quick and passionate and full of fearless life. I guess there was a certain sibling rivalry between us and we both laughed when I told her recently that my strongest memory of the first four years of my life was the fact that she bit the nose off my brand-new celluloid doll! My mother had saved up for this special present and there she was, the largest doll I had ever had—about the size of a real baby and carefully dressed by my mother. I called her Lauris.

Within days of Lauris's arrival, Carmyl picked her up and firmly bit off her nose. My mother said, 'Never mind, dear, I will fix it.' But of course she couldn't really. Lauris's nose always looked battered and the wrong colour. I remember thinking seriously about whether I could bear to look at her anymore but decided that the doll would be really hurt if I cast her away. So I carefully included her in my family of dolls and returned to my old doll Glinda as the one I carried around all the time. It concerned me deeply that I could not enjoy Lauris as she might expect to be enjoyed. That was me, a three-year-old who felt guilty about not being able to love a damaged doll enough!

During the storms and drought and doll dilemmas, I knew where I could go when I had had enough. I would retire to the tree in the paddock with the cow and join Christopher Robin and his friends. My parents read books to me from my earliest days. My rather reserved and undemonstrative father loved all the A.A. Milne books and came alive when he read them to me. He became all the characters: funny old Pooh bear, clever Rabbit, wise Owl, vulnerable Piglet and funny Tigger. He was the king who just wanted a little bit of butter for his bread and the little girl who didn't want rice pudding. I would sit on his knee and listen entranced to the adventures of Christopher Robin in the wood and knew lots of the stories and poems by heart. So, having heard the worst about life, and having had a moment of probably well-hidden rage with my sister, I would withdraw into the land of books where no-one could touch me, carrying my beloved teddy bear. With some variations, this is probably not a bad summary of the way I have lived my life since.

On my fourth birthday, we left Beulah. On the way to Hobart, we paused to visit the zoo in Melbourne. Somehow, in all the excitement, I left my cherished teddy bear at the zoo. It was too late to do anything by the time we discovered the loss. My mother told me that my bear was bound to be very happy living with real bear friends in the zoo and bought me another bear. Although none of that was any real comfort—not for a child who was already learning that, just as you make friends with people and places, you move on and leave them behind.

Hobart

We arrived in Hobart and climbed what seemed like endless steps up to the huge house in which we were to live for the next three-and-a-half years. In those days the Methodist parsonage in North Hobart sat among grand houses built on the high side of Swan Street. Our poor mother had a hard time dragging prams and pushers up the steps to the house, climbing stairs within the house and then more steps up to the back garden.

It has been interesting to return to Hobart many decades later and see what a beautiful city it is. My childhood memories are largely limited to around the house, the church, my school and a couple of friends' houses which we visited. We still didn't have a car so, quite apart from the distorted reality of the views which are taken in by a young child, we really didn't travel far. I think we must have borrowed a car for holidays from some kind parishioner.

It is interesting how church cultures become relatively set. It is as though certain sorts of people form a church and they attract others rather like themselves, and then invite people to minister to them who will generally fit in. I recall the people of Swan Street Methodist Church as absolutely kind and accepting—gathering in we parsonage kids with generosity and without any pressure to be particularly special.

My mother and father blossomed at Swan Street. My father seemed to move with confidence and enjoyment around his work and to grow as the people affirmed him and received what he had to offer to them. He was obviously very busy and if my account of life in Hobart is often focused on my mother, I guess the truth is that we saw relatively little of him as well as being of the age when more attention was provided by mothers in most cases.

This was the time when I first began to observe what other people looked like and became more fussy about how I looked myself. I remember my mother wearing the smartest dress I ever recall her owning. It was black and decorated with beautiful bright flowers. She wore it with a big black hat and I loved seeing her in that outfit. This was unusual as my mother was not known for showing any interest in clothes or her appearance in general. Not that she looked untidy or particularly awful, she was just not interested and she didn't give clothes much of a priority in her slender budget. She would buy a special outfit about every five to seven years and wear it out. She would purchase this outfit by deciding on a good shop (sometimes led by God to this shop) and then, as she used to say, would 'put myself in the hands of' a good saleswoman for advice. She would then be guided through the entire outfit, including accessories.

In her youth my mother had fluffy, curly hair. By the time she married she had a bob and her hair was pressed into rows of waves which she disciplined with bobby pins after she washed her hair. She did that all her life and died with exactly the same hairdo as she had when she was first married. Mother didn't wear corsets like other women at that time, or make-up, and was quite unselfconscious about her body in general. My sister Carmyl inherited this strength, unlike me.

In the end I was the only member of our family without curly hair and I could never understand why Mother didn't let her hair curl softly around her face. My father's hair went prematurely grey, as did most members of his family, and I thought he looked very distinguished with almost white hair by the time he was in his early thirties. Our time in Hobart was the era of Shirley Temple with her curls and tap-dancing shoes and most little girls tried to look like her. I had my long straight hair plaited during the week and on Sundays my mother wound it round her finger and set it in curls with bobby pins. She thought this made much better

The whole family in our Sunday best, 1941

curls than having your hair set in pieces of rag like most other little girls. I did too and tossed my Sunday curls proudly while longing for a pair of tapping shoes.

Thaïs, my younger sister, was born while we were in Hobart. My grandmother, Maggie McRae, looked after us while the birth took place. I think I only ever met my grandmother about five times in my life. She was a gentle and strong woman, born in Glasgow, and had a beautiful Scottish accent. My mother respected her greatly and asked us to call her 'Mother', instead of Mummy or Mum because that was the way my grandmother was addressed by her own children. I think she was a wise woman and I regret that I never really knew her as an adult or saw enough of her to receive more of this wisdom. She had a hard life, raising her six children on their farm with no running water in the house. As children we really didn't get to know any of our blood relatives because they lived in other states and none of us had the money to travel to see each other. My mother would tell us that 'Auntie someone' was coming to visit and we would ask whether it was a real auntie or just a pretend one. It was virtually always a pretend one.

My sister Thaïs was named after Massenet's beautiful 'Meditation from Thaïs'. She spent a good deal of her time later saying, 'My name is Thaïs with two dots over the I' (which it did have in its Greek form). Our mother loved that piece of music. Thaïs was a remarkably beautiful child with big brown eyes and fair curly hair. She was full of life and confidence and I can always picture her as a two-year-old performing for visitors when Mother gave afternoon teas.

There was a real routine to these afternoon teas. Mother would make asparagus rolls by wrapping asparagus in thinly cut buttered brown bread with the crusts cut off. She always bought a special sponge cake (she was not a sponge-maker) with cream on top and little bits of cracked toffee scattered over the cream. All would be arranged on the traymobile with the best china plates and cups ready for the guests. I would play a sort of quiet hostess role, looking after people. From my earliest days, I recall looking at people very carefully to see how they were feeling. While I wouldn't claim to see auras around people, I did experience some sort of sense of how they were through a sort of air around them of sadness or stress or pain or happiness or peacefulness. I just assumed that everyone could feel this and I would study each person with interest and sometimes concern and go and stand by them if they seemed upset.

Carmyl would worry my mother with what she was doing or saying or would energetically help with fetching and carrying. She was prone to say things like, 'Why is that lady so fat?' or 'What are those lines all over that lady's face for, Mother?' in a loud voice. Or she would have a significant tantrum lying on the floor and screaming or biting. I would watch anxiously as this happened and try to care for everyone, including Mother. Those who captured Carmyl's love and dealt calmly with her found themselves engaging with a highly intelligent little person whose quick mind and honest response to everything was very touching. She was full of passionate life and her tantrums passed like brief thunderstorms which turned into equally sunny enthusiasm for things.

Thaïs, in the meantime, would be busy charming the whole company with dimpled welcoming smiles. When the guests were assembled, she would find our whalebone stool (made by our father from a real vertebra of a whale with upholstery over the top) and then stand on it in the centre of the gathered company and make up a song, creating her own words and tune as she went. She would smile in delight as everyone applauded.

We three girls were very different and did our share of scrapping, but I always felt that we were loyal to each other; absolutely trustworthy when it came to the crunch.

In spite of my virtuous behaviour, or perhaps because of it, I do remember one moment of rebellion against Mother. By this time I was a keen member of the Brownies. I loved dancing around a toadstool and being assigned to the Pixie Six. I loved all the little rituals and the uniform. Alongside this, I hated porridge. And porridge was a very important beginning to the day in the McRae household. The oats would be soaked overnight and my father would begin its cooking first thing when he arose in the morning. The day when the pinch of salt was forgotten was regarded as very serious! One Saturday I decided that I would no longer eat porridge. I sat before my full plate and refused to take a spoonful. Mother was not into smacking so she said that if I didn't eat it I could not go to Brownies that morning. I weighed things up and decided that even Brownies was not worth more than taking a stand on the porridge. Perhaps I recall this incident because my child's mind realised that both my mother and I regretted having painted ourselves into a corner, but neither of us could work out a reasonable way of compromising. In the end, I did not eat my porridge and I missed Brownies. I never ate porridge again and was never pressed to do so.

Mother had a very hard time when I began school because in one year we all had two lots of ordinary measles, German measles, chickenpox, mumps and finally a mild form of whooping cough. She spent all her days running up and down stairs trying to care for three sick children. We were unlucky to get whooping cough as we had been given two vaccinations after sharing a holiday with another family and caught whooping cough from the children there. I must say, if what we had was mild whooping cough, I hate to think what the full dose would be like. I can still see each of us struggling to breathe as our mother or father held us anxiously.

I began school at Elizabeth Street School in Hobart. I was very shy and found the beginnings of school a real ordeal. I was helped by a marvellous teacher called Miss Rowntree. She was part of the famous Tasmanian Quaker family which developed Rowntrees chocolates. I mostly remember her because she had one brown eye and one blue eye, could play the piano for us remarkably well and was very understanding of my fears.

I don't recall much of my kindergarten year in school, probably because I was away sick so much! My proudest moment in second grade was being given 11 marks out of ten for a composition. I loved learning to read and write, but from the earliest days disliked arithmetic. All the children in our family loved reading and were always saving up our penny a week pocket money to buy the next on our list of Whitcombe and Tombs little storybooks.

By this stage the Second World War had broken out and my next year as I moved into primary school, which was across the road from the infants school, was lived with a very strong awareness of this. Hobart had a particular experience of the war as the huge British warships used it for docking and supplies. We had a full blackout each night, with proper blackout curtains over our windows, and practised taking shelter when the air-raid signals went off. Because we had a two-storey house, we all huddled under the kitchen table on the ground floor in response to the sirens. Our parents tried to make a bit of a game of it, but I didn't feel particularly safe under the table. I had enough imagination to think about a bomb falling on our house and us being squashed by the second storey as it fell upon us.

We had rows of trenches dug in our school grounds and all had to wear a little pouch held across our shoulders by a strap, provided by our mothers. Inside the pouch was a piece of rubber to put between our teeth in case a bomb went off, some cotton wool to put in our ears and a barley sugar to eat. When the sirens went off during school time, we all filed out of class and sat in the often muddy trenches, put the rubber between our teeth and the cotton wool in our ears and waited for the all clear to sound. I'm not sure when we were expected to eat the barley sugar! It all felt scary but exciting and I will never forget the sound of the sirens. As you sat in the trenches you imagined that maybe one day a bomb would really go off and it was always an enormous relief to hear the all clear.

My first friend at school was a little boy called Alan Hopgood. Our mothers were close friends and he started out as my school companion because I didn't know anyone else. I was grateful to gravitate to female friends relatively soon as Alan had the talent which later made him one of Australia's most distinguished actors, starring in *Evil Angels* and *The Blue Lagoon* and playing leading roles in *Bellbird*, *Prisoner*, *Halifax f.p.* and *Neighbours*. At five years old he had an amazing capacity to invent and act out terrifying scenarios, and I was a very satisfying audience because I was easily scared!

Mother liked to encourage us to perform, reciting poems or singing songs to people in various environments. She loved to sing and play the piano (when we had access to one) and had a good true contralto voice. Very early in life we learned to harmonise and spent a lot of time singing around the house. I recall being taken with Carmyl to sing on a local religious radio program on one occasion. Carmyl remembers that we sang a song called 'God make my life a little light within the world to glow'. Later on my musical performing days came to an abrupt end when Carmyl and I were to perform a duo act, clad in crepe-paper costumes for the annual Sunday school concert. I was supposed to be a violet and Carmyl a snowdrop and we each had a song to sing about those flowers. I think mine was about being a modest little violet. I went out onto centre stage, had stage fright and had to be carried off. While much later I learned to speak in public and I have sung in many choirs over the years, I've never tried to sing a solo again.

One of the best things about living in Hobart was that Jessie Castle joined our household. She was the first of several young women who lived with us over the years and helped Mother with us and household things in general. Jess was a gentle, light-hearted young woman, very intelligent and endlessly patient with us all. She read us stories and played with us and was like a special family member. I still love visiting her when I go to Hobart.

# 3   Launceston

In 1941 we moved to Launceston into a rather different environment. Our new home was in many respects even grander than our one in Hobart but it was set in a very different type of area. I realised, when I visited it 50 years later, that Invermay was a working-class area of Launceston. It helped me understand why my father helped to set up a branch of the Labor Party there, a move which I understand was not very popular with his congregation who thought clergy should steer clear of politics.

The parsonage was nothing short of astonishing. Apparently, many years before, the Rooms family had settled in the area. They had built a mansion for themselves and about five other mansions for their children, each set on an acre of land. These houses were built in a row, backing onto a street which carried normal traffic and fronting onto Rooms Avenue which ran between large oak trees and had a stile at each end. By the time we moved into one of these mansions most of them were fairly rundown and few people owning them could manage the care of the huge gardens.

Our house had a ballroom, a formal lounge room, large dining room with a servery into the kitchen area, servant accommodation at the back and several bedrooms. We girls slept in the ballroom which was big enough to house our three beds, with masses of playing space in the middle. There was a walled kitchen garden, a massive front lawn surrounded by all manner of shrubs and numerous fruit trees—peaches, apples, plums and pears. Even though our father was a keen gardener, no busy clergyman could attend to this huge area of garden. Dad mowed the lawns, grew his vegetables in abundance, established the chookhouse and simply did his best with the rest. Mother had a ball making jam, plum sauce and various other goodies from the fruit off the trees and the raspberry canes.

As for me, I decided that I was really the heroine in my favourite book which by this time was *The Secret Garden*. Quite apart from its wild beauty, the garden often felt a bit mysterious with its rambling ivy, gnarled trees, mushrooms and toadstools and all sorts of overgrowth and undergrowth. We were always establishing cubbyhouses in secret places and living a make-believe life. Rooms Avenue felt like our personal lane from an old English story with its oak trees meeting overhead and the stile to be climbed at each end. We all had our own bits of garden for planting things like mustard and cress and radishes. We rode our various second-hand tricycles, scooters and finally, to my great joy, a real two-wheeler bike around its garden pathways and up and down its wide driveway.

We bought our first car in Launceston—a second-hand Austin Tourer. When you started the engine you had to set the choke lever on the steering wheel and then Dad would crank the handle at the front. We liked sitting behind the steering wheel ready to give the engine more choke when Dad got it going. If you moved the choke lever one way the engine would roar louder. It had no synchronised gearing so the driver had to judge when to drop the engine into the next gear and then double declutch. Dad loved this car and was very proud about how smoothly he could change the gears. The car had a top speed of about 24 miles (50 kilometres) an hour. When we went on trips and came to the top of a good long hill, Dad would cut the engine and we would cruise down silently to save petrol. I hated him doing that because the car felt as though it was out of control—which it was, of course. I knew all these details because Dad thought we ought to know such things and was keen to teach us how to handle a car as soon as possible. At quite an early age he would let us sit on his knee and steer the car to get a feel for it. He drove quite fast and later in his life in country Victoria was caught speeding, but was let off because it would have been too embarrassing to have the local minister fined for speeding!

Unfortunately most of us were carsick regularly when we went on winding roads, especially Thaïs who used to feel sick as soon as she got in the car! We would carry an enamel potty with us in case we left it too late or couldn't conveniently stop to let us out to be sick. Mother used to encouragingly tell us we were 'nearly there' almost as soon as we left our own driveway.

Apart from our life at home, my memories of life in Launceston are very focused on the school and Sunday school. Both of them were associated with a sense of anxiety. The school was built around a large quadrangle which was used for the morning assembly. The entry to the quadrangle was through a very large sliding door and this was shut when the bell for the beginning of school stopped ringing. It was always my fear that I would be one of the ones left outside the door and punished for being late. I don't think I ever was late, but I felt as though I might be. My other two strongest memories of this time are both very different. The first is linked with my then intense dislike of knitting (unlike now!). We had to knit a tea-cosy. Mine was fawn and green with some sort of square pattern on it. One of my friends offered to knit it for me if I would do her spelling homework and I agreed. We never got caught but I lived with years of regret as Mother regularly brought out the wretched tea-cosy and showed it proudly to her friends as my splendid work.

The second strong memory is of an incident which happened in fifth grade. Our teacher was a large woman to whom we mostly gave great respect. One day she was standing out the front of the class and, as we watched in amazement, her bloomers slowly descended below her skirt. Obviously the elastic had broken. We watched in silence as she calmly took them off, gathered them up, told us to continue our work with a 'No talking!' and left the room. We all looked at each other and did what we were told—such was the obedience in those days of the threat of caning. A short time after, she returned and the class went on. Of course, we could hardly wait to get into the playground to laugh and tell the story.

One thing which really affected my later life was the school method of teaching us to swim. We were taken to the public baths and lined up on the edge looking down on the ice-blue water—and it was icy, too! When it came for my turn, a belt was placed around my waist that was attached to something which looked like a large fishing line. Then I was dropped into the deep end of the pool and instructed to swim! I was in no real danger because of the line which was attached to me but that was not how it felt. I sank in the water and then rose panic-stricken to the surface. I did actually learn to swim later in the Tamar River but I have never really liked swimming and never have managed to do any stroke which involves putting my face under water. Such were the rigours of Tasmanian education in those days.

On the other hand, as in Hobart and later at Sandy Beach, I have great memories of the walk home from school. I feel sad that so few children have this experience now because of the rise in anxiety about their safety. Walking home was the time when you gossiped with your friends, explored the environment and made your assessment of people's houses, their cats and dogs and possibly them. We ran rulers along fences and walls, kicked stones along, avoided cracks in the pavement, skipped and hopped, ran or lingered. We were the marble-playing generation. We all had our bags of marbles which we cherished and even named. At home and school we played bangers—throwing the marbles against a wall or fence and trying to get them within a handspan of the other person's marbles. As we walked home we often played runners—bowling our marbles along the footpath to achieve the same aim. Walking home was a whole culture in itself.

My sense of the Invermay church was that it was fairly rigid and conservative. Sunday school felt a far more threatening place than it had in Hobart. I would look at the picture of Jesus with children gathered at his feet which graced the Sunday school wall and wonder how that fitted with the rather punishing God I was sometimes hearing about from my teachers, although never at home. I became far more aware that parsonage kids were expected to be an example to all and I found this oppressive, even though I was mostly still a very good little girl. My father didn't seem as happy here as he had been in Hobart.

Mother had by now become linked with an international organisation called Moral Rearmament. Some of the features of this movement were a commitment to spend part of each day participating in 'quiet time'. The idea was that you listened to God rather than praying to God and then wrote down what you understood God was saying to you that day. There was also the belief that if all the leaders of the world were converted to Christianity most problems would be solved. Its proponents tried to place themselves in situations around the world close to powerful people to influence them to convert. I recall the gratification in the movement when Chiang Kai-shek, the Taiwanese leader, was converted to Christianity. The people who did the overseas work often 'lived by faith' relying on the gifts they received from supporters of the movement. They also encouraged young people to move around the world in groups singing and playing to audiences to tell of their faith.

At this stage we had a couple of women living with us—'Auntie' Elsie who was a friend of our mother's and Peggy who helped Mother. She was a fairly vulnerable person, I suspect, and I remember when Carmyl put a life-size rubber rat in her bed she had hysterics. We were amazed as we watched her, finding it hard to understand how a grown-up could be scared of a rubber rat. Very briefly we also had Coral staying with us who had been recently released from prison, I think. She didn't stay long as Dad caught her one night on the front lawn 'with a man'.

Auntie Elsie used to share the 'quiet time' with Mother and they would tell each other what God was saying to them. I remember Mother's annoyance when Elsie told her that God wanted Mother to let Elsie use her best china teacup and saucer every day for breakfast. I think there was something else about particular food which God thought Elsie was due for as well. There was a distinct cooling-off period from listening to God at that stage!

However, it was during this time that I realised that Mother was committed to prayer for healing and that sometimes the prayers of those she led were answered. I am sure that I remember a woman coming to our home in a wheelchair and walking out. Certainly I realised that Mother took prayer very seriously and was absolutely disciplined in praying every day about all aspects of her life and ours. Dad obviously prayed in church but, even then, I realised that while he deeply respected Mother's faith, he had a somewhat different approach to things.

Life out of school now carried with it greater awareness of the war. I don't remember trenches in the school grounds and there were no air-raid sirens, but many things were rationed. I also now knew that school friends and others I met had fathers or other family members away at the war. I listened to the radio a little and people sang songs about the war. You couldn't buy things like chocolate and ice-creams anymore but the woman who owned the local shop managed to enthrall us with Blue Heaven iceblocks which she made herself. Goodness knows what was in them but, whatever it was, it made our mouths all blue and we would exchange viewings of our blue tongues.

By this stage, I was a very keen Brownie indeed, accumulating proficiency badges in large numbers. I was a gardener who could grow radishes, a cook who could make custard, I could tie knots and give directions to people. I also could do washing and ironing—I think that was a laundry badge. Mother also thought it was a good idea to train her children to be as independent as possible and we all had our domestic tasks. However, Mother had a major disagreement with the Brown Owl (Brownie leader) after she informed me, during my test, that socks should be hung on the line with a peg at both their toe and heel, instead of just at the toe as my mother had taught me. I must say I have never ever met anyone who would agree with the way my Brown Owl hung socks. Funny the things that stick in your mind!

Our brother John was born in Launceston—a beautiful, gentle little boy. Carmyl remembers when Mother went to hospital to give birth to John, Auntie Elsie said that she would look after me and Thaïs, but not Carmyl. She was rescued by another of Mother's friends, Betty Ling, who loved Carmyl and had gained her trust. We all helped to look after John as by this stage we girls were nine, seven and five years old.

After much agonising and receiving a white feather in the mail, Dad decided in 1944 that he should join the army as a chaplain and he was sent to Papua New Guinea. The rest of the family moved to Sandy Beach, a small place not far from Launceston, down the Tamar River. We settled in a rented holiday house together with another of Mother's young helpers, Dulcie Pickett. We were no longer in a parsonage and we were no longer 'the minister's children'.

Sandy Beach

I suppose we did realise how serious it was that our father was now engaged in the war, but our life went on and Mother clearly protected us from focusing on the worry and fear which she must have experienced. Things went on in a new way as we adjusted to having a greater space between us and the church. We did, of course, go to church and I even taught a kindergarten class in the Sunday school—which was a bit odd, given that I was only 11 years old! However, this felt entirely different to me compared to life as the minister's daughter. It was as though people didn't have their eyes on us all the time.

Our house was significantly smaller than those we were used to and it had two attic bedrooms. I loved that. I pretended I was Milly Molly Mandy or someone in an English storybook. I shared a bedroom with John who said funny two-year-old things in the night. I was recently reminded that he once asked our mother, 'Muvver, do fish have eyebrows?' Mind you, he had a fairly hard time with three older sisters. Mother at one stage told us to stop saying, 'Oh John!' in critical voices to him so often and to remember that he was just a little boy. We rather liked reading him stories and watching for his emotional response to our dramatic reading. We all remember the one about the poor little green grasshopper who was shut out in the cold. We read this in a mode of sadness and pathos and watched for his eyes to fill with tears, at which point we would mock him. The cruelty of children! For all that, we did love him and spent a good deal of time watching over him when we were not at school.

We went to the state school in Beaconsfield and travelled there in the school bus. This 'bus' was really a truck which was used for carting timber when not in use for school transport. It had four wooden benches which ran down its sides and back to back in the middle. The children who sat on the outside benches used to hold up the canvas blinds which covered the top and sides and were held down by a piece of wood at the bottom. We held onto the piece of wood so we could see out and get some air. We met the bus beside the Tamar River and played around there as we waited or when we alighted from the bus after school. We slid on the ice which coated the pavements down to the river in the freezing winter and tried to fend off chilblains and numb feet and hands. We didn't have the use of our car as Mother couldn't drive.

Perhaps because I was more aware of things, or perhaps because it was a very strict school, I recall being very conscious of the tough discipline in my classes. If you as much as talked uninvited in class you could get six cuts of the cane, delivered in front of the class. I think in my previous schools it was only the principal who administered caning and not in front of the class. I remember keeping very silent indeed and flinching as I watched the cane swish down on other children's hands and heard them cry. I was surprised to find when I recently went through some old school reports that I was actually dux of grade six. I had no perception of myself as academically proficient. I think the teaching was probably excellent and education in Tasmania in general was of a high standard, with pupils moving to Victoria being regularly assessed as one year ahead of their Victorian counterparts.

Beaconsfield was an old mining town and in our lunch break we sometimes roved around the mine sites and occasionally climbed down into them. They were old gold mines which had been closed due to rising water. We always expected to come across a hidden gold nugget and make our fortune and took considerable risks in our search! We also spent much time shouting abusive jingles across the road at the kids from the local Catholic school. I must say that neither my father or mother approved of this activity as they, unlike most Protestants of the day, respected the Catholic Church.

My sisters and I didn't get to go down the street in our lunchtimes as much as other children because we were only allowed to buy our lunch once a term. This was the grand day when we ate bought pies or pasties. What bliss! Our mother went to great trouble with our sandwiches, making all sorts of imaginative and healthy fillings for us while we longed for jam sandwiches and white bread and sometimes swapped with others in order to achieve that.

We didn't have a refrigerator but in the winter we sometimes put out a pie dish of milk and sugar which froze by the morning. We would cut it up and make our own iceblocks. Milk was delivered to the door and poured into the billies which Mother left out. She would then scald it and let the cream rise to the top which we had on our fruit. We also were able to buy cheap fish, even crayfish and scallops, from the local fishermen direct off their boats.

By the time I was 12, my friends were beginning to ponder on which boys they would like to have as their boyfriends. I knew that I didn't want any boyfriends and recall running for my life from two brothers who wanted to kiss me.

We loved our life at Sandy Beach as we had many freedoms. We roved around the area and into the bush behind our house. I used to write plays, mainly about Cavaliers and Roundheads, and we three girls would dress up and perform often on the top of a cliff nearby with great dramatic effects. Someone had given Mother a largish satin padded evening jacket and we had it in our dressing-up box. It was always known as the 'Cavalier coat'. Other notable events were Thaïs being chased by a bull up the lane near our house and my finding a baby penguin on the edge of the river and bringing it home. I was told to take it back at once and it paddled out into the river with great relief! We also had a couple of blue wrens who came each year and nested low in some vines at the front of the house. They became quite tame and let us come close to see their eggs hatch and the chicks learn to fly.

One of our favourite games was knucklebones. These days kids have the plastic version of this, but we used real knucklebones from the joint of a

Dressed up with Dulcie Pickett and our wigwam

leg of lamb (mutton in our case). You cracked the joint, extracted the knucklebone and cleaned and polished it to add to your collection for the game which involved throwing the knucklebone in the air and catching it on the back of your hand. If you were really good at it and had nice big hands with a flexible curve down the middle, you could catch several at once and become the winner. I had small, stiff hands but I still liked playing the game and collecting my 'best' knucklebones.

We spent a good deal of time in the bush, often pretending to be native Americans with tents like wigwams and bands around our heads with feathers stuck in them. We were always lighting fires to sit around and then carefully putting them out and burying the coals and ashes as we had been taught in Brownies. We did not have many toys but we were very used to living through our imagination and from our reading of endless books. I used to read all the way to school on the bus and back again and was always getting into trouble for having my head in a book when I should have been doing my household chores.

A key person in all this was Dulcie Pickett who simply joined us in our activities and watched over us without diminishing our play. Dulcie was a critical figure in my life at that time in a multitude of ways. While she deeply respected and loved Mother, she knew that when you are 12 you need to feel like other children. Over and over again she smoothed my path through life with sensitivity in this direction. We were only allowed to listen to the ABC children's hour, the ABC news and *The Lawsons*, a long-running radio serial of the time. Mother thought that soapies on commercial stations were not suitable for us. All the kids at school talked about the way the soaps were going and Dulcie would casually feed me bits of information about some of these things so that I could pretend to be like everyone else.

We also did not go to the movies like other children, who mostly seemed to go on their own to the local picture theatre every Saturday afternoon. The only movies which mother thought suitable for us were the Walt Disney ones. Ironically, I had nightmares about the Wicked Queen in *Snow White and the Seven Dwarfs* and was distressed by the sadness of *Bambi*. Mother did relent and let us see *For Me and My Gal* near the end of our time at Sandy Beach and that was great. The lesser feature on the night was a relatively adult one (in our terms) called *One Dangerous Night*. We discussed that long after!

Kids at school were always talking about movies and we even had a playground game called 'film stars'. I forget how it was played but you needed to be familiar with the names of the most prominent movie stars of the time. And everyone had their favourite stars which they compared with others. Dulcie gave me a 'signed' postcard of Clark Gable—such an early one that he didn't even have his famous little moustache. I still have that card cherished in a special box of treasures. She also gave me one of Joan Fontaine. I had never seen either of these stars in movies but I could flash my cards as my favourites and pretend I knew all about them. She also sang some of the popular songs of the day so I could sing along with everybody. She talked 'girl-talk' with me about life and love and we discussed the fortunes of the players in *The Lawsons* as though we really knew them. We even sent off for some photos of the wedding of two of them. Dulcie made it possible for me to feel normal among my peers which was very, very important to me.

On the day the war ended we were on our way to school on the bus when the news came through. The bus was stopped and we were returned home. Mother decided to take us all into Launceston so she and Dulcie could be with friends and celebrate. She packed a picnic and we all piled onto a real bus. Mother and my sisters and brother gathered in someone's home to enjoy the day. I stayed with Dulcie and we went dancing down the streets with the cheering crowds. Then she caught up with a friend and we all went to see the movie *Gone with the Wind*. That was quite a distance from Walt Disney! There was my hero, Clark Gable, in the flesh, so to speak, and me transfixed by a truly adult movie. I thought about that for a very long time indeed and later bought the book and watched the movie twice more.

For some children I notice that it doesn't matter too much if their home experience and cultural world is different from others'. Perhaps they have a certain sort of confidence or simply don't care. I did care very deeply and Dulcie's careful and sensitive awareness of what I needed to know and to talk about was quite critical in my life. She was a generous mentor to me. She had a wry sense of humour and taught me to laugh and be romantic and fun in ways which I can't really describe. I guess she simply made me more human and more part of the human race for that period of my childhood. She was, and is, a wise woman.

My father returned from the war about eight months after it ended. He looked so handsome in his uniform and I recall finding his identity card and finally discovering how old he was. When asked he would always say, 'As old as my tongue and a little older than my teeth.' I asked him whether he hated the Japanese and he replied, 'No, Dorothy. I don't hate the Japanese. I hate war.' The period of his war service was the only time he actually had any money as chaplains were paid at the rate of officers in the army. At home, clergy were paid below the basic wage of the day so that they wouldn't be richer than their parishioners. It was called a 'stipend' which was intended to cover costs rather than actually be a salary. At that stage I didn't have much sense of being poor, although I wished I had as many clothes as other children. We didn't wear school uniforms to primary school and I was rather conscious that other people had more variety to wear than I did.

The next place we moved to was Ballarat. Because Dad knew that he may never have the money to do so again, he and Mother decided that we would fly to Victoria rather than go by boat. Most of us were travel sick all the way in the unpressurised Douglas plane, but it was an adventure! I was very sad to leave my special friend Dulcie in Tasmania.

# 5 Ballarat

Ballarat was a shock after the freedom and relatively relaxed lifestyle of Sandy Beach. Dad was home and we were once again the minister's children. When we arrived at the huge two-storey brick house which was to be my home for the next five years, and longer for the rest of the family, I immediately checked it for any secret passages or hidey-holes. I knew from my reading that old houses may contain such exciting things and that you tapped the walls for any hollow sounds to discover them. We had a moment of hope when we found a hollow sound under the pantry floor and joy of joys, we could see evidence of a trapdoor there! Disappointingly it turned out to be nothing but a tiny cellar space for storing, presumably, a small number of bottles of wine. Nevertheless, we raced up the sweeping staircase and slid down the curving bannister and generally gave approval. Our poor mother sighed as she faced a huge, rather rundown house to clean, sparse old furniture, fairly grotty mattresses and threadbare carpets. She hated all the moving, especially the inheriting of parsonage furniture which stayed with the houses in those days.

We claimed our bedrooms and I delighted in the fact that the light switches were operated by long cords from the ceiling. In a short space of time I had ours rigged up so that I could switch it on and off without getting out of bed. John was my bedroom companion again and I knew he would go off to sleep and I could read on until Mother discovered that the light was still on. I thought she had extraordinary hearing when, as I gently clicked off the light, I would hear her voice from downstairs saying, 'I heard you switch the light off, Dorothy. I thought I told you to do it ages ago!'

My religious history in Ballarat was related to a number of influences. The church at Pleasant Street was conservative in the very literal sense. The rather constant comment when Dad or anyone else suggested anything new was, 'It was good enough for our parents and grandparents, so why would we want to change?' We had some very long-winded conservative lay preachers. I recall one who used to rise on his toes and sway threateningly over the high pulpit. It was a day of great glee when a bunch of wild cats who lived under the church started howling during his sermon. The door stewards rushed out and poked around but the cats kept up the noise—in wonderful style, we thought. We lived next door to the church and decided that we would support these cats as far as possible!

The church had a great tradition of performing musicals like Gilbert and Sullivan's and its huge hall was used for performances. Singing was a good feature of church life. We had Sunday school anniversaries when we all stood on a specially erected platform with seats which tiered up to the ceiling from the large stage. This was the day when you were supposed to have your annual new outfit, with hat, bag and gloves included. Mother made most of our clothes, including our hats, herself and had to work very hard to achieve this for us as our finances were seriously stretched during this period.

Sunday school was a very mixed experience. Every year, being Methodist, we had Temperance Sunday when there was a special study on the evils of consuming alcohol. We habitually received a pamphlet which had two drawings in it—one of a handsome, strapping young man who never let alcohol pass his lips and another of a weedy, unattractive young man who drank! One particular year we also had the methylated spirits demon-stration. A piece of bread was placed in a glass of methylated spirits and another in a glass of water. We were then instructed to feel that the bread in the metho went hard and the bread in the water swelled and remained soft—such were the dangers of the demon drink. After that we were invited to sign the pledge which was our commitment to remain a total abstainer for the rest of our lives. 'Temperance' was a misnomer for this Sunday!

I took home my pledge form and, being virtuous, decided to sign it and return it to our teacher the next Sunday as requested. I proudly told my father I was doing this, assuming he would be gratified seeing he was a total abstainer himself. I was amazed when he insisted that I print a qualifying statement on the form which read, 'until I am 18 years of age'. He said that although he did not drink himself because he believed that some people found alcohol destructive in their lives, and he would not want to be part of their temptation to drink, he did not believe in asking children to make a decision for the rest of their lives. He thought it was manipulative and that we were not mature enough to make such a decision. The Sunday school staff were very disapproving when I returned the form and Dad was given a hard time. I was proud of my father and decided that I wanted to have that sort of courage and ethical behaviour.

On Sundays we were not allowed to play with other children; we had to stay home and play. There was some sense that we had to do relaxing and very wholesome things as a family but we mostly messed around playing the piano and singing or playing various board games or card games. One day we were all playing cards when some parishioners dropped in. They were deeply shocked and offended that the minister's children would be playing a card game on a Sunday! We saw it as their problem and continued our card playing.

We also had state-run Sunday school exams and the minister's children were expected to study hard for them and do well. I hated learning all the texts by heart and complained to my mother that they would never be of use to me. She said, 'Dorothy, one day you may be in some terrible and tough situation, maybe even in prison, where you have no access to your Bible and these texts will be your comfort and will help you survive. Or you may be dying and unable to read and these texts will come to you.' I thought to myself that this would never happen and I would have forgotten the texts anyway by then. I have never had that sort of memory and I am not sure that texts have been the first thing to come into my head when under pressure, anyway! However, we did do well in the Sunday school exams and had to come forward to receive our prizes. I hated this because I could hear the other kids saying scornfully, 'Minister's kids! They always win!' Little did they know that it was a no-win situation. We were awarded vouchers to buy books and I always hated the books we had to 'choose'. They were mostly very boring indeed.

Luckily my last Sunday school teacher was a very special woman who stood out in the congregation as wise and open. She was a retired school-teacher called Miss Stubbs and handled her somewhat unruly bunch of early adolescents with calmness and competence. She did not disapprove of my father either. On one occasion she invited the class to afternoon tea at her house. We were all very toey but sort of excited about this. After all, adults were invited to have afternoon tea, not children. When we arrived, she sat us around her polished table and solemnly served us tea and delicious food. We all pretended that of course we drank tea and attempted a grown-up sort of conversation led by her. She talked with us as though we were significant, as though we might have opinions worth listening to, and we were very impressed.

All the time we were eating she played some music to us on her gramophone. I had not heard this type of music before as we didn't have a gramophone and although I had heard some music on the radio, it was mostly singing. I sat entranced and as we left asked her what it was. 'Bach', she told me. I decided that it was my sort of music but didn't really connect with it again until about 30 years later. When we left we walked self-consciously down the street as though we were very grown up. Then, all of a sudden, we all started laughing and leaping around and became adolescents again.

By now I was becoming much more aware of the difference between the spirituality of our parents. Mother would sit us down on many occasions and tell us to 'listen to God' and write down what God told us. After this we were asked to join her in praying. I always envied Carmyl and Thaïs who seemed to frequently have marvellous messages from God. Mine always seemed very ordinary and my prayers began to form into a pattern which I thought covered most things. I can still remember roughly what I prayed: 'God bless Mother and Dad, God bless the sick and lonely and those without mothers and fathers and help me to be good and loving. Amen.'

Apart from prayers for others, I remember Mother praying that we would be given some way of having a holiday and that someone would give us enough money to pay our debts before we left Ballarat. Someone always did offer us a loan of their holiday house at the right time and, as in previous parishes, the gift which we received on our leaving did cover our debts to local shops and tradespeople almost exactly, as Mother pointed out. Once we sat down at the table and she said, 'Children, we haven't quite enough for dinner tonight. We will ask God to send us more food.' Shortly afterwards there was a knock at the door from someone carrying a casserole for us!

Dad was always engrossed in his study when he was home and I often talked with him about life and faith and found him challenging and informing. He would make me think through all sorts of things which I was accepting without criticism. I talked with him about my concern about a God who would send people to the fires of hell. He would say to that, 'So, you think you are more loving than God, do you, Dorothy?' I would realise what he was saying—that if I longed for more mercy it was unlikely that God would be less merciful than me. I knew that the punishing God of that sort of hell was not his God and said, 'No.' And he then replied, 'Good. If you ever think you are more loving than God, you are on the wrong track.' He would then tell me how to look at the Bible in the light of biblical scholarship—to see the themes that run through it and the human material that is there alongside the wisdom of God. I have carried that with me for the rest of my life.

If I said things about people who didn't believe in God, he would say, 'So, how do you know God exists?' I would tell him that the Bible said so. He would then ask me how I knew that the Bible was true and eventually take me through to the realisation that there is no proof of the existence of God. It is always a matter of faith in the end. He never let any of us stay with sloppy thinking. If we were to hold to any world view, we had to strip it right back to its roots and face its ambiguities and/or certainties. He was never other than a man of deep and abiding faith, and he inspired that in his children. I remember once saying to him, 'I wish you were like other people's fathers and just told me what to think and do!' He looked at me wryly and said, 'One day you may be grateful that I am not like that, Dorothy.' And I was.

In spite of this rather mature and radical religious influence, as a 16-year-old I accepted an invitation to go along to an evangelical rally held by a group called Campaigners for Christ. During the meeting we were handed every last manipulative hell and damnation threat. This included the thought that unless we gave our hearts to Jesus that night, we might be killed by a bus on the way home and go to hell. Then they played what seemed like 100 verses of a hymn called 'Just As I Am Thine Own to Be' and urged us to come forward and witness to our salvation. I did have a deep sense of making a personal decision to be a Christian, but I sat there desperately fearful of going to the front. I was very shy and wearing hand-me-down clothes which made me feel very self-conscious. I hated the thought of everyone's eyes upon me as I walked to the front. I shut my eyes and made a bargain with God. I said to God that, because I couldn't go forward and 'witness to my faith', I would earn my salvation by giving up all sorts of things and being very good.

I decided that I would give up make-up, swearing, drinking and gambling, going to movies and that I would probably be a missionary when I grew up. I wasn't actually doing any of these things at the time, so I decided that I would also be especially pious as well. My changed attitude to life in general was obvious and after a while my mother sat me down and asked if I really thought that this was Christianity, given that it was so miserable. Clearly what she was picking up was that I was refusing to enjoy myself in any way and was probably being judgemental of others who did. I told her that I had been saved by Jesus and that I would pray for her salvation. Fortunately this stage of my faith did not last in most respects as I returned to the greater maturity and wisdom of my earlier learnings, but I did continue to close my eyes for the prayers in church as a sign that I was born again! The hangover from this part of my spiritual journey, which lasted for ten years, was a profound sense that I must do lots of good works in order to learn the love of God. Having said all that, it was a moment of real decision for me and taught me that often we receive things from unexpected people, even if the gift comes with all sorts of less helpful things attached.

Although in many ways Dad and Mother allowed me my own life and faith, they both had their subtle ways of telling us what they really wanted us to do and be. Mother was either stern or rather manipulatingly tearful and I could tell from the discussions we had what Dad's real views were on things, even if he couched them in indirect language. Like me, beneath his peace-making exterior, there could be fairly formidable anger which he mainly projected onto justice causes. He hated anger openly expressed by us, and there were times when I wished he or Mother would just be overtly angry. We became excellent over-the-dinner-table debaters, carefully avoiding words of abuse or anger, but decimating each other's arguments nevertheless. This skill has often stood me in good stead in later life. However, the expression of non-overt anger in relationships has not been a good inheritance.

Both my parents were, as many people of their day, inhibited about any discussion of sex. We weren't given the sense that sex was 'dirty', but that it was too holy for words. At least Mother did take me aside and in her 'important' voice, which always told me that she was rather embarrassed, gave me real information about menstruation in plenty of time, unlike the mothers of many of my peers. However, I had a real laugh years later when she came to me when my first daughter was about five years old and solemnly presented me with a copy of a book called *The Cradle Ship*. She said, 'I guess Lindy is about ready for this book now, Dorothy.' I asked her what she meant by 'ready'. She said that it was the best book to inform children about where babies came from. Then I remembered that while we were at Ballarat she used to insist on reading a chapter of this book to us all on Sunday afternoons and recalled that she used her 'important' voice as she read it. It was a very boring book, all about pollen and plants—literally about the birds and the bees—and none of us had got the message. In fact, at the time she was reading to us about pollen and birds I had already read, from cover to cover, *The Mastery of Sex* by Leslie Weatherhead from the shelves of my father's study!

Dad and Mother said that I could either join the church youth group or the Girl Guides, but not both as it would mean too many nights out. I chose Guides, mainly because there wouldn't be any boys there, and entered into it with the same enthusiasm as I had for Brownies. Guiding had a real impact on my life. We had a leader who convinced us that girls could do anything and, what's more, they could do most things all by themselves. We went camping and carried our own heavy tents and put them up. We could do an excellent job with the right sort of knot for any occasion. I was the patrol leader of the Magpies and proudly wore about 16 proficiency badges on my uniform. I was one of the Guides chosen to shake Lady Baden-Powell by the hand when she, the founder of the Guiding movement, visited Ballarat.

When I was nearly 15, our brother David was born. Mother had had a miscarriage between the birth of John and David, but we were not told about this at the time. When she had David, mother was 43 years old and she told me she had definitely chosen to have another child. I well remember the day on which David was born. I can see my father preaching, obviously stressed, as he knew that our mother was in some danger as she fought to give birth. David was eleven-and-half pounds in weight at birth and his big head became stuck somewhere in the birth process. She had been in labour for at least 48 hours and was very weak. At last the doctor managed a forceps delivery and not long after the church service was over we all went to the hospital to greet our new brother and see our mother. She looked so pale and tired that I remember being scared that she wouldn't recover. However, she did and both she and David thrived. From the moment of his birth, David was a cheerful, assertive little boy with a large presence. He was also very clever indeed. I will always remember him standing at the top of the stairs at the age of about three and calling us all to hear his major pronouncement. We all came out to see what he was about and he announced firmly, 'God is a germ. God is everywhere and germs are everywhere, so God is a germ.'

John, meanwhile, had created a whole imaginary place for himself to play in called Pookey Land. There he had friendly companions who didn't tease or oppress him. Of course, we used to tease him about Pookey Land, but he had found a place under some bushes near the back door where he could get away from us. He was also connecting with the musical soul which he would later develop as a fine musician. Mother would play the piano and he would sing and move and enjoy himself hugely. He especially liked her rendition of a piece called 'Napoleon's Last Charge' and would play out the Battle of Waterloo to music in fine style. We all loved singing around the piano and by now could naturally harmonise. I began to learn the piano but never really had big enough hands to play and as my teacher used to hit me over the knuckles, I didn't look forward to lessons. In the end, we couldn't afford for me to have lessons anyway.

We had a big backyard which Dad quickly turned into a vegetable garden with a chookhouse and cubbyhouse for us to play in. There were lots of trees and when they shed their leaves we would rake them up and light our camp fires outside the cubbyhouse. After a while we began to value-add to this and threw on some potatoes to cook in the embers. Then we decided that our leaves didn't burn long enough and added wood. After that, we thought that potatoes covered in charcoal were not up to our standards so we began to cook chips in a pan with dripping. Of course, we had long ago learned to chop wood. In almost all the parsonages there was a wood stove and open wood fires for heating. From our earliest years, we could chop kindling—we developed the chopping of kindling into an art form. We all knew how to set a fire, taught by our father who was the main lighter of the stove in the morning. As we didn't have a toaster, we toasted our bread on a toasting fork before the open door of the stove or in front of the dining room fire. We were always poking away at fires in some form or another.

We still didn't have a refrigerator but Dad had acquired a large army box like a travelling trunk which sat on the dining room floor with a drip tray underneath and we put ice in that—a sort of homemade ice chest. We thought it was pretty terrific. We were also gratified when Mother made a friend of a neighbour opposite who had a refrigerator. On special occasions she would let us make homemade ice-cream in her fridge. We would mix up the recipe in trays, take it across to her and then collect it later when it had crystallised enough for beating and take it back again until the special meal.

Mother was interested in health in general, especially in natural remedies and vitamin-filled food. She almost never used medication or things like pain-killers. For some years we had quantities of cod-liver oil mixture every day. I am sure this was actually good for us, but we tasted fish in our mouths all day—there were no capsules in those days. Then she decided that molasses was a beneficial health supplement and we were required to drink a tablespoon of that each morning mixed in hot water. It was revolting! We also had a handful of borax in our bathwater. I didn't like the gritty feeling it gave the bath. Mother also used borax in hot water to soak our feet to prevent chilblains and I must say that did seem to work. We were mostly healthy, so maybe her methods were effective.

Part of Mother's health routine was her rest after lunch each day when she stretched out on her bed for about an hour. Whoever was living with us looked after the younger children while she did this or we looked after ourselves when we were old enough. Mother was often tired. She did have heavy responsibilities as the minister's wife which she largely enjoyed and she may well have been already suffering from a degree of angina. Her tiredness always made me feel as though I was letting her down in some way, as though I should be caring more for her and doing more to help.

We couldn't afford shampoo so we just used ordinary soap to wash our hair, especially Velvet Soap which was normally used for washing clothes. I used to add some vinegar to the water because I believed it made my hair

A studio photo of the family in Ballarat

shine. Our clothes were washed in soap which Mother made from dripping. She would collect the clarified dripping in kerosene cans and then boil it all up with additives in the copper and chop it into pieces when it cooled. The women of the church used to collect dripping for her and she made the soap for fund-raising as well.

They used to say that tramps (as they were known then) put a mark on the gatepost of houses where it was worth asking for support. I never noticed any marks on our gatepost, but I suspect that the word was around that my dad was a soft touch. Mother also liked to help all sorts of people as best she could. She was never shocked by people and in some ways exercised the qualities which would have made her a good nurse—had she had the opportunity. We often had tramps at the door and, in spite of our not having much money, some often changed hands. We were also used to having people sleep in the sheds at the end of the back garden.

Holidays were mostly spent at kindly loaned holiday houses. We still had the Austin Tourer at a time when almost everyone was driving sedans.

For holidays we would all pack into the car with luggage tied on the carrier at the back and on the running boards. We took the side window curtains off the car to climb in through the window openings and then we would chug off. I remember once we were all loaded up and Dad had to deliver something on the other side of Lake Wendouree before we left. On the way, a gust of wind blew the entire roof off the car and we had to gather it up and secure it down with upholstery tacks before we could go on our holiday! As we went, Mother would give a running commentary of the scenery to try to divert us from being sick and I recall her saying how she didn't envy all those cars passing us as they really couldn't enjoy the scenery like we did. One thing about Mother was that she always found something good about everything, which was intensely irritating when things were deserving of anger or grief and sort of noble when she was showing courage and helping us all to survive. She was a genuine survivor and I forgave her many things much later when I saw her in life's larger perspective—as I hope my kids will ultimately do for me.

Ballarat was another mining city. Its glory had been many decades before and most of the mining was over in our day and the shafts filled in or covered over. The mullock heaps remained and we would rove around them after school. The history I loved most in the story of Ballarat was that of the Eureka Stockade. This was the story of the battle between the miners, led by Peter Lalor, and the soldiers who were sent to collect the money for the mining licences which the miners thought was exorbitant. The victory of the miners and the lives of the people lost in the struggle were celebrated with a monument and a park. We used to go there sometimes to swim and I would read the inscriptions on the monument and feel a sense of deep connection with that brave battle. I wanted my life to be linked with people like Peter Lalor. I love the Eureka flag with its white cross and stars on the blue background and when that flag arose before me, carried by neo-Nazis decades later, I found myself filled with rage at the betrayal of what I believed was the real message of the Eureka

Stockade struggle. I felt like seizing it from them and saying, 'This is my flag. I am a Ballarat person and I know better what this stands for. Don't you dare hold it high!'

It was in the five years at Ballarat that my political ideas were largely formed. Without remembering specifically how, I knew that Dad had socialist leanings. He regarded his Methodist heritage as the origins of this thinking and I certainly absorbed the belief in the levelling out of society in terms of rewards for work done, all of which was fundamentally equal in importance. I really believed that the rubbish collector was as important to society as the prime minister or business leader—that they had differing talents but each should be respected for their own sake. I believed that, at its best, society is very corporate, owning things together and distributing resources according to need.

I do remember Dad sitting me down beside the radio and saying, 'Listen to Mr Chifley, Dorothy. He is a good man and the way he speaks is the best way of debating things. Listen. He never attacks other people personally, just their ideas. That is the way good debate takes place anywhere.' He pointed out that, by contrast, Robert Menzies attacked his opponents personally. I did take that to heart and have always tried to stick to that rule in debating environments. When I visited Old Parliament House in Canberra not long ago, I found myself buying a postcard with a picture of Ben Chifley on it to keep on my desk and I often make a point of having coffee in Chifley Square in Sydney where I can look at the huge statue of him. I am not quite so convinced a socialist these days but the principles which underly that ideology still shape my ideals about human community.

One of my keen interests at this stage was cricket. I can't remember whether Dad also liked cricket, but I used to sit and listen enthralled by the radio. Of course, my main interest was in the Tests between England and Australia. I loved hearing the broadcasts where the commentators would sit in a studio with an audience and relay to us what was happening in England, including making the sounds of balls hitting bats and wickets falling. I remember that every time a wicket fell to us, the studio audience would sing a little ditty called 'Rickety Kate'. I haven't met anyone else who recalls this, but I am sure it happened. My favourite cricketer was the bowler Colin McCool. I never actually saw a match until very much later. Even now, I love going to Test and day matches with my daughter Melissa who is also a keen follower of cricket.

Alongside all of these activities much of my life was, of course, lived at school. Ballarat High School was on the then outskirts of the city and we rode our bikes there and back each day. It probably stirred our bodies in the freezing inland cold of the Ballarat winter—much more severe than the insular frostiness of Tasmania. It was a coeducational school, although boys and girls sat on different sides of the classroom, had different playgrounds and were not supposed to be seen talking with each other when in uniform. Despite all this, neither gender grew up with too many romanticised views of the opposite sex unlike, as we thought, the kids who went to the private single-sex schools.

In many ways it was a fine school with some great teachers, most of whom had taught there for a long period. It was a good, solid building at the end of an avenue of cypress trees with a grand assembly hall, extensive playing fields and a small swimming pool. I was very grateful to spend all my secondary schooling there, even if it was a mixed experience. Obviously it was the critical schooling which shaped my expectations and perceptions of life and myself. I was still an anxious student—keeping very quiet in class and not putting my hand up to answer questions in case I was wrong.

This was not helped by an experience in about fourth form. We used to sit in class with particular people and I decided to sit with a girl called Doris. I rather liked her because she was fun and a bit cheeky and I felt for the fact that she was known to be a ward of the state living in foster care. My closest friends had been allocated to other classes and I spent my time with them in the playground and after school rather than in class. While Doris was sitting with me, she continued to be her own somewhat rebellious self and I would watch her daring responses to teachers. After some months, I was called up to the headmistress's office. I went in fear and trembling trying to think what I could have done. Miss Vickery sat me down and said, 'Dorothy, the staff of the school are all very disappointed in you. When we noticed that Doris was sitting with you we thought that she would change and become a good girl and we now see that she is just as difficult as before. Given that your father teaches scripture at the school, we thought you would do better than that.' I cried and was sent back to class. At the same time, I was devastated by the degree of injustice as I reflected that the teachers couldn't control Doris and yet I was expected to do it.

I had two special friends with whom I spent my time outside classes. Val McKenzie lived a few doors from us. She was a wonderfully cheerful soul, a tonic for my serious self. Her dad bred Dalmatian dogs and I loved watching the puppies grow. Val was not very academically inclined and studied the 'commercial' subjects at school, like typing and shorthand, and left school in fourth form. She had a fine singing voice which was being trained and she competed, often successfully, in what was called the South Street Competition each year—a prestigious feature of life in Ballarat where many fine singers had their beginnings.

My other friend was Jean McDonald who also left school early and became a secretary. She was a Presbyterian minister's daughter and we would often compare stories of our lives. She lived in Learmonth, a small country town not far from Ballarat, and came to school on the bus each day. This meant that we didn't share much life other than in school hours, except when I went to stay with her. I would then marvel at her capacity to cook scones all by herself—she had all the skills of a farmer's daughter. I didn't like her father or his sermons though. We kept in touch for many years afterwards and I was matron of honour at her wedding.

The principal of our school for many years was Mr G.A. Simcocks, predictably known as 'Gas'. He was a large, odd man with somewhat bulgy eyes and he had the habit of coming along the central corridor which separated the classrooms and flattening himself against the wall to peer in at a class. Not only could this be seen from the classrooms on the other side of the corridor, but we would come out of a room during class time and there he would be doing just that. We thought it was a great joke. He was not known as an inspiration and we all knew that the school was really run by Miss Vickery the headmistress and Mr Ainsworth the deputy principal.

Four teachers added significantly to my life. Firstly, there was Miss Cotton who gave me a love of history; a fascination for the journey of humankind down the years. She deeply loved her own subject and brought it alive. She was a fine teacher who invoked respect in us all and showed us that this is often gained by showing a deep respect for others.

Mr Loyd Jones taught me English over several years. Quite apart from conveying his love of words and poetry, he also taught us logic. Not only did he teach the process of good thinking, he made us anaylse the daily newspapers as part of searching for the truth. He would invite us to ask, 'Who benefits from this point of view and who loses? How does this thinking enhance power or disempower people?' No-one played around in his classes because if they did, he would calmly sit the offender in the wastepaper basket in front of the class for the rest of the lesson.

Mr Sheehan was another English teacher who later became the Labor member for Ballarat in the Victorian Parliament. He was very political in his approach to things and began to teach us formal debating. As one who never spoke in class, the thought of being in a formal and adjudicated debate was one of dread. One day, Mr Sheehan announced that the next subject for debate would be the White Australia Policy. I went home and said to Dad that I really wanted to have my say on this but I was too nervous. By this stage I was 16 and in what was to be my last year at school. Dad said, 'Well, Dorothy, when you care enough, you will find a voice.' I decided that I did care enough about the issue of the White Australia Policy and volunteered to speak against it. I prepared my case carefully, trying to strike a balance between facts and attitudes, and Dad helped me in my efforts. I was sick the night before and went to school wondering if I would get more than a squeak out of my mouth when I rose to speak.

However, with trembling knees and feeble voice, I found I could do it! I discovered that my heart could carry me beyond my nervousness, just as my father had suggested. Mr Sheehan made some applauding comments and our side won the debate. It was to be many decades before I became more confident in public speaking, but after that, I knew I could do it.

I'm not completely clear about why I have always felt so strongly about racism. Perhaps it is because we sometimes had people from other races and cultures to stay with us—people from the Pacific Islands and Asia. I had experienced them as beautiful and gracious people in every case, especially the Pacific islanders who were so warm and who seemed to love children. Certainly we were brought up to challenge racism. When we remarked on other children calling out 'Ching chong Chinaman' jeeringly to a local Chinese merchant, or indicated that we might have joined in, Dad would tell us very firmly they were not a 'Chinaman' but a Chinese person who was to be respected at all times.

Under the tutelage of the deputy principal and art master, Mr Ainsworth, I found I had a love of art. He died in my last year of school but not before he had convinced me that I wanted to be an art teacher myself. I did have a good eye for reproducing images and designing things in general, but I am not sure this would have been the best vocation for me.

By the time I was in my last year at school, I was recognised as being quite good at athletics and some sports. I was captain of the school running team which made the zone finals and a good hockey player. I would have been the school champion high and long jumper also, but in my fourth year of high school we were suddenly told that jumping was not desirable for girls as we might injure ourselves in some unspoken way which we gathered had to do with fertility!

I also involved myself with the musical life of the school and conducted my house choir. The election of school prefects involved students voting to elect six boys and six girls for the year. Ten students were elected from sixth form and two from fifth form. I was the girl elected from fifth form. I was surprised when this happened and somewhat uncomfortable with the role of prefect, which meant I sometimes had to supervise the behaviour of the younger students. I knew that people liked me because I was nice, agreeable and supportive, but I didn't feel like a leader.

I felt self-conscious at school with my homemade uniforms, or ones passed down from someone else. I also wore unfashionable and drab makeshift dresses when we had a school dance or on other occasions when we didn't wear uniforms. At my last school dance, I desperately slaved away trying to transform an awful out-of-date olive green dress which had belonged to my aunt and which, although perfectly good as Mother said, was meant for a middle-aged woman. The other problem was that I didn't know how to dance. As a Methodist I was not allowed to dance until there was a policy change by the church when I was 16. I hated waiting on one side of the hall in my embarrassing clothes to see if a boy would ask me to dance. Occasionally they did and once I even 'walked home' with a boy. He gave me a peck on the cheek and my father appeared in the doorway. The boy hastily exited the scene and Dad joined me in the dark beside the church near our front door and warned me that, although dancing was now allowed, it really was a very risky activity as it involved a degree of intimacy. Boys might get the wrong idea and think I wanted to marry them; I might be compromised! This warning didn't bother me too much as I didn't have a boyfriend and didn't want one, other than to be like everyone else my age.

Our family's lack of money for new clothes, outings of various sorts and other things which I felt set me apart from my peers, did have an effect on my life. I felt quite fundamentally unattractive and self-conscious for many years. And I still stock our pantry shelves as though I might be in for a siege and mostly over-cater for guests. If I am asked to contribute food to something, I am very fussy about what I take as I remember always bringing dry biscuits with cheese to everything as a young person while other people brought cream cakes. It was interesting to discuss with some of my siblings how our lack of money affected them. I voiced my sense of deprivation. Carmyl thought we were very clever because we managed to pull off all sorts of things with very little. John thought we were noble! Of course, although we were money-poor, we had a big, secure house, vegetables in the garden and most important of all, books and a love of education.

My academic life in high school was set in a more competitive environment than Beaconsfield State School. I mostly came somewhere in the top ten in all subjects, except for one year when something was obviously bothering me (maybe Doris!) and I sank down the overall list. I loved working with words in any context and that carried me through in most subjects. I hated maths but still managed to do quite well.

If I mention all this it is to make the point that, when I was awarded the prize for Best All-Round Student in the school in fifth form, I had very little sense of satisfaction. I felt I was probably moderately good at many things and excellent at nothing. This was partly because by now I had two sisters who were clearly brilliant students—dux in every subject every year. I remember sitting in on Carmyl's maths class when my teacher was ill and there she was saying to the teacher in her enthusiastic, assertive voice, 'You're wrong, sir!' He looked at what he had done and reluctantly agreed that he was indeed wrong. I marvelled at her cheek and envied her brain. Thaïs also was starring in all she did. Both of them went on to be school captain when we later moved to Geelong. Carmyl was brilliant at all things mathematical and excellent in every other subject. Thaïs excelled at everything—music, art, sport and all school subjects. She could have chosen to pursue any career.

Fifth form was my last year at school. I mentioned to my mother that I would like to be an art teacher, which would have involved another year of school and going to university. She said that art offered very little to the world and that she thought I wouldn't cope with university. She told me that I was very good with small children (which I had to be, given how much I looked after my siblings) and that it would help the family's stretched finances if I got a scholarship to go to the Kindergarten Training College in Melbourne. I don't recall feeling that I had much choice in this. I also imagined myself dealing with small children and decided that I wouldn't feel inadequate with them. Mother had the conviction that all children should leave home at about 16 or 17 years of age. She clearly didn't want me to go on and matriculate as that would have been a waste of time and I couldn't think of anything I really wanted to do of which she would approve.

I don't remember my father saying anything about my future at this stage. I always assumed that if Mother was saying something important to me, she and Dad would have discussed it and agreed on the matter. I knew that Dad was committed to education for his daughters as well as his sons—something which was not common at the time. I felt that if he wasn't pushing for university for me, then maybe he also thought I wouldn't be up to that level of education. So I qualified for a health department scholarship and headed for Melbourne to train as a preschool teacher.

*Part* 2

Growing Up

# 6   Kew

The Kindergarten Training College was in Kew—an elite suburb of Melbourne. In those days it was made up of a smallish series of demountable lecture rooms alongside an old mansion called Mooroolbeek in which the residential students like myself were housed. I arrived carrying my fairly small supply of luggage, aged not quite 17 and on my own in the big city.

The student hostel was really a good place to be because it felt secure, predictable to a point and our meals were provided. The sleeping arrangements by today's standards were rather astonishing. First-year students were invariably assigned to sleep on the verandah. Each of us was also given a small desk and a wardrobe in a room shared with other students. The balcony ran across the back of the old house and was about two-and-a-half metres wide. Its roofing cover was probably about three metres from the floor, there was a low wall on the edge of it about a metre high and, apart from that, it was open to the elements. This was really something in the cold and wet Melbourne winter! Our beds had canvas covers to keep them relatively dry—but very heavy to sleep under. Possums frequented the balcony and were often to be found sitting on the end of our beds. About eight of us were accommodated like this, lined up dormitory style. Oddly enough, I rather liked sleeping there once I got used to it and actually chose to do so for a second year. Somehow it felt better than sharing a very pokey room with another person or being lined up dormitory style in one of the larger rooms inside.

One of the features of life sleeping on the balcony was that during our first year there, we occasionally had nocturnal visits from enthusiastic medical students who would come up the fire-escape stairs at the end and be let in by some of the young women. I don't know why they were always med students, although they did have quite a reputation in those days. I viewed this with interest but wished they wouldn't do it. Somehow the hostel staff got to hear of this activity and they announced that they were concerned for our security and would therefore put an alarm on the fire-escape door. No mention was made of the med students, but everyone got the message!

There were about 30 students in each year—about nine in residence and the others living at home. Training for preschool teaching was at that time regarded as an excellent preparation for marriage, and the college had something of the atmosphere of a finishing school about it. Having said that, the three-year course was actually of a very high standard and covered the teaching of children from birth to about seven years of age as well as children with special needs. It was a very holistic approach to education and child development and I have never regretted doing it, even though it was not my chosen vocation.

There were only two women in our year who had not spent their schooling at one of the elite private schools of Melbourne or Geelong. I was, obviously, one of the two. As we mingled on the first day, the introductory question was almost inevitably, 'Which school did you go to?' When I said, 'Ballarat High School', the response would be, 'Oh', in dismissive tones. Unlike most Australian cities, Melbourne in those days really did have a class system in regard to education. If you attended a private school then you were 'in' and looked after each other's welfare. You usually had a distinctive accent to prove it too.

I believed that I could match it with this lot academically, but socially I was on the edge, especially at the beginning. These young women were mostly wealthy, had the very latest clothes and were used to attending balls and socialising with 'desirable' young men mainly from Melbourne University. They drank, smoked and played cards and generally carried themselves with huge confidence. I was very daunted by all this in the early days, but after a while, although I envied their supreme confidence, I could see that these young women were as diverse as any other group of people. Some of them were happy and mature and others were not. Some of them were good people and some were very superficial. Some were quite sad young people who had lived in boarding school almost all their lives and felt deprived of family life. Interestingly, although they had all attended church schools, only one of them ever attended church. So much for the effectiveness of religious education!

I immediately made friends with Gwyn Sommerville, the other non-private school student, and we stuck together for the next three years of our training while enlarging the group of women with whom we moved. I had one go at smoking and felt sick so gave that up. I learned to play five hundred and solo, which we did between every lecture, and I made a name for myself as the one who never let alcohol pass her lips! I had the huge sum of four pounds a week as the living allowance from my scholarship. When I graduated as a kindergarten director, I earned the massive sum of 17 pounds a week! The community has never really valued preschool teachers, even though we trained for longer than most primary teachers in those days and had the responsibility for the care of children during their most formative years.

The first things I spent my money on were a bra, some deodorant and a lipstick—none of which I had from home. After that, I used to save to buy material to make myself what clothes I could. The college had a ball a couple of times a year and of course I had nothing remotely like an evening dress or shoes. I also tried to study what make-up the other girls put on their faces and then bought some cheap version of it. It was all very exciting and alarming at the same time!

I loved all the lectures including continuing to study English. We had a teacher called Mrs Riley who brought the poetry of Gerard Manley Hopkins alive for me. She moved away from the high school approach to poetry which often involved taking a poem apart and analysing it to bits. She invited us to let the words flow into our souls as we listened and to move past whether Hopkins was 'correctly' using words or grammar to enjoying the wonder of his images and language. I still love his poetry and studying it this way gave me the freedom to simply let words almost attach themselves to thoughts and images as though they have a life of their own. I developed this much more deeply when I began writing books of liturgy and rituals much later in life.

For our practical work we were assigned to various kindergartens for periods of time. In those days, the inner city of Melbourne was regarded as a slum area and indeed most of the people who lived in areas like North Melbourne, Carlton and Fitzroy were poor and their houses were often rundown and tiny. The kindergartens in which I did my practical teaching over the next few years were attended free of charge by children who were supplied with lunch and milk and who often came from quite struggling families. I only taught in one outer suburban kindergarten and didn't like that at all. I loved working with children who challenged me to give them experiences which they often lacked at home and whose tough exteriors invited me to gain their confidence and love. I really felt I could make a difference to their lives and give them a flying start for school. Whether this was true was another matter, but I enjoyed watching them gain confidence and skills.

I also learned that while the children often came from homes very different to mine, that parents who spoke in tough terms to their children or boxed their ears didn't necessarily love their children less than did my parents. I saw that sometimes the children in apparently better circumstances whose mothers spoke to them in more objective tones longed for an active warmth and closeness. I especially loved working at the Lady Gowrie Centre in North Carlton which was a large preschool which had a research component in its work. It had observation rooms for students from the university and others to watch the play of the children, and its staff were often included in various types of research.

While the course I was doing was focused on preparing us to teach children, it also invited us to reflect on our own upbringing and maturity. One of our first lectures was on child psychology. Our lecturer, who was also a university lecturer and psychoanalyst, asked us to write down a description of the way our own parents disciplined their children. I wrote that my parents didn't need to discipline us. They gave us a careful and mostly unspoken understanding of what they expected of us and we followed that expectation. For this reason they never needed to smack us or raise their voices. I indicated that I thought this was an excellent way of disciplining children. The lecturer wrote on my paper that she would be interested to know if I still held this view later in life. I thought that was a bit rich—she was obviously implying that this might not be the best way to discipline children. She was, of course, right. While I now think that my parents were not too bad in their mode of discipline, I think they were using all sorts of subtle methods which invoked guilt rather than honest, open negotiation. Mind you, I am not one to judge as I no doubt reproduced some of that in my own parenting.

We were trained at the time when preschool education was just moving past the conviction that all children needed to 'express themselves', whatever form that took! Our formula was more like 'I know what you are feeling but you may not do that'. We were warned that if a child had painted or drawn something, not to ask, 'What is that', because the child may have simply been doing an expressive work of art which was not a depiction of anything other than their feelings. We were told we should appear very interested in what they had done and say, 'Tell me about it'. We were to encourage a love of learning but to avoid moving into formal reading and writing. The child was to enter school bursting to learn these things having expanded themselves with all sorts of creative play. Our graduates found formal school pretty tough sometimes because they were so lively!

After two years the hostel accommodation at the college was closed as the number of students grew and more lecture space was required. I went to live with my aunt Chris McRae, in Kensington. She was my father's sister, the daughter who remained single and shared life with their parents on the farm outside Echuca. When my grandfather died, she and Grandmother couldn't look after the farm and they moved to

Melbourne. I am not sure why this was—possibly because my father's two brothers then lived in Melbourne. Grandmother died not very long after the move. The house in Kensington was a tiny terrace with an outside bathroom and a toilet right at the end of the small backyard. I loved living with Auntie Chris and having a bedroom to myself for the first time. She was a wise and loving woman who was a mentor to me in many ways during that year.

While in Kew, I joined the local Methodist Church and its youth group. It was there that I met Barrie McMahon. He invited me to a birthday dance of a friend and we went from there. I invited him to the college balls and he took me to university balls. Neither of us were much good at dancing so we bought a Victor Sylvester book of instructions with diagrams of little feet moving and practised while playing one of his records. He was the first young man I ever went out with and, apart from one trip to a movie with a young man from Geelong during the holidays at home, I didn't go out with anyone else before we married.

Barrie was an engineering student at Melbourne University—a pragmatic, direct sort of person, very different in personality from me. We had our politics and our life in the church in common. I liked his parents, especially his mum. I appreciated the say-it-like-it-is style of relating of his parents; their capacity to be somewhat rude to each other. I found it refreshing after my parents. We never had much money to spend and, although Barrie could drive, he only had access to his father's car on very rare occasions. He later bought a motorbike—a large Bsa on which I occasionally rode pillion. Barrie's parents were quite comfortably off—his dad was the senior investigating engineer for the Victorian Electricity Commission, but they believed in living frugally. They sent Barrie to Wesley College in Melbourne for his last years of high school, but I would have to say that the private-school education did not rub off on Barrie. He refused to be other than his homely self. His two older sisters, Barbara and Marjorie, I grew to love and admire.

Apart from the occasional balls, we basically spent our time going to church youth group activities and pottering around the Yarra River which flowed through Kew. Barrie had a largish canoe and we would paddle as far as we could up the river and walk around the lovely environment. Mind you, Barrie's mother warned me about what could happen to girls who went in canoes at night with young men. I was rather surprised that she was warning me about her own son. At the youth group we had participated in a session on sex. The young men were separated from the women for these lectures. We women were told that we were responsible in the end for the sexual behaviour of men as they couldn't really control themselves like we could. I recall people spending lots of time both around the church youth group and at the college discussing how far you could go before it was too far in sexual situations. Most people saw anything before penetration as permissible.

There were what were called 'parking spots' along the river where people could park for kissing in cars and whatever else they chose to do. Barrie and I were part of this activity and I recall feeling quite anxious about it. I also dreaded the last dance of each ball, usually accompanied by the song 'Goodnight, Sweetheart, Goodnight', when you danced much closer to your partner than earlier in the evening. I still feel my stomach tightening when I hear that song. I was aware of all this going on for me and assumed that it was because I was shy. Barrie remarked on my lack of initiative in our relationship and I tried to respond to his comments. I did like feeling that someone loved me and regarded me as attractive.

I ended my training one mark off being awarded the prize for being the most outstanding student in the college, which confirmed my view of myself as nearly good enough, but not quite. I gained the highest mark for prac teaching and was one mark behind on the academic work. Our graduation was pretty amazing. We were all clad in white evening dresses (mine homemade, of course) and wafted down the staircase of Mooroolbeek like debutantes to receive our diplomas in early childhood education.

When I said goodbye to my close friend Gwyn she said, 'Goodbye, Dorothy. What will I do without you to say "yes" to me?' I laughed and hugged her but felt troubled by her words. Was I really a 'yes' person? Was that who I wanted to be? I knew that she was largely right; that I was agreeable to the point of adapting myself to everybody's needs and opinions. Nothing was too much trouble if the other person wanted me to go that way. I wouldn't compromise my principles but, other than that, I was everyone's faithful servant. I read later about adaptive personalities and could see some of myself there. I also knew by now that I was the sort of person who sat on buses and trains and found complete strangers telling me their troubles or life stories. I felt overwhelmed by this and wore brown clothes and retired into corners in the hope that they wouldn't notice me.

I was offered a staff position at the Lady Gowrie Centre, but Mother thought I should come home to Geelong, where the family now lived, and contribute to life there. I did what I was told, as usual. Before I left Melbourne, Barrie asked me to marry him. He asked me if I loved him and I said that I did and we went from there. I knew that I did love him as a person, but felt somewhat uneasy about the idea of marrying. I decided that this was my problem, as indeed it was, but I hadn't the faintest idea of the nature of that problem. I left for Geelong while Barrie finished his honours degree and did his three months of required military training as an airman.

# 7     Geelong

The family home at Belmont in Geelong was really quite small for a parsonage. It had four not very large bedrooms, one of which had to be assigned for my father's study, a modest lounge room, a small dining room and a galley style kitchen. Carmyl and I shared a room, Thaïs was in a very small bedroom with our cousin Pat Wenn, Mother's niece, who was down in Geelong to attend a private school, and David was in with Mother and Dad. John, who slept on the front verandah with a canvas blind to shield him from the weather, once had a fright when he awoke to see a strange man looking at him. The toilet was out the back, as was the laundry, and the bath had a gas heater which spat and fumed with alarming enthusiasm. We finally had a proper ice chest and later, a refrigerator.

Every Saturday morning we girls would be lined up and assigned our cooking tasks—cakes or biscuits to fill the tins for the week's after-school consumption and guests. The boys did the lawns. We grew to be quite competent cooks. We also made ginger beer and were used to the tops popping off the bottles in the cupboard where they were stored. The laundry was still a major exercise of boiling the copper, rinsing in troughs, putting things through a mangle, hanging them out to dry, damping, ironing, airing and folding before putting away. Dad always helped Mother with this task which seemed to go on for the first three days of every week.

The church in Belmont was very different from the one in Ballarat. It was full of open, loving people—many of them young. During my father's ministry they built a new, larger church and I suspect it was his happiest and most successful ministry. Mother flourished as she gathered her prayer group together to pray for people in general and for healing in particular. There appeared to be numbers of healings associated with her prayer group which I remember as an adult rather than wondering about childhood recollections of people getting up out of wheelchairs. One I recall in particular, was a case of a baby boy being born with an inoperable cleft palate. This was very serious for the child because he couldn't chew properly and was unlikely to ever be able to speak. The group prayed for him and the cleft palate slowly grew across and joined. The specialist attending the child could not believe what he saw. While Mother gained appreciation for her leadership in this area, she never really drew attention to herself or made any claims other than that connection with your God in faithful hope may bring creative and new possibilities, the nature of which we may not determine.

I enjoyed church life in Belmont and played tennis with the church tennis team. Carmyl and Thaïs starred at Geelong High School and John went to the primary school across the road from our house. We all loved holidaying around the coast when people were kind enough to loan us houses in the little places along the Great Ocean Road west of Geelong. The Austin Tourer had finally been laid to rest and we enjoyed our new sedan. We swam and walked and played on the promenade by the bay, watched the Head of the River rowing races and became fans of the Geelong Australian Rules football team and were there for its premiership win (a truly rare event!).

After they finished high school, both Carmyl and Thaïs went to Melbourne University. When Carmyl applied for a course in physics, she and Dad had an interview with the dean of the faculty. He advised that girls did not normally do physics, but my father insisted that she be enrolled in the course. She lived at Women's College and graduated as a physicist with an outstanding academic record. Thaïs also lived at Women's College and completed an Arts degree and a Diploma of Education. She was awarded the university prize in biology, majored in French and went on to be a high school teacher. By the age of 22 she was a state examiner in French. While Carmyl and Thaïs were at university, Mother became very involved in raising money for and setting up St Hilda's College which was the second residential college for women at Melbourne University.

I don't remember feeling resentful that they went to university, although I always envied them, especially their experience of university life which sounded exciting to me. It was obvious to me that they were outstanding students and I recall feeling proud that Dad fought for Carmyl to do physics and gratified that she did so well and showed up the prejudice of the dean of the faculty.

During this time I was offered the position of director of the Corio Preschool Centre in North Geelong. This was a health department kindergarten which was located in Osborne House, an old mansion on the bay, the upper floors of which were used as local council offices. It was near the public housing and industrial area of Geelong and the area where newly arrived migrants often settled. It was the other end of Geelong from Belmont and I travelled on the tram right through the city and out the other side to get to work. So there I was, not quite 20 years old and in charge of a kindergarten. I had one untrained staff person and responsibility for about 50 children overall. At the time, I thought this quite appropriate. These days I would wonder!

We were expected to have a careful plan for each week with story, music and discussion groups each day and to keep the indoor equipment clean and in order. We mixed paints from powder, made our own playdough and often had to prepare clay from powder. We were trained to tell stories rather than read them as eye contact with the children as we related the story was important and, if we couldn't play the piano, we had been taught to play the recorder. We ran regular parent groups as well as teaching and sometimes did home visits. It was all a challenge, to say the least.

The worst thing about the job was the daily lifting of heavy outdoor equipment. There was a basic fixed wooden climbing frame and then all these trestles and huge boards which I had to carry in and out of a shed each day and arrange in creative ways for sliding, jumping and other activities. Since the untrained helper didn't arrive until the children did, I had to do the lifting and carrying by myself.

In the second year of work, Mother decided that it would be good if David could have some preschool experience and so she asked if I could take him to kindergarten with me. He and his friend Johnny came on the tram with me and were picked up by Dad at lunchtime as it was a sessional kindergarten, not an all-day centre. I didn't mind this too much as, although David and Johnny were very lively little boys, they were fun and generally agreeable in class. However, it did add to my responsibilities and there were times when I could have done without it. It was also a bit odd having a teacher relationship with my own brother. At least I got to know David better as I had missed a good deal of his early life being away in Melbourne and I don't think the interlude has really affected my relationship with him in later years. He certainly doesn't see me as his teacher now!

During these two years, Barrie came and went and we corresponded. I don't recall ever going to Melbourne to see him. During his visits to Geelong we began to plan our wedding for March 1956, a few weeks before my twenty-second birthday. Not long before the end of the year in 1955 I became quite ill—unable to get out of bed or keep food down. After my whole body turned bright yellow I was diagnosed with infective hepatitis and had six weeks off work. This was rather a sad way to end my work in Geelong, but I had planned to finish in that year anyway.

I had been taking sewing lessons so that I could make my own wedding dress and going-away outfit and achieved both goals. One of the features of my wedding dress was that it had an 18-inch waist! The church folk prepared plans for the wedding breakfast for us in the church hall and Carmyl and Thaïs were looking forward to being bridesmaids. Mother was rather doubtful about the whole exercise—she wasn't sure that I was old enough or that Barrie was the right person for me. She may well have been right, but not in the way she could ever have imagined, and since she always had negative things to say about my friends and tended to disapprove of any young men who approached her daughters, for once I decided that she was wrong and proceeded. I was a strange mixture of maturity and immaturity—like a child in the ways of the world but with political and religious convictions beyond my years and a strongly

Our wedding day

developed sense of responsibility. When I look at photos of myself then, I appear to be 22 going on 13!

Our wedding was a happy affair with a guard of honour of my preschool children ushering us out of the church. Like most principals in a wedding, I can't remember much of it, other than the photographer doing daring things hanging over the pulpit in order to get unusual angles of the ceremony. We stayed in a hotel in Geelong overnight and were embarrassed to find ourselves with some of Barrie's relations in the dining room over breakfast the next day. You were supposed to disappear after your wedding in those days! Then we boarded the bus to Lorne for our honeymoon, with

Thaïs with her fiancé, John Worner, on graduation day

me hoping I wouldn't be sick on the bus as we wound around the Great Ocean Road. We stayed at a guesthouse in Lorne and were assigned to a meal table with two elderly women who engaged us in playing card games at regular intervals. We left Lorne a couple of days early as our funds were running low. We had put everything we had, plus a generous gift from Barrie's father, into buying our first house at Oak Park, a new suburb of Melbourne and not too far from Essendon Airport where Barrie had his first job designing a helicopter.

Both Carmyl and Thaïs also married before the family left Geelong for Hamilton in the western district of Victoria. Carmyl married Don Winkler whose family was connected to the Belmont church. Don had left school early but worked his way through to an adult matriculation, completed an arts degree and diploma of education at Melbourne University and become a high school teacher. Carmyl worked for a while at the Peter McCallum Cancer Institute in Melbourne while Don completed his study. Then she and Don joined what was then known as 'volunteer graduates' and went to Kutaradja in North Sumatra to teach at the University of Aceh for several years. They spoke fluent Indonesian and made lasting relationships with the people there. Their daughter, Bronwyn, was born while they were there.

Thaïs met John Worner while she was at university. He was a brilliant young physicist whose father was Dr Howard Worner, then Dean of Metallurgy in the school of engineering. John, at the age of 22, was made a fellow of the Royal College of Physicists in London for his research in relation to cancer. He and Thaïs settled at Albert Park in Melbourne.

John and David were still at school and, of course, went to Hamilton with our parents when they moved on from Geelong. The family was gradually separating, but we always met again at Christmas and kept in touch through Mother's weekly letters.

*Part* $3$

Married Life

Oak Park

When we began our married life, Barrie and I moved into a spec-built house in Oak Park, eight miles from the centre of Melbourne. This was a relatively new suburb, although there were a few houses which had been there for quite a while. The railway station had just been opened and some shops established, although there were few sealed roads and no sewerage—we didn't even have septic tanks because the clay soil was too heavy. We had a 'pan service' which meant a truck came and collected the toilet pan from the outside toilet once a week.

Living in a spec-built house meant that a number of your neighbours had exactly the same house and you found yourself planting gardens, putting names on your house and generally doing things to distinguish your own home. Our house had unpolished floors which we planned to seal and polish ourselves. We had a table and four chairs, an ice chest, and a large radio which stood on the floor in the eat-in kitchen. We had some second-hand lounge furniture given to us by Barrie's parents and a bed base, which Barrie had made, and mattress in the bedroom. That was about it, but we felt quite fortunate and gradually added things as the seven years of our living there went by. There was nothing in the garden when we arrived as the house was just set on bare land so we started by planting some native trees and defining the back and front lawns.

Barrie used to walk miles up and down hills to Essendon Airport for work as we had no car. After a couple of years, just after the prototype of his helicopter was built and he had designed possibly the first aluminum tankers in the country, he moved to Commonwealth Industrial Gases

Our spec-built Oak Park house

which was a much larger company—an off-shoot of British Oxygen. At this stage, he was given a utility van for going to and from work and was on call to deal with emergencies which involved him in a good deal of out-of-hours work.

I finished my three-year scholarship bond with the Victorian health department by doing a year's work as kindergarten director of the Baptist kindergarten in Aberfeldie, near Moonie Ponds. I quite enjoyed my time there but already knew that, should I keep on in paid work, I would need to retrain in a different profession—I thought possibly social work. As it happened, according to our plans, I was pregnant a few weeks after I completed my year at Aberfeldie. It was just as well that I had not planned to work while pregnant as I was sick for almost the entire pregnancy, as I was with all four pregnancies.

Christopher Barrie was born on October 16, 1957, after 36 hours of labour on my part. As I began life as a parent, I found myself thinking how sure I had been when giving advice to mothers of small children as a teacher and how much more complex it was to actually be responsible for one full-time. I found just how tiring it is to be the one who feeds

The bright and beautiful Christopher at nine months old

and cares for a young baby. In fact, I seemed to be permanently tired. However, I also discovered the joy of watching Christopher grow and learn each new skill. He was a beautiful little boy—quite serious and intelligent with big brown eyes and dark hair. He went through all his stages quickly and I remember being so proud of him as I mingled with other young mothers and we compared notes about progress. I loved seeing him pick up something and earnestly examine it—often taking things apart and carefully putting them back together again. I imagined him being an engineer like his father. He was walking by the time he was 15 months old and was talking in sentences when his brother Robert Anthony was born almost exactly two years later.

Robert was more like Barrie's family with fair hair and blue eyes. He, too, was a gentle little boy. Weeks after Robert's birth, Christopher went into a total autistic withdrawal and never spoke again. He also acted in constant distress, banging his head on things, crying, throwing himself on the floor and sleeping very little. I am always sad when I think how little attention Robert had as a young baby as a result of this.

We were devastated, of course, and took Christopher to the most prominent pediatric specialists in Melbourne. One of them asked us if he had a difficult grandfather and had the theory that there was some connection between what he saw in Christopher and that fact. We were not prepared to say that either grandfather was particularly difficult, but no other suggestions were offered by this doctor.

Other doctors indicated that he may be having an extreme response to the arrival of Robert or that we were in some ways not handling him well at home. When I indicated concern because he was not saying a word at age three, when he had been speaking well before, our GP said cheerfully that he himself had not spoken well until he was five years old. The suggestion was that we send him to kindergarten where he would make progress among other children. The only person who really stood by us was the health centre sister who had seen him from birth and knew that something was seriously and suddenly wrong.

As a competent preschool teacher, although I realised by now that parenting by anyone was far from easy (not quite as clear as I had been telling parents when I was a young teacher!), I did not believe that we were causing Christopher's problems. I knew he wasn't spoilt as one specialist suggested and I didn't think he was responding traumatically to Robert's birth. Although Christopher was a little younger than we had planned for beginning preschool, we decided to send him there so he could be seen by skilled professionals in the context of normal children and some assessment could be made. It took almost no time for the teachers concerned to tell us that they believed that, whatever the cause, there was something seriously wrong with Christopher and they referred him to a health department psychiatric centre for further assessment.

I was very grateful that by now I could drive and we had a little lime green Mini Minor to carry us into the psychiatric centre for what was to become a weekly visit. Christopher had therapy with the psychiatrist there, I had counselling about parenting and my own life with a psychiatric social worker and Barrie had the same once a month. The diagnosis was still that we were dealing with something behavioural. This went on for a couple of years. Robert, meanwhile, was the gentle and compliant little boy in the middle of it all—the one who had never really known the full attention of his parents as we tried to cope with Christopher. I realise that I have few memories of what he was like, apart from the recollection that he was a dear little boy and no trouble. I think now that he suffered much in all that and it is a miracle and a great tribute to him that he grew up to be a gentle and gracious man.

Oak Park was a friendly place to live and we had very special neighbours—Anglo–Australian on one side and Italian–Australian on the other. We swapped resources, supported each other and compared notes on the raising of our children. Nick and Alda, our Italian–Australian neighbours, had three little girls and then finally a much-desired son. Their son was born on Christmas Day and Nick came running in to tell us with great joy. He said, 'We need an Australian name for our son. We thought we might call him Mario Josephus. What do you think?' We murmured that Mario Josephus did not exactly have an Australian ring about it and he said, 'Well, what have you called your new son?' We said, 'Robert.' 'That's great!' said Nick. 'We will call our son Roberto!' and off he went to celebrate.

I also remember Nick asking our permission to hide behind a bush in our front garden in the early hours of the morning so he could catch a boy who was stealing milk money from the gateposts. It seems absolutely unbelievable now that people left cash to pay the milkman on their gateposts when he delivered the milk early each day. We also left money in the meter box for the baker who delivered the bread and no-one nicked this readily available cash—that is, until a naughty boy from down the road got the idea of doing so. Nick did hide behind our bush and, when the boy appeared, rose roaring out of the bushes clad in his nightshirt. The boy ran for his life and never stole our money again. I often wonder whether that boy thought he had experienced a visitation from some ghoulish creature!

Because of the lack of sealed roads for some years of our time there, I learned to push a pram through wet clay until the wheels refused to move because they were too clogged up. I also learned how not to spin the car wheels when bogged because you sink further into the mud. All very helpful skills which I thankfully have never needed to use since!

Being earnest young Christians we made connection with our nearest Methodist church at Glenroy, which was situated in a demountable building. The members of the church consisted of six young couples who, like us, had just moved to the area, and one older couple who had been there longer. Within the seven years that we were at Oak Park, we built an all-purpose hall for our church and then a church building as the congregation grew.

We were a very close-knit group and much of our life was spent involved in the church and its activities. We prayed and studied together and gradually developed relationships with the community around us. I was still working out my debts to God for not having gone forward at my conversion and so, even with two little children, I worked endlessly for the church and its causes. I was Sunday school superintendent, a choir member, president of the ladies' guild and finally, the big honour, I was asked to be one of the church's trustees. This was unusual for a woman at that time as the trustees were the real power group in the Methodist local church system. I recall awaiting my first meeting—wondering if I should do some special training or preparation. The big night came and, to my amazement, the trustees spent a whole hour discussing the size of the proposed cement pavers to be placed between the hall and the toilets. I was both disillusioned and relieved. I could cope with that sort of stuff!

Then, one Sunday, as I was sitting in church and the minister gave the Bible reading, I heard the words of Jesus, 'I am come that you might have life and have it more abundantly'. All of a sudden I thought to myself that what I was having was not abundant life. It seemed like an endless struggle to please God. I realised that I had been wrong about this God; that life might be a gift. I sat there and looked out the windows and the grass looked greener and the sky looked bluer. I didn't even hear the sermon. We came to Holy Communion and the minister, Bruce Silverwood, who was a very radical man, said, 'Perhaps there are people here today who would like to make a renewed commitment to their faith. If anyone would like to symbolise that by coming forward to the communion rail first to receive the bread and wine, feel free to do so.' I thought, with a great sense of freedom, that I did not need to go forward to earn my salvation. I also realised that I had grown up a bit and was in a loving environment, and that I felt quite able to go forward, which I then did. I asked Bruce afterwards why he had made the invitation as it was totally uncharacteristic of him. He told me that he had no idea why he did it—he just suddenly felt that he should. That began a real moving on in my life—a true moment of liberation.

The original group in our church was still the core of its organisation and leadership, even though the church was growing fast in numbers. Most of us had begun our families together and discussed our children and their developing life. When Christopher suddenly changed, obviously for the worse, they didn't know what to do or say. We prayed for his healing and it didn't happen—my mother prayed too and it was always one of her sadnesses that she couldn't be part of the bringing of healing to her own grandson. One of our church friends asked me what I thought we could have done to have this happen to our child. I was both angry and grateful that the theology which I had been taught had not included a God who would so punish a vulnerable child for the sins of his parents. It was a time when I realised on several fronts how ill-equipped most people are to respond to real trauma in the lives of others.

I also experienced a terrible silence from our friends. We were used to asking after the progress of each other's children and swapping ideas about parenting. That all stopped when Christopher was making no progress at all and they obviously felt it was not appropriate to ask after Robert either, in case I had to compare his progress with Christopher's. I guess they also thought I might become emotional. At that time, I didn't know how to initiate such a conversation and maybe I thought that if I started to cry I might never stop. So I went on being a shining Christian, full of life and hope and joy.

Looking back now, I suspect that many people who live with trauma and daily stress have little option but to press on and survive. There is a sort of numbness which descends upon you which covers over the ongoing questions and pain. Barrie and I rarely talked about the whole situation. I don't think we knew how to do that in our relationship, and Barrie has always been a person to deal with what needs to be done rather than reflecting on things. He was still on call for work which took him away from home a good deal, even on weekends, and I had to take most of the load with our children at that stage.

One thing I was really grateful for was that people in the church simply received and loved Christopher as he was. When he made various disturbances in the church service, they simply said, 'Bless you, Christopher.' You might think this was little enough, but I assure you, this was not always our experience in other places.

One of the great gifts which I received from our friends at the Glenroy church was a powerful moment during a Bible study. We were earnestly studying a little book called *Calvary Road* and we came to a chapter on selfishness. There, listed under the sins of selfishness, was the word 'self-consciousness'. As one who rarely spoke in the group because I felt self-conscious, I found myself feeling really angry and I burst out and said I thought it was very inappropriate to have that on the list as a sin. There was an absolute silence in the group instead of the reassurances I had expected. Then someone cautiously said, 'So when you are not speaking or acting because you are self-conscious, who and what are you watching?' I thought for a moment and then admitted that I was watching the other person's or people's response to me. The group then gently suggested that I might think of watching other people to see what was happening for them and forget for a while what they might be thinking of me. I said no more but went home and reflected on this for a long time. I decided that they were right and so was the book and that it was high time I started watching what was happening to other people and not worrying so much about what other people thought of me. This is not to say that I have no sympathy for people who lack confidence for all sorts of reasons. It was just a salutary truth for me which changed my life. It was not an easy change to make as I still felt anxious about people's responses to me, but I learned to override that by shifting my focus and watching others to see what was happening to them, rather than focusing on their response to me.

In seven years, beginning a few years before we arrived in the area, 75,000 people had been resettled there, some from the slum areas of Melbourne and some as they arrived as migrants. The suburb of Broadmeadows was completed while we were at Oak Park. Much of it was formed by identical houses or a series of houses repeated. There were no hotels, churches or hospitals and not nearly enough schools, even though every family was required to have children to live there. Later we built the first Methodist Church in Broadmeadows and began what was to be the foundation of community work within the suburb.

This was undoubtedly the most radicalising period in my life as we saw first-hand the reasons why the poor get poorer and the rich get richer. We watched the big companies in the area put workers on and off according to their own interests. The casualisation of work has now become the norm but, in those days, you did not expect that when sales dropped a bit a huge company like Ford would simply lay off its workers and then put them on again when convenient. We joined the picket lines outside the factories in support of the struggling workers. We saw how harsh their lives were when we visited their houses—often almost empty because furniture had been repossessed after one default of payment. We knew, on the other hand, that those of us who lived on 'the other side of the tracks' would be given time to pay. We would visit people's houses where apart from the absolutely bare necessities, the only bit of furniture left would be a bookcase containing the *Encyclopaedia Britannica*. The person who lived there would tell you that it was critical to keep the payments up on these, even though they might lack a table for their meals, because the salesperson had told them that those books would give their children the chance they never had.

We noted that people who lived in the housing commission area had to pay up front before they could see a doctor, no matter how serious their situation, while we would be sent an account. We watched as Waltons department store would deliver unsolicited articles to the door of people in the area with a letter which said they could look at them and either pay for them or send them back by a certain time. In response to this disgraceful situation, a group of us developed the 'Waltons Defence Kit' and trained a woman from the area to introduce people to it and advise them how to get the better of Waltons.

We saw people who had been removed from their networks of support in the inner slum areas struggle to survive, even though their housing may have been better. We realised how significant community relationships are in the battle to survive. People told us of young teachers sent into the few schools in the area being unable to handle the large and difficult classes so that children who were keen to learn were unable to get an adequate education. I remember one young teacher who didn't know how to control his class simply making the class stand with hands on heads for the whole lesson. Because it was a tough area for teaching, many experienced teachers didn't want to go there, so many were straight out of training college. I suspect nothing has changed about that pattern.

Perhaps most of all, I realised what real poverty is like. We were relating to people who were economically poor, who had problems in the handling of the slender finances they had and who, for generations, had not had access to more than a minimal education. Often there were few cooking skills so that people bought expensive and less healthy takeaway food rather than cooking at home. We began some cooking classes in the area and people were really glad to have the chance to learn. I saw that even their expectations of relationships were low. If there was a fight, more often than not, that was the end of that, whereas we would have tried to negotiate. It was as though expectations on all fronts were lessened in response to little hope about most things in life. I saw that my experience of financial stringency was nothing compared to the struggles of many people in Broadmeadows. Of course, it rapidly became a 'problem area' with high petty crime rates and, no doubt, violence in the home, although that was a hidden problem in those days. I grew to love the people there and longed to defend them and to try to help bring in the systemic changes which would give them a chance.

In the years when Christopher and Robert were very young, and I was fairly confined in my care of them, given Barrie's demanding job, I felt as though I had little stimulus in my life. I decided to begin my matriculation by correspondence and work on that in the evenings. I studied English and modern history over two years and completed both subjects quite successfully. Apart from the stimulation of the study, I was, of course, proving to my mother and satisfying myself that I could have matriculated. After the two subjects, I decided that I had made my point.

I was also beginning to expand my life into political arenas in a new way. In choosing to do this, I discovered that when your life is pressured by things which must be done, the way you survive is not necessarily by cutting back on other things, but by adding things. In terms of life in general, I have almost always re-energised and restored myself by expanding rather than diminishing my activities. It has some connection with a fundamental optimism rather than pessimism and a sense of claiming life rather than relinquishing it when signs seem to be telling you otherwise.

Bruce Silverwood, our minister, was radical in many ways—theologically and liturgically. He conducted worship in a style rather like Anglican worship which was very 'high' for a Methodist. He was also politically radical and active. Barrie had a keen interest in removing the White Australia Policy and became a foundation member of the Immigration Reform Group which campaigned for an end to the policy. I decided that I was interested in peace and disarmament. I had joined the International Fellowship of Reconciliation some years earlier—a Christian pacifist network, formed during the Second World War—but I wanted to be more directly involved than that. Bruce was a socialist and a member of the peace movement which at that time was usually called the ban-the-bomb movement. He was a leading light in the local branch of that movement and introduced me into its life. Of course, we were all proud of our radical Methodist heritage as the descendants of those who formed the British Labour Party and labour unions.

In joining the local peace group, I met my first communist. She was a middle-aged woman and we met in her house. I remember her well because I found her so impressive and informed, and because she had a German shepherd–corgi cross. This dog had legs the size of a corgi and a body the size of a German shepherd. Its special trick was when you gave it a raw egg, it would make a careful small hole in the eggshell with its teeth and suck out the egg. All very memorable! We talked about world issues and, although I listened, I was careful to separate out what I thought might be communist propaganda and what was likely to be fact. Actually, I rarely found she said anything other than obvious truth from verifiable sources. What we would do with that truth from our differing ideologies might be at variance, but I could see that she was certainly not the devil incarnate as some people would have liked us to believe.

I went on my first peace marches through the city of Melbourne, following people like Jim Cairns who was our local member of parliament. People hissed, booed and threw things at us and shouted that we were communists or pawns of communists. Some of us were indeed communists, but I never met any pawns. We had clear and honest differences within the movement and were very careful to check information we had—more careful than those who did the shouting, in my view. I read a good deal and went to hear various speakers. In the very early 1960s our peace group was already talking about the Vietnam War and forecasting that it would lead to much dissent and disaster for Vietnam.

Meanwhile, the British were conducting atomic tests at Maralinga and the United States wanted to expand its military bases in Australia. We had much information from good sources about the risks involved in all this and raised them in our protest rallies. They were vehemently denied by the government authorities and other leaders in the relevant fields. Carmyl, in her work as a physicist, was doing checks of the air over Melbourne at the time of the atomic tests at Maralinga and she noted a significant rise in radiation as the wind blew the air from the tests over Victoria. She reported this, but the information was suppressed. Of course, the authorities were lying about many things, as was revealed much later. This made me very cautious about trusting politicians when they had much to gain, especially economically and by raising the fears of the electorate. It also made me very wary about the trustworthiness of Britain and the United States.

One day when I was at home, I received a phone call. It was from Auntie Chris. She said cautiously to me, 'Are any of you girls travelling at the moment?' Immediately I knew that something had happened to Thaïs. In fact I sensed that she was dead. The police had apparently been looking for relatives to notify, had somehow connected the name McRae with Thaïs (who no longer bore that name) and had found Auntie Chris and given her a bit of information to see if she was a family member. Recognising that she was not an immediate member of the family, they didn't give her anything definite, but I knew that Thaïs was away and likely to be on the road. A couple of hours later, Mother and Dad, and I think David and John, arrived. They had been on holiday and the police had finally found them to give them the news. I was very glad that I already knew when they arrived and they didn't have the terrible task of telling me. Carmyl was far away in Indonesia.

Both Thaïs and her husband, John, were killed in a road accident as they drove from a Christian youth conference in Adelaide, where they had been singing in the choir, to John's parents who now lived in Newcastle. There had been a storm and the car had run off the road, hit a tree and they had been killed instantly. They were both only 22 years old. We were very fortunate that they were found relatively quickly as the car ran off in an isolated spot and could not be seen from the road. A minister from New South Wales was travelling the road and, after passing the spot, had some sort of instinctive feeling that he should go back and have a look around, which he did in the pouring rain. He then saw the car and its tragic inmates and notified the police when he arrived at the next town. Thaïs had been driving and we will never know if she went to sleep or whether they were simply caught up in the storm and went off the crumbling edges of the road. John's father was notified first and did the brave job of identifying them. Three weeks before they died, they had taken out a life insurance policy to cover them if they died together. Most of that went as a gift to further the work John had started in cancer research.

Three days after Thaïs died, before we had the funeral, I was walking to the local shops with Robert in the pram and Christopher alongside me. Christopher threw himself down on the ground and was screaming and banging his head. I stood and said to myself, 'O God, what will I do?' Thaïs's voice came to me as clear as a bell and said, 'Dearth, take Christopher to see Laura Nesbitt in Collins Street.' (Dearth is my family nickname derived from the young David calling me Dearthra because he couldn't say Dorothy.) I looked around to try to see her because it was all so real. I went home and looked up Laura Nesbitt in the phone book and, sure enough, there was such a person listed in Melbourne's Collins Street. I tentatively rang the number and the phone was answered by Laura herself. I said, 'I feel a bit silly asking, but what sort of a doctor are you?' She replied, 'I am an allergist. Are you, by any chance, Thaïs Worner's sister?' I told her that I was and she said, 'The presence of your sister came to me this morning and told me you would ring.'

As it turned out, Laura Nesbitt was not a doctor but a nurse who had studied with Sister Kenny, the renowned expert on polio, in the United States. She had built up a reputation as an allergist and, unbeknown to me, Thaïs had been referred to her when she had an allergic reaction to the Salk polio vaccination as a young teacher. We took Christopher to see her and she examined him and asked if he had been given an electroencephalograph. When advised that he had not, she suggested that we should ask the psychiatrist who was treating him to authorise one. She believed that Christopher had what she called a 'stabilised allergy' due to his response to his polio vaccination. I recalled that Christopher had been given the booster dose of that vaccine shortly after Robert was born and had been dreadfully distressed after receiving it. We had been told to expect some distress, so I had made no association in my mind with the advent of his autistic withdrawal.

When we asked the psychiatrist if Christopher could be suffering from a stabilised allergy and whether he would be prepared to authorise an EEG, he looked distinctly disturbed and authorised one immediately. We prayed the EEG would at least clarify for us what was wrong with Christopher. The test was carried out at one of Melbourne's main psychiatric hospitals by several neurologists. After it was over, they told us that Christopher was definitely brain damaged. They said that the picture they were getting was 'typical of an allergic response to the Salk polio vaccine'. One of them told me that he would never let his children have the vaccine because he believed that about one in 10,000 children suffered from brain damage after it. We asked further questions about what sort of allergies would cause such a thing and they talked about overly strong antibodies. They advised us that a smallpox vaccine could be fatal—not that Christopher was ever likely to need one. However, we needed all of this information to help us work out how we dealt with vaccines for Robert and any other children we might have.

The diagnosis of brain damage meant that nothing could be done to heal Christopher, but the relief of knowing at last what we were facing and being released from the responsibility for his distress was huge. Christopher has never spoken to us again and I will carry within me forever the grief for the bright little boy he was in his beginnings. We had none of this diagnosis or advice in writing. It was not in the days of high litigation and, even if it had been, I doubt whether we would have gone in that direction. I saw Christopher as a casualty of progress. Almost every school class I had attended as a child had a child afflicted by polio and I knew what a terrible thing that was. I am not an opponent of vaccinations, I just wish the medical profession could find a way of giving tests to children before they are vaccinated. The year after Christopher was brain damaged, the parents of babies arriving for vaccination were asked whether their children showed any sign of asthma or eczema. If they did, they were given a small trial dose, but this was not enough to pick up children who showed no symptoms of allergic response.

This method would not have saved Christopher as his allergies lay in the area of antibiotics and a whole range of food intolerances, which we discovered later. I knew that my mother had an intolerance of antibiotics and obviously Thaïs had had a severe response to the polio vaccine. We can now see it running through my family, including two of my four children. Later, when we had our next child, Lindy, I contacted the NSW health authorities and asked their advice about vaccinations for her. They said that we had a hard choice to make—to risk brain damage or the various diseases covered by vaccinations. That was in fact not a hard choice for us, given our experience with Christopher. I have always thought that Thaïs's love for Christopher possibly saved us from having two brain-damaged children. I am deeply grateful that so many children can safely have vaccinations so that some diseases can be virtually stamped out and members of my family saved from them.

Thaïs's voice of love coming to me after her death convinced me of several things. It confirmed my belief that there is some ongoing after death, at least for a period. It told me that we know more after death than we know before it because Thaïs had obviously not known the connection between her allergic response and Christopher's illness before she died. It affirmed for me that love is stronger than death and reaches towards us from the life beyond us in the universe. When I went to the huge funeral for Thaïs and John, I looked at their coffins in front of us and felt that there was nothing of them there. Thaïs and John were hovering over us in love, free to surround us all in ways beyond our understanding. I felt the presence of Thaïs around me in our house for several weeks after that and then she went.

We sadly sorted through their belongings in the little house at Albert Park and each took a memento of our beloved family member. I still have on my dressing table the little rose-red vase which I selected. Mother tried to cheer us up by saying that our family had really had a favoured life, full of blessings, up until then. I reminded her of Christopher. Dad was full of grief as, in some ways, I think Thaïs was always his special little girl who could break through his reserve. He wondered if he had actually told her he loved her and determined to make sure that he said things like that more directly in the future. All of us, I am sure, were intensely aware of our own mortality and I wondered what it would be like for people to sort out my messy things if I had died then. I still have that thought now and again and get rid of things which will be of no value to anyone else. We had a record of the Melbourne University Queen's College choir in which both Thaïs and John sang and persuaded ourselves that we could hear their voices when we listened to it.

However, life went on and there were battles to be fought and children to care for. When my brother John had his sixtieth birthday last year, his daughter Sally played a piece of music called 'In a Monastery Garden', which Thaïs used to play a lot. To my surprise, I found myself filled with grief, much stronger than at the time of her death and over the years since. I suddenly realised how much I had missed her over the decades— a missing which had probably been clouded by my gratitude to her for the message she gave me about Christopher.

In 1963 Barrie was invited to move to the head office of CIG to become the company's safety engineer, and we were off to Sydney where we knew no-one and had never been. We sold our house, farewelled all our friends in Oak Park and Glenroy and Barrie's family who were in Melbourne, then packed up the Mini Minor and the furniture van and headed to Sydney. It seemed a very long trip up the Hume Highway.

# 9 Greenacre

After a few days in a motel in Ashfield, we found a house to rent in Greenacre which was not too far from where we hoped to buy a house that would be accessible to Barrie's workplace. We once again enjoyed having Italian–Australian neighbours. Our house was owned by the family who lived next door. The owner was a greengrocer who literally trod grapes to make wine in the huge glass containers under his house. The fruits of this activity he then enjoyed with his friends as they played Italian bowls on the little alley which ran behind the block on which our house was built. We felt rather vulnerable so far from our old friends and family.

Our first task was to follow up the referral which we had to the North Ryde Psychiatric Centre in order to find a day-care centre for Christopher, who was now nearly seven years old. We were surprised to find that, unlike in Victoria, there were no such government-run centres for children with intellectual disabilities. We were told to simply pursue the privately run centres of our choice, most of which were managed by the Sub-Normal Children's Association. Quite apart from not liking the name of the organisation, the centres which we explored appeared to have no trained staff and those in the area of our interest had closed waiting lists.

We stayed in Greenacre for six months while we sorted out Christopher's schooling and got to know Sydney a little better. We loved the people of Greenacre who were homely and friendly and we attended the local Methodist church. This was a bit of a shock to us after our Glenroy experience of fine worship, radical and scholarly preaching and the focus on social justice. It was not that the people at the Greenacre church were other than good and kindly people, it was that we were now in another church culture. The church in Victoria, for probably 100 years, had required its ministers to be graduates. They were expected to have at least a primary degree in some discipline and then to become Licentiates of Theology. This applied to all three churches that later formed the Uniting Church. They had long-standing theological halls which accommodated all sorts of university students alongside the people training for ordination. In NSW, the Methodist Church had its own theological college removed from any university. It was exceptional for its ordinands to be graduates and the college library was little larger than my father's personal library at home.

The worship in Greenacre was informal—so informal that on one occasion when our minister was performing a baptism he arrived at the centre of the liturgy and realised that he had forgotten to bring in the baptismal font from the vestry behind the church where it was kept! Not all Methodist churches in Sydney were quite so casual, as we later discovered, but compared to Melbourne it felt like a different church.

We joined the local branch of the Labor Party and that was an eye-opener. At one of our first meetings, we were addressed by the local state member who told us in no uncertain terms why the Labor Party firmly supported the White Australia Policy! We realised that we were in right-wing territory and tried to understand that working-class people might feel as though their jobs were threatened by immigrants. However, why they felt particularly threatened by non-white immigrants, as against others, was hard to defend. We probably stopped being romantic about the ALP at that point, while still committed to it.

At the end of the six months at Greenacre, we decided that the best arrangement we could make was to send Christopher to Inala, a Rudolf Steiner school in West Pennant Hills. We chose this school because the staff were trained in the education of 'children in need of special care' and were seriously interested in the nature of his disability. We had not given any of his history to the school prior to our interview with its principal, Dr Pohl. When we entered her office, she drew Christopher towards her, put her hands on his head and said, 'Brain damage caused by his polio vaccine, is it?' I was astonished and asked how she knew. She said she had struck such cases before and had a sense of who Christopher was.

Rudolf Steiner and his followers believe in a form of reincarnation in which people choose after death which part of themselves they need to develop in their next life. Thus they believe that people who have an intellectual disability may have been a genius in their previous life and now wish to live life without the advantage of a strong mind. Whatever you think of this world view, what it produces is education which is respectfully and carefully planned and which is given by people who choose to spend their lives giving that care as part of their incarnational journey. There was a strong focus on music, art and drama and a love of the natural environment. In the seven years of Christopher's life at Inala he made more progress in emerging from his autistic withdrawal than at any other stage, but was still in need of constant supervision.

# 10 Eastwood

In order to make it possible for Christopher to attend the Steiner school and qualify for state-provided transport there, we found a house in Eastwood which was to be our home for the next 25 years. It was in this period of our life at Eastwood and later, Chippendale, that my life expanded and changed in many ways.

Our house was in the centre of Eastwood, a few doors from the local state school. As Robert was nearing school age, this was very convenient. Barrie was a fair distance from his workplace, but later his firm fortuitously moved to a nearer suburb. Our house was a solid brick Federation one on a large block of land with a lovely garden at the back. There were initially three bedrooms but we added another later. Again, we had Italian–Australian neighbours who became good friends to us, our children and our cats!

We joined the local Methodist Church which had a largish congregation of people, many of whom had been there for several generations. When we attended for the first time, Christopher made a few noises during the service and I was tapped on the shoulder and told that there was a crèche in the Sunday school hall. It was probably a kindly offer, but it felt as though children's noises were not acceptable in this church and I knew that the crèche volunteers would be unlikely to be able to handle Christopher. We gradually moved to taking it in turns to go to church, with one of us staying at home with Christopher.

Soon after, I approached one of the church leaders after a service to ask if there was any way I could be of use—did they need another Sunday school teacher or any other form of helper? Having been so much involved in our church in Melbourne, I wanted to get my usual life in place again. The person replied firmly that they didn't need anymore people—they had plenty of teachers and other helpers! Of course, all that changed later, but it was a signal for me to find my place in groups outside the church in political and community life.

Within a few weeks of moving to Eastwood, I was pregnant again. Not really knowing anyone well in Sydney, we planned for Barrie's mother to come up from Melbourne to look after the children while I went to hospital for the birth. Within days of the due date, Barrie's 95-year-old grandmother was hospitalised and close to death, so his mum couldn't come to us. For some reason, my mother couldn't come either, so Barrie had to take time off work to look after Christopher and Robert. On the morning when I went into labour, Barrie came out with masses of spots which were diagnosed as chickenpox! He dropped me at the door of the hospital with as many nightclothes and other resources as we could muster and went home to suffer from the awful experience of adult chickenpox. Our daughter Lindy Louise was born on August 30, 1965 and we celebrated, if apart!

Lindy came into the world looking carefully around her. She was a quiet and cautious little girl and because Robert was by now nearly five years old, she had three devoted carers. She was very artistic and was always watching people and things and making drawings of them. At three years old she was doing drawings of people in profile which is rather exceptional. She was quite reserved and rarely moved more than a metre away from me as a young child. I took her everywhere with me—including to meetings.

However, anyone who underestimated Lindy soon learned differently. She would observe the world, make her judgements about it and then act or speak, no matter what it cost her. She might then be upset at the response of others, but that didn't stop her doing exactly the same brave thing the next time she thought something should be challenged. She was later renowned for fronting up to teachers and schoolmates alike if she thought justice needed attending to. I used to watch her with some anxiety

The troubled face of Christopher, 1968

because I could not imagine having such a level of courage as a child. I also remember an occasion when we sang a hymn at church which had words including, 'Nothing is impossible with God'. Lindy came home and advised us that she would never sing that song again. When asked why, she said that, if nothing was impossible for God, why didn't he make Christopher better? Good question!

Three years later, on May 10, 1969, Melissa was born. She came into the world in such a rush we barely made it to the hospital. From the beginning she looked expectantly at everyone and assumed they were her friends. She was adventurous, lively and very bright. When we were out I always had to watch her as she regularly headed off to explore the wider world. I was always chasing her around supermarket aisles and she was not nearly as peaceful as Lindy if taken to meetings. I remember once coming to a street corner in the Eastwood shopping centre and seeing a promotion was taking place with a huge green St George dragon. I had Melissa in her pusher and I thought to myself that I had better quickly move in the other direction in case she got a fright on seeing the dragon. I looked down to see if she was anxious and then realised that she had already climbed out of the stroller and was running towards the dragon.

Robert, Melissa and Lindy near their cubbyhouse, 1972

By the time I caught up with her she was standing holding its hand and looking into its face with great interest!

Of course, all three younger children had to grow up mighty fast as so much of our energy and time was taken in caring for Christopher and they had to adjust to life lived with his behaviour. They all had school reports which commented on unexpected maturity for their age. They looked after each other a good deal. Robert was always having gatherings in his room and generally entertaining his sisters. Melissa took it upon herself to do quite a bit of supervising of Christopher. I can still hear her saying firmly, 'No, Chrissie. Don't do that!' I remember once, when there was a partial eclipse of the sun, Lindy heard about the dangers of looking at the sun while in class. Lindy was so concerned that Melissa might come out after school and look at the sun, that her teacher finally let her go over to the infants school to warn her. The first I knew of this was Melissa coming out of her classroom with her head facing the ground hardly able to see where I waited for her in case she got a glimpse of the sun when she raised her head to look for me!

The three of them did well in school, all qualifying for the area's selective opportunity class which was situated in their school. Being the ideologues we then were, and sometimes still are, Barrie and I decided not to let them enter that class because we felt it was discriminatory and would separate them from the wider range of children. That may well have been the right decision for Robert and Lindy who, at that stage, seemed to do better with encouragement rather than competition. However, I think it was probably the wrong decision for Melissa who thrived under extra pressure and stimulation. She almost defeated us anyway by choosing all her friends from the opportunity class and then getting higher marks than any of them. The opportunity class teacher took pity on her and invited her to various outings and extracurricular activities.

They each made their own mark in school—Robert with his art, Lindy with her music and leadership and Melissa with her imagination. I recall being shown Melissa's essay on pets which her class had been asked to write. She chose to do it on relief teachers as pets and described in detail how to handle and train them to do your bidding!

Even on holiday, Barrie and I had to share what amounted to 24-hour care of Christopher. Barrie's job as an engineer entailed fairly long hours and much responsibility, but his care of Christopher when he was home was exemplary. In some ways he was better with Christopher than I was, even though I obviously had to take the major load at that point as the one at home. He was endlessly patient and attentive and took the initiative in changing and bathing Christopher ahead of me.

Christopher was a major responsibility in those days. He was not toilet-trained and was unpredictable and lively. He engaged in all sorts of activities like a toddler, but with the enhanced capacity of a growing boy. He once took a canister of flour, tipped it into our wardrobe and then mixed that with a jar of honey! He would empty the rubbish bin over the fence into our next-door neighbours' place, so we quickly added some wire netting to our side fence. He took all our wedding photos, apart from those in an album, and threw them into the burning incinerator. He would run off down the street, diving into shops and seizing a sweet bar or two and just keep going until either we or the local police picked him up. At one stage he liked stroking and tapping shoes and when he found the shoe shop he went in there and moved around stroking all the shoes on display! People didn't know quite what to do as he appeared to be fairly normal and was almost adult size at 14 years old. The house became like Fort Knox, but of course there was always the time when someone forgot to secure all the locks and off he would go.

Christopher ate everything in sight with quite unpredictable selection—any sort of food was rapidly consumed and we needed to keep the kitchen cupboards locked. On top of that he like chewing up paper, including the homework of his siblings, books were fair game, soap, anything at all that he could get in his mouth. I will always remember three-year-old Melissa coming to me and saying urgently, 'Mum! Mum! Come and stop Chrissie! He's eaten the shepherds and the wise men and now he's going to eat Mary and the baby Jesus!' Sure enough, Christopher was busy consuming her cardboard nativity scene. You have to either laugh or cry with things like that happening around you.

At one point Christopher was at Inala, Robert at Marsden High School, Lindy at Eastwood Primary School and Melissa at the local preschool. To do my duties as a parent in all these schools was a challenge; however, I did do my stint at the tuckshop at Marsden High, attended parent open days and created numerous outfits for Easter bunny parades and Library Week events—with some success, I might say! One of my better efforts happened when my mother was staying with us and, as Lindy was about to step out the door and walk the 100 or so metres to school, she suddenly said, 'Oh, Mum! I forgot, I have to be dressed as a rabbit at school this morning!' I calmly and quickly resurrected some rabbit ears from somewhere and on the way to school we bought a bunch of carrots. When I came home, Mother told me firmly that none of this would have happened if I wasn't a feminist and not paying due attention to my children and, what's more, it was wasteful to buy a whole bunch of carrots for Lindy—a single one would have done! I must say I took all this with a grain of salt. I was beginning to appreciate what I could affirm in my mother and told her how lucky I was to have a mother who when visiting would do some ironing and clean the windows. We raised funds to support Inala, as well as paying fees, and I was in charge of the children's wear stall for the annual fete. I recall in one year sewing nearly 100 items of clothing for the stall as well as making virtually all the clothes for our children.

We tried to interest our children in the scouting and guiding movements—Barrie had been a very keen Scout and his father a commissioner in the movement. Robert was briefly a Cub, Lindy joined the Brownies and Guides for a while, but it was little like the experience which I had—the local Guides seemed to be concentrating on etiquette! Melissa decided very quickly that she wasn't going to dance around any toadstools and polish badges. We faced that the new generation was different to us and enjoyed less ritualistic activities.

Cats were part of our life for all the years at Eastwood and cat stories abound in our family. There was the cat who stood beside Lindy and made a howling sound every time she played her flute—we never knew whether it was agony or ecstasy! There was the kitten who loved to sit on top of the piano and play with the nearby light cord until she, by some amazing process, got the cord knotted around her tail and we found her swinging by her tail to the tune of loud screeches. There was Megsy, a large dignified ginger tom, who was with us for a long time. One day we came home to a neighbour who had to break the bad news that Megsy had been killed after being run over by a car and was lying on the road. We sadly picked up what was left of him and gave him a special burial ceremony in our back garden. We then retired to the house with tears and stories of Megsy. As we sat there, all of a sudden, in walked Megsy. He surely was amazed at his welcome! Obviously we had buried someone else's ginger tom.

Sausage was the most memorable cat of them all. He was a very ordinary tough tabby tom—fiercely territorial at all times. He assumed that his territory stretched widely in the area and woe betide any other cat who crossed into it. Our next-door neighbour, an elderly woman, was fond of Sausage and gave him quite a bit of her attention. However, I was very surprised when she leant over the fence one day and asked whether I had noticed how fussy Sausage was about his food. I said that we only fed him very common tinned cat food. She said that she liked to give him snacks and had found that he mostly preferred a little 'lightly cooked whiting and eggflips'. The next development came from the neighbours two doors down who said they were getting quite attached to Sausage because he came in their cat door each night and slept with their cat on the sofa—rather than our garage. Sausage was undoubtedly a very well-organised cat. One day I was looking out the kitchen window and, to my surprise, I saw Sausage sitting in the middle of a circle of six cats eating his breakfast. When he finished eating, they made way for him and that was the last time that any of us saw Sausage. The mysteries of life and death and cats are boundless!

In the early days, when the children were very young and most of my time seemed to be spent at home, I felt as I had in Melbourne. I knew that nothing could be changed in relation to my responsibilities, but I needed a greater challenge to expand my life. I racked my brains for something meaningful which I could do. Christopher was only in care for a few hours in the middle of the day and in those hours I needed to get the housework and shopping done and fit in anything else that I wanted to do, so there wasn't much time. I decided to go in two ways. I joined up with two other women, one from our church and one from the Baptists, and every month we held a lunch in our homes for a handful of elderly or incapacitated women referred to us by the local community centre. Two of us would pick the women up and the other would cater for a simple lunch. Then we would all take them home. We did this together for several years.

I also decided to become a Life Line counsellor, volunteering to go on the phones at night when Barrie was home caring for the family. I did the basic training and worked on the phones and later as an emergency face-to-face counsellor for suicidal people for the next seven years. When I did the face-to-face work it was as part of a pair who would be available to be on call through the night and into the early morning for emergency visits. One of my partners in this task was Sergeant John Avery who was later to become Police Commissioner for New South Wales. He did this as a volunteer to balance his police work and was a great partner—a fine and gentle man.

If I learned anything in this work it was that when people are suicidal, they have usually lost any sort of sense of their own worth; they feel there is nothing of themselves worth saving. They may be full of anger, of pain, of guilt or despair, but underlying all this is a profound lack of worth. In the deep of the night, when energy for survival is at its lowest, we would sit with them and try to find one thing that we saw in them which they might value in themselves. We never knew whether they survived past that one night, but it was our task to bring them to a level of hope which would inspire them to voluntarily come with us to get professional help. We mostly managed that.

I will always remember trying desperately for hours to find something for a lonely middle-aged man to celebrate in himself. In the end, we uncovered that he had worked in a chicken factory and could kill more chickens in one day than anyone else. That memory was enough to save his life that night. Another time, we noticed that the man we were counselling had a carefully folded coloured handkerchief in his pocket and had well-groomed hair. I pointed out how good those things looked and he straightened himself up and said that he had tried to look dignified through all the struggles in his life. He decided that he was worth saving at least for that night. Of course, I know that to hold onto life for one more night is only a beginning. In every case, I pondered the aloneness of so many people and felt deeply grateful for being loved.

Eastwood at that time was an upper working-class and lower middle-class area. Its people were often tradespeople or public servants—solid, steady and conservative in every sense of the word. Their votes rarely shifted by more than a couple of hundred for the whole 25 years we lived there—two thirds Liberal–National Party and one third other parties. We were among a very small handful of people in our church who voted ALP and the only ones who had membership of the party which we now moved to the Eastwood branch. We were both active in the party, which was relatively easy, given that the structure and processes were almost exactly the same as those in the Methodist Church. The followers of the founder of Methodism, John Wesley, who started the Labor Party also saw his careful agendas for meetings, prepared for the guidance of working-class people, as very suitable for a political party.

In 1971 Barrie stood as the Labor candidate for the state seat of East-wood. I was campaign director on a couple of occasions and once stood for preselection for the seat of Parramatta. I have to admit that I had no intention of actually getting up. I had agreed with our left faction to see if I could split the vote in order to bring forward a centre candidate. I 'ran dead' apart from addressing the local branches, but gained just a few too many votes to make our numbers game effective. The priests in all the Catholic churches in the Parramatta area were instructed to tell their people that any ALP members were not to vote for me because I was a feminist and would support abortion. I must say that, as I glimpsed what it would cost to get up as a candidate, I didn't feel like proceeding anyway. I was active in the Labor Women's Conference and met many fine women there. I left the party in the early eighties because I became fed up with endlessly trying to push resolu-tions through a system which I felt simply gathered them all into a file in the NSW head office. I also had an altercation with the chairperson of the local branch who insisted that we rise to speak in a meeting of about six people. It seemed to me to be a ridiculous formality.

In that period, possibly because I was seen as active in the ALP, I was sometimes asked to speak alongside the state member for Eastwood, Philip Ruddock, at things like the local school Anzac Day service. I recall coming home from one such effort and saying to Barrie that knowing Philip Ruddock had forced me to recognise that there were some people with integrity and a commitment to justice and human rights in the Liberal Party, even if their ways of achieving that might differ from mine.

I look at Philip Ruddock, now Attorney General in federal parliament, and wonder where that man went.

Both Barrie and I were connected with the radical church movements which had as their slogan 'Live simply that all may simply live'. Barrie was a very keen member of Action for World Development and I did my bit through the Ecumenical Council and its overseas aid work. I was never very good at living simply—I think I felt I had done enough of that in my childhood. Not that I lived extravagantly, but there was a contrast in degree between Barrie and myself—Barrie has always been a person who lives with absolute frugality while giving generously to those in need, both in money and time.

My ideological commitment to living simply, such as it was, was challenged by two events. On one occasion a devotee of the movement introduced me to someone as 'One of the McMahons who bought the carpets'. We had indeed bought some modest carpet for our lounge room to replace the layers of threadbare bits and pieces that were there and obviously this was seen as not living simply enough. Then one of our children spoke of some good friends as being less than acceptable because they 'had a big car'. I really didn't want to raise children who judged people like that. To me it smacked of the fundamentalism of the left and self-righteousness. I made real changes in myself and my attitudes to others at this time.

My belief has always been that if stressful things cannot be changed, it is best to expand rather than diminish your life if possible. However, I am aware that this expanding outward into a myriad of things may well have been my way of refusing to face things in myself of which I was afraid at that point in my life. Perhaps, had I been able and prepared to do that earlier, I might have saved myself and those I hold dear some pain later.

Mrs Martin was a wonderful older woman who lived locally and was prepared to babysit our challenging family. She was quite a small person, but she took on Christopher which meant we could go out at night for meetings. I don't recall doing much else—so serious about life were we!

No-one had ever offered to babysit for us and we had always hesitated to ask people, knowing what was involved. We could at least pay Mrs Martin and that made it possible for us to feel free to ask her whenever we needed her. She got to know the children very well and they loved her. Later on a young woman called Ann-Maree Codrington, whose mother had been one of the women with whom I had shared the providing of the monthly lunches for 'shut-ins', also babysat for us.

In spite of this help, we were still moving towards the difficult decision of Christopher's future. By the time he was about 14 years old, he was bigger than me and still not toilet-trained. He was every bit as active and although Inala School was doing a great job with him, they felt they would not be able to cope with him in residential care. Barrie and I knew that whatever else happened, we should make provision for his future care in a way which ensured that the other children would not have to bear the burden of that. We were aware that the friends of our other children were loath to visit because Christopher acted strangely, even though he was no danger to anyone, and that he had a considerable impact on their lives every day. We also knew that unless he was in a state institution by the time he was 16, the only option for Christopher even a few years later would be admission to a psychiatric centre in a ward for old people with psychiatric problems or dementia.

In the end, we went through the state assessment system and Christopher was placed on the high-priority list for placement into care. Just weeks before his sixteenth birthday he was admitted into residential care at the newly established Marsden Hospital in Westmead. Marsden was a new way of setting up institutional life in that it was a large hospital but built in smaller cottages around a campus. It was new and attractive and Christopher seemed to make a fairly good adjustment to his changed situation. Christopher is in some ways well suited to institutional life as he is rather obsessive. He likes to live in a ritualised manner and is disturbed by change. At Marsden he could no longer have access to food other than what was put in front of him at mealtimes. The staff quite quickly managed to introduce a measure of toilet-training, which made life easier for us all. He was also medicated for the first time and that made him much calmer. We had him home for one weekend in each month at that stage. Even though we could see no other positive way forward for us all, it was still a very tough decision and had a number of ramifications.

We explained to our other children as best we could why we were sending Christopher away. However, you can never really adequately explain to a seven- and a four-year-old why you are sending their brother away. Robert grieved for the brother he never really had, but I hope understood our decision. Lindy attached herself as firmly to me as possible, presumably so that we would never send her away. Much later, when she was doing her personal therapy in preparation for registration as a psychologist, Lindy told me of the separations from me which she needed to make. I think that Melissa subconsciously decided that she would excel at everything so that she would meet our standards for staying. I realised that there is always a cost, whatever decision you make in these circumstances, and who can tell which is the greater? In some ways, it may be most honest for me to simply say that I needed Christopher to go because I couldn't cope any longer with devoting my life to him. I say that with grief, but not guilt.

The response of some of our church friends was interesting. Most of them had not really taken any notice of Christopher and had certainly not shared in his care in any way. However, when we sent him into hospital, one of them said disapprovingly, 'I thought if God had given you Christopher, God would have given you the strength to care for him.' I told her that I thought that Christians lived corporately and that Christopher had been given to us all. I indicated that I had not noticed much of the church gathering Christopher into its embrace and that I was grateful that some people in the community had a vocation to be psychiatric nurses and would share with us in his care.

You never really recover from sending away one of your own children, no matter how necessary it seems to be. When I was writing my previous book, *Rituals for Life, Love and Loss*, I found myself crying as I prepared a meditation on loving a child with a grave disability and a ritual for sending someone you love into care. I watch with deep respect parents and other carers who give their lives for another. That is really what it is—a giving of one's own life. When people ask why we should sustain the lives of people with severe disabilities, I admit that I can see no real point in Christopher's life beyond what he calls forth in others in love and care for the vulnerable. I hope and believe that one day, when his broken life joins universal life, he will have a chance to live in some way which gives him all that he is due for, or that his vulnerable life is gathered into the fuller life of some other person who comes into being in the future.

Christopher went into care at the same time as Melissa began preschool. So, after 16 years, I was suddenly on my own for a good deal of the day and with what seemed like almost no responsibilities. At first I felt desperately tired. I think that, when you live from day to day basically surviving, you can't afford to really feel what you are experiencing because you might go under. When it all stops, you can then let yourself feel both exhaustion and relief. After I had a brief rest, I found that I had this huge and quite unfamiliar energy. So, what would I do with it? I thought I might try relief preschool teaching. I did that for one day and knew that I had been right the first time; that it was not my real profession. Besides, I had just lived through 16 years of caring for a child who never grew beyond early pre-school in development and that was enough.

Just at that time, my good friend Jean Skuse, who was Executive Secretary of the NSW Ecumenical Council, had to enter hospital for significant surgery. She asked me if I could go into the council for several hours a day and help with the work related to the Christmas Bowl Appeal. I agreed to go for a few weeks and ended up staying for eight years—as Associate Executive Secretary for part of that time. This decision was to change and influence my life in many ways.

Our children went on to Marsden High School which was a good co-ed school with children from differing socio-economic backgrounds. Robert, a rather small, quiet little boy, grew tall and slim. He achieved an excellent matriculation mark and his major work for art was chosen for the state exhibition. He decided to do a Diploma in Fine Arts. Lindy was school captain and did equally well. She also had her art major work in the state exhibition and played her flute in the Sydney Youth Orchestra.

By this time, I had completed my training for ministry in the Uniting Church and was ordained and appointed as minister with the Pitt Street Uniting Church in central Sydney. We stayed in Eastwood for a couple of years and I remember driving Melissa to school one day and having her ask me to drop her a block before the school so that she wouldn't be embarrassed by her friends seeing her with a minister. She got over that later!

As I reflect on my life from 1970 to 1985, I can only imagine what I did to myself and everyone around me. There I was, passionately participating in all these movements, travelling overseas to various conferences, working and studying part-time and finally ministering with a challenging parish, and caring for the three children who remained at home and sometimes Christopher. I recall one salutary moment when I was sitting at the table having a cup of tea. I came to to hear Lindy's voice saying, 'Mum didn't hear you, Melissa. She might look as though she is just having a cup of tea but she's really thinking.' I also remember Lindy saying one day that she sometimes wished I was home all the time like her friend's mum, but then she thought about it and realised that she would like to have a life like mine when she grew up.

Barrie was a real example in the days when very few husbands had wives who went to work, studied, travelled overseas alone or were politically active. He bore the load of that in many ways and I will always be grateful for his generosity and respect. I think now that I asked a great deal of our relationship in that regard and a lot from our children. I sometimes wonder whether I was really cut out to be a mother, although I did my best and I am grateful that our children are still my friends, even if they have told me the hard truth about some aspects of our relationship over the years.


The last ten years of our marriage were full of the signs of its ending. In 1975 I knew that I was attracted to women. In the mode of the period,

I told myself that this was just an honest admission of impulses that possibly lie in most people. I congratulated myself on my self-awareness and refused to face that this had any real significance in my life. Running alongside that was the conviction that I was not happy in our marriage and that as our children left home, I felt I could not spend the rest of my life alone with Barrie—not that he was anything other than a good man, but I felt that we were not sustaining a life-giving relationship.

I am sure that some people will blame the fact that I was an enthusiastic feminist for these developments in my life. This is only partly true. Certainly we feminists were challenging the traditional views of marriage and working towards more mutuality and equity. However, I was not part of the women's movement which thought that marriage in itself was wrong for women. I believed in marriage and I still do. Where my life did interact with the women's movement at that stage was in the belief in 'consciousness-raising'; in the deep reflection on the realities of our lives, in ways which we may never have done before. Indeed, I doubt that I ever had time or given myself time to do that before. T.S. Eliot once wrote in his *Choruses from the Rock*: 'Where is the life we have lost in living?' I know now that I did indeed lose a lot of life in the living. Once I stopped and gave thought to what I felt and reviewed my life, I knew that I was in trouble. I only shared these thoughts with a couple of close friends and I couldn't even really put a name to what the central issues were.

Instead, I began thrashing around trying to find my way through to what I wanted or needed. This sounds very self-focused and in some ways it was—I have observed that most of us become self-focused when we are in trouble. Perhaps we have to do that to survive. Obviously in other ways my behaviour was not so self-focused. It was about the future of my marriage and how I could make my way towards something real, something true and something as good as I could achieve for everyone concerned. At a few points I tried to engage with Barrie in achieving this, but now I know that my heart wasn't in it and he found it hard to understand where the problems were lying—understandably, as I wasn't clear about that myself.

In the journey towards the ending of our marriage, I guess I did no better than most and worse than some. I related to Barrie and to other people in ways which became very significant parts of my life journey, but which were wounding and betraying and messy. In some ways, I betrayed my own ethical standards. I recall my dear friend, Jean Skuse, who by this time was General Secretary of the National Council of Churches, taking me aside to ask me what I thought I was doing to myself, and she was right to do that, even if I fended her off at the time. Barrie responded in ways which asked for more honesty than I was offering and in ways which gave him self-respect, even if they didn't solve our problems anymore than I was doing. All this taught me that I am as messily human as anyone else and now, when I see relationships breaking down and think that people should sort out the primary relationship before entering others, I know that this is likely to be harder than we might think. Most of us fear to be alone. Some of us don't really know where we are in the middle of a relationship breakdown and, as we clutch at people, we think we can survive in ways which often do harm to others.

# 11  Chippendale

In the middle of all this chaos, in 1985 we left Eastwood for Chippendale. Melissa was in Year 10. We looked at high schools around the area and found that none of them carried the range and level of subjects she was doing. We applied for her entry to Fort Street, an elective high school, and she spent her last two years there where she blossomed and gained an outstanding Higher School Certificate. Robert had left home by this stage and was working as a public servant for Legal Aid. When he was offered the position of office manager he decided to leave and spend a year travelling overseas before returning to follow a career in the arts—in music, art or drama. Lindy began her honours Arts Degree majoring in psychology and later moved into a household with student friends just down the street from our house.

We loved our house in Chippendale—a modern terrace and very convenient to the inner city. As it had many bedrooms and bathrooms, we were joined there by our young friend Christine Ledger who was working for the Student Christian Movement and, for a time, my nephew Michael Winkler.

Part of my problem in working out my own life at this stage was that, in spite of my earlier perceptions about my sexual orientation, I genuinely did not recognise what lay at the centre of the conflict, pain and disturbance. It was not until 1986 when I got to know Jenny Chambers, that I at last faced where the problem lay. I was really a lesbian; that was my true orientation. When I later reviewed my life, I could track the signs going right back to my adolescence and could see that much of my activity had

Melissa, Robert, Lindy, me and Barrie at Chippendale, 1986

been a flight from this truth. I knew that I had never really enjoyed heterosexual sex. I used to read the many books on frigidity which were around in those days and simply assumed that I had a problem, possibly caused by a fairly inhibited approach to sex in my family. I wondered if I was with the wrong man. The truth was, my feelings of attraction to women in 1975, which I then put to the back of my mind, were not some complex part of most people—they were absolutely central to my identity and life.

The fact that it took me almost half a century of life to discover who I am surprises many people. In some ways it doesn't surprise me. I am of a generation and culture which didn't even say the word 'homosexual'. I must have heard of people who were attracted to people of the same sex in my younger years, but I have absolutely no recollection of this. Looking back, I certainly recall people saying things about single women living together like, 'Mary never married. How sad. But isn't it wonderful that she has a friend like Jane to live with'! Of course, no men would have ever lived together—after all, they had the choice to go out and get a wife.

I was trained by my parents and the church to turn my eyes away from myself and look after the interests of others. I am not sure that I did this so very well, but it certainly used up my energy and time. The 16 years of looking after Christopher at home diverted me and soaked up my life and when he went into care I raced out into the world and put all my passion into struggles for justice. While the women's movement brought me into much closer encounter with myself, it also placed me into contact with lesbians for the first time. Not that they in any way tried to seduce me into their lifestyle. I had a couple of lesbian friends, quite by chance, among the many women I knew and not one of them ever invited in me the possibility that I was of their orientation. Some straight friends from that time told me afterwards that they knew before I did that I was probably a lesbian. Apparently I wrote a poem for one of our publications which revealed me as one.

Just weeks ago I was asked for an interview by a great young student from one of Sydney's high schools. She was doing an HSC project and had the transcript of a women's 'speak out' from the heady days of the women's movement, when women met to speak out on a particular theme. It was from the time when lesbians were just beginning to challenge other women to let them take their rightful place. There I was, telling the story of how some women might think that I was a lesbian because I had written a love poem about women in general. It should not make people assume that I was a lesbian because straight women could write such poems, I told them all. Well, maybe they can too, but I wasn't one of them! Looking back, I wonder how on earth I could have been so unaware. I guess, in some respects, I took a long time to grow up.

I want to affirm with great conviction that homosexuality is not caught. A tiny number of very radical women made deliberate choices to relate to women rather than men, but I was not of their number, and nor were my friends. After all, why would I be seduced into becoming a lesbian? What did I have to gain other than the truth about myself? There I was, married to a good man and with four children. I was also a minister and a minister's daughter. What would be the rewards in pursuing some ideologically driven lifestyle in the face of that? I can never understand why people ever consider that people are persuaded to identify as homosexuals for the fun of it. The greater truth is that some people die rather than do that because of the hate and rejection which surrounds them.

Most certainly I had nothing to gain but my authentic life and I found that this was everything. Once I really knew who I was, there could be no return. I could do no other than deal with it and put the future in the hands of God. I remember saying to my God that what I was about to choose felt like jumping off a cliff. I would now say that when I jumped off that cliff, I had a clear sense that the hands of God were beneath me. This is not to say that I had some wonderful, calm and well-handled exit from our marriage and before I moved into a new life. I wish I could say that, both as a person and as a minister. The only thing I can say is that the whole process which followed was brief and I had no intention of anything other than immediately sorting everything out.

Barrie guessed I was involved with someone and that it was a woman and challenged me. I think he still hoped to save our marriage. We went to relationship counselling and the very fine counsellor, Michelle Webster, had my measure in a flash. She would not allow me to give double messages about commitment to Barrie and my determination to leave him. She also made it clear that I could not comfort him and care for him while I was the one ending the marriage.

I am sometimes asked whether I regret those 32 years. No, I don't. I don't think of life as something which could have been more perfect had I known what I know now. I rather think of life as a journey which winds around, makes detours and passes through all sorts of wonderful countryside on the way, even if it is not as direct a path as we might choose. This doesn't mean that I do not regret thousands of things which I chose to do and be along the way. It just means that I know I am human like everyone else. I am not sorry that I met Barrie McMahon and I hope and believe that he is not sorry that he met me, even though he is now married to the special Sara who invites in him things which I did not do.

Our marriage was made difficult by the power battles and the correcting which I offered into it, quite apart from the limitations which must be there if you marry a non-heterosexual. I know now that, for the whole of our life together, I was keeping my distance from Barrie—creating an indefinable space between us. I am enormously grateful that I had the chance to have children, in spite of being just a 'good enough' mum. (I am told by my children that this is so!) Had I claimed my sexuality 50 years ago, I am sure that I would not have had children because that would have been impossible for me in the cultural climate of that time.

I am also glad that I had all those years to contribute to the life of the church so that, when I 'came out', the church would at least have to ask the question about how it had recognised my life and ministry even during the period when I was a lesbian.

Was our marriage a lie? On one level it was. It was never a true marriage of body, mind, heart and soul and I knew it wasn't right from the beginning, without knowing why. However, there was much love within it and as two people we chose to share life together for all that time. Our children were conceived in all the love we had for each other and we wanted to have them. None of it was anywhere near perfect, none of it was as it should have been. We both love our children and our little grandchildren and step-grandchild and care for them together. What we were unable to give them was a good picture of two heterosexual people deeply in love with all the intimacies that give evidence of that in everyday living—the touching in love as you pass, the obvious warmth and delight in each other, the shared laughter and confident flowing of a relationship. I hope they see that now in our present relationships and in other good marriages around them.

*Part* 4

# Choosing a New Life

# 12 Coming Out to My Children

I took so long to come out to myself that I thought it would not be surprising if my kids did not believe me when I finally told them that I was a lesbian. By the time I had sorted myself out I was more than 50 years into my life and 32 years married.

Some years before I faced my sexuality, I recall Lindy standing at the foot of our bed and saying, 'Mum, are you and Dad in love? I am trying to work out what being in love is like and when I look at you and Dad, I am not sure you are in love. Sometimes I think you don't even like each other very much.' I mumbled something about there being many different sorts of love and ways of showing it. I should think it is rarely the case that when anybody comes to the point of breaking the news to their children that they are lesbian or gay in their mature years that those children will be shocked to realise that their parents have not been in a wonderful marriage. However, it is a very different thing to see weaknesses in the relationship between your parents and to be told that their relationship is at an end.

Barrie and I decided that we needed to wait for the end of Melissa's Higher School Certificate before we told our children. We also agreed that we could not face waiting until after Christmas to do so, even though this was only a matter of weeks away. Somehow, the thought of going through a family Christmas as though we were still a happy family seemed impossible. Both these decisions were, I think, the right ones, although Melissa told me later that she had said to a cousin that she suspected she was about to become the child of a broken home before she began her exams. Obviously the stress in the house was clear to her even though we had not made anything explicit.

Barrie and I had brought our children up to respect differences in people—racial, cultural and in sexual orientation. They had met people who were gay or lesbian and therefore I knew I would not be facing homophobia when I revealed my own sexuality. There had been a period, several years earlier, when I had noticed that someone in our household regularly turned the spine of a large book named *Homosexualities* to the wall when inviting friends to visit. I believed that had more to do with earlier dealings with puberty and wanting to avoid embarrassment rather than lasting personal views!

The plan was for all of our children to hear the news at the same time. However, there was one moment which I later regretted initiating with Lindy. It was one of those moments when you feel so close to your child that you forget they are your child and offer information which does not belong to them at that stage. Before I had gone through all the appropriate processes with Barrie, and some months before I was ready to tell everyone in the family, I had said to her, 'I think I might be a lesbian.' I was so self-focused at that stage that I failed to even notice how shocking and significant this information was. For me it had been a moment of self-reflection which I felt free to share with her. For Lindy, even though there had been a sense that all was not well in the marriage, it was a dreadful moment of truth about impending divorce. It also affected the balance of relationships—between parent and child, between siblings and between parents—in a most damaging way.

Later, as an older and very self-respecting person, Lindy rightly faced me with my lack of appropriate boundaries. So great had my self-absorption been at the time, that when I was told about how that breach of boundaries had felt, I couldn't easily remember having said it at all. In fact, what I had done was to ask one of my children to carry a burden of knowing something very important alone, before I had properly dealt with knowing myself and before I had gone through carefully prepared ways of telling our children all together.

Lindy did not know whether her father had been told what was in my mind and, being a responsible person, was scrupulously careful not to share my information with others. This meant a lonely journey indeed. I will always grieve this, even though I think we have now sorted things out between us. It alerts me to the fact that, when I am in high trauma myself, I am often out of touch with reality. This is understandable, but a warning to me that I need around me trusted people who will help me to be more aware of my state of being. I suspect that I am not the only one who has this experience.

The level of my trauma at that time was evident when I came to write this story and could not bring to mind exactly how I told our children that I was a lesbian and was ending my marriage with their father. So great was the pain that I had blocked the details from my memory, even though I can remember the feelings I had, gentled though they are now. I certainly remember that I believed it was my responsibility to break the news, seeing the decisions were mine. One of the critical things was that there were two bits of news and they were both traumatic. The fact that your parents are leaving each other is one thing. The fact that your mother is a lesbian is another.

I am reminded by one of my children that I broke the news of the ending of our marriage and my sexuality when all the family, plus their cousin who was living with us at the time, were together in a friend's house. My son was looking after the house while the friend was away. We sat around the table and apparently I said that our marriage was ending and that I thought I was lesbian. Robert, I think, was the only person who said anything. He said something like, 'You should have done it long ago.' The others were numb with the shock of it. Robert said later that he had long sensed that all was not well. In some ways, I suspect it freed him up a little to talk about how he had experienced his parenting in general. However, I could see that he had not guessed that I was a lesbian. This did not seem to bother him, even though it might have been a surprise.

Lindy didn't say much at the time, but I knew that she was really hurt by it all, even though as a person who has always been very committed to the truth, she knew there was no other way forward. She had naturally hoped for a united family in her future. Because she was more closely related to the church than my other children at that time she was more aware of the possible consequences for me and my work in the church and there were more people around her with whom she could not share the truth. Ten years later, when I very publicly announced that I was a lesbian, she was one of the first to phone me and say how very thrilled she was because now she could talk about me with church friends. I had not really considered this aspect of having a lesbian mother.

Melissa, in spite of her earlier comments about being the possible child of a broken marriage, tells me that she was very shocked. She felt that the whole marriage had been a lie. Even though she had not seen ours as an anywhere near perfect marriage, we had been telling her by implication that we loved each other and now she wondered if she could trust anything about us and relationships. She wondered whether, when I said that I loved her, she could trust this to be true. Was this also a lie? She wondered whether she had been conceived in love. She felt that, in waiting until after her exams to tell the family, we were implying that people who have finished their high school years are to be regarded as adult and therefore able to cope with things, while she felt still like a child. All this disturbed her deeply, far more than the news that I was a lesbian. In fact she told a friend at the time that she thought my being a lesbian was 'glamorous'!

We were very fortunate indeed about Christmas. We had some good friends, John and Norma Brown, who we told about the situation and they graciously included us all in an invitation to join their family Christmas picnic in the Botanic Gardens. While, of course, we still could not play happy families, it meant that we could all be there together outside our home environment and do the best we could while being cared for by others. Even the fact that it was an outdoors picnic somehow helped because we could spread out and go for little walks and focus on the beauty around us.

Within a few weeks, on New Year's Day in 1987, I gathered some things together and left home to stay with a friend while I found a house of my own. Barrie was away and that made it a little easier but I would honestly say that ending my marriage was the hardest thing I have ever done. Thirty-two years of life is not easily laid aside and in one sense, I never have laid it aside, just moved on from it. The family home was almost immediately placed on the market.

When Barrie and I had settled our affairs (Barrie doing so very generously), I bought my little town house in Leichhardt. I will always remember walking in its doors and knowing with a sense of wonder that this was the first time I had really wanted to go home for a very long time. While I would never want this to be seen as a negative comment on Barrie or our children, it just framed the truth for me that I had never really been at home in heterosexual marriage and that, whatever it cost, I had now come home.

Melissa moved in with me for a few months and then she took off for Paris as she had said that she would do from about year four!

When she said she was going at the age of not quite 18 and all by herself, I pretended to myself it might not happen if I did nothing much to assist. She finished school, set to work to earn some money, told us that she assumed that we would add to that the allowance that we had given to the others, arranged for her visa and ticket, connected with a student hostel in Paris, packed significant amounts of op shop clothes and off she went!

Melissa was the one who was closest to the reality that I was a lesbian as when she returned home my partner, Jenny Chambers, was often in our house and regularly staying the night. It is one thing to know in your head that your mother is a lesbian, quite another to live with it. Although my children all had to make the adjustment to relating to another person as part of our family (indeed two extra people when their father remarried two years later), Melissa was much more directly connected to this at that early time. She did it very gracefully in my view, while astutely seeing that it was probably not the relationship which would ultimately be the right one for me.

One of the things I found hardest to cope with was the newfound need I had to explain both my sexuality and the ending of the marriage. Most parents of any sexual orientation do not discuss their sex lives and relationships with their children. We certainly never did with our parents. Some of this reticence is usually appropriate and some is not. I imagine that in the ending of any marriage, no matter how mutual, most parents feel a desire to explain their side of the situation. This inevitably seems like an attack on the other side. My children would agree, I think, that I veered between a sense of responsibility for it all, a sense of guilt, and a need to defend myself.

If I could have the time over again, I would try to be much more aware of the level of shock I was giving my children about a whole range of things. I would also be much more careful about discussing with them the ways I was handling the situation myself—how confidential my life was, who I was telling about things and what my hopes were for how they would handle it. I would then talk about how my decisions related to their interaction with others and their support for themselves.

I had also simply assumed that my children would share the truth with their closest friends at least. Indeed a little later, I asked one of them about dealing with having a lesbian mother when it came to friends. I was told that the strategy was to judge which friends could cope with it and tell those who could and not tell the others, and that this was fine.

In all, I would say that my children were truly remarkable in their continued love and support for me, and also for their father. We didn't talk much about the situation—regrettably, we never did have the habit of doing that in our family. In fact it is writing this down which reveals the conversations we never had and the misinterpretations we had at the time. In spite of this, their care and respect for both Barrie and me was marvellous, something for which I will always be grateful. Lindy, not very long after receiving the news, was applying for her first job. When the second interview was offered and it looked as though the job might follow, she made it clear to them that, if there were homosexual clients, their lifestyle would be affirmed. This was said knowing that the institution concerned was not normally affirming of homosexual lifestyles. I am relieved to say that the job was still offered.

Of course, when my marriage ended, I needed to advise my parish, which I did. They stood by both Barrie and me, and Barrie, understandably, moved to another parish. I also told the parish leaders and, over a time, most of the members of the parish, that I was a lesbian. They stood by me in a way which moves me still when I think of it.

My children went through at least two major phases in dealing with my sexuality. The first was when I came out to them. The second was when I came out to the world ten years later—indeed it was literally a national and international coming out because of my role in the church by then. I regret to say that in spite of the reflections above, I was still my often unaware and inconsiderate self as I handled this new state of our life. Perhaps because they were all older, I assumed that what I had decided about my life and my ways of handling it would have little impact upon their lives.

A few months after I came out publicly, I was approached by the producers of ABC television's *Australian Story* to see if I would be the subject of a program. I was warned that it would be an intrusive process and was invited to think carefully. I figured that I was experienced with the media and that anyone else involved could decide if and to what extent they wanted to participate—after all, I said to myself, they were all adults. Wrong. Yes, they were all adults, but I had produced a situation where my choice significantly reduced their real freedom to choose.

As Ali, my partner pointed out, if my husband agreed to participate, it was very hard for her to refuse. As my children demonstrated to me, if one of them decided to participate it made it very hard for another to refuse in case that was misinterpreted, and if all of them refused people would almost certainly interpret that as disapproval of me. Being the loving and loyal people that they are, all of them agreed to participate and we went through more than 30 hours of filming for the program and waited anxiously to see what the producers would do with it. To say that it was harrowing would be putting it mildly! Each of my children had said that they needed to be very honest. A couple of them decided to tell me some of their thoughts before they went to air, so that I would hear them personally before I heard them publicly. Until a few hours before the program was shown, none of us knew what it would look like. Ali and I watched the advance copy with a bunch of good friends for support.

Most of us sat there with tears in our eyes as the program unfolded, and I gave thanks for having, in spite of my far-from-adequate parenting, fine children. They were prepared to stay with me on my rackety journey through life in ways far beyond my deserving. They did not avoid calling me to account as an ordinary failing human being, but they called me back to my humanity in honest and healthy ways. They refused to participate in making me a heroine or taking me too seriously. They were cheeky and fun and revealed themselves as mature and healthy human beings. They challenged those who would elevate hate as an appropriate way of life, especially the church. They supported me as a lesbian with firmness, courage and pride.

No children should ever need to produce courage in themselves in order to claim and own their own mother. Even my writing of this story asks my children, yet again, to bear some of the weight of my choices; to be exposed in what are really private journeys in order to challenge the attitudes present still in society. One day there will be a world where no child is required to do this simply because their mother is a lesbian or their father gay. In this new century, some of us will work to bring about the changes so that we are all included in society as diverse and wonderful human beings who have a right to love as we were made by God. May that be so one day, and may that day be soon.

In the meantime, for the last two years, we have all celebrated Christmas together—Barrie and Sara, Ali and me, with all our children and grand-children. We had always done that for birthdays, but Christmas is another thing—and we've made it!

# 13 Owning My Sexuality

I suspect that there is a continuum of sexual orientation. The people at each end of that line could not imagine having a sexual relationship with, in the case of a heterosexual person, a person of the same gender or, in the case of a homosexual person, with people of the opposite gender. They actually speak of being revolted by the idea. Then there is everything in between with bisexual people in the middle, which is possibly the hardest place to be. While this is my view, I believe we have much to learn about sexual orientation. Using this theory of the continuum, I would place myself somewhere maybe about 75 per cent down the line—well and truly homosexual in orientation but not at the extreme end.

Perhaps this is why it took me so long to decide who I was. I can only say that when I dared to claim homosexual orientation, there was not one shred of doubt in me. I am a lesbian and, whether I realised it or not, I always have been. People, especially in the church, often talk about sexual orientation as though it is about sexual activity alone. They see it as some sort of temptation to a particular type of sexual activity and you just have to decide to stop doing that and all will be well.

In fact for people like myself, and many others with whom I have spoken, the reality of our orientation is absolutely profound. When you 'own' your orientation it is like finding yourself and coming alive in ways which are impossible to describe. It is like at last fitting into your own skin. When I finally came out publicly, I bought myself a brooch depicting a flock of birds flying high because that is how I felt. I was flying free in the universe and claiming my real place in it. I was soaring into the clouds in joy and peace and moving into my future as a whole person at last. It felt as though all the fragments of myself were finally coming together and I was settling down into a serene peacefulness. Nothing could touch that, no matter what lay ahead, and I have never had a single moment of regret that I chose to live my life as I believed it was truly meant to be.

I felt a wholeness of body, heart, soul and mind in this relationship which was something I had never known before. As a person who had lived all their life in the church, I was in no doubt about the fact that some of the church would disagree with my joy and my understanding of the leading and grace of God. I knew where those people were coming from, especially in their approach to scripture, but I disagreed with their views and believed that, in doing so, I was being more true to mainstream biblical scholarship and theology than they were.

The churches which formed the Uniting Church in Australia (Methodist, Presbyterian and Congregational) had not trained their clergy in a literal view of the Bible for more than 70 years. In this, we were and are part of a whole respected stream in the church internationally. As the daughter of a Methodist minister who was a fine theologian and biblical scholar, I had never been raised to view the Bible as a literal document. It was always presented to me as open to interpretation and answerable to the witness of Jesus and the Gospels—neither of which even mention homosexuality, which is very strange if it is such a deadly sin.

Gradually I informed the church about who I was—person by person, group by group, and then publicly at our assembly in 1997. Knowing the church very well, I was not really surprised that I had no option but to resign my job as National Director for Mission at that stage. The church in general has, of course, ordained thousands of faithful priests and ministers throughout the centuries who were lesbian or gay—some celibate and some not. I believe that it would prefer us not to reveal ourselves because, in its heart, it knows that we do indeed have the gifts and grace to be ministers and priests and this challenges the view that we may be 'abominations'. I also believe that the Holy Spirit is challenging the church to change on this issue and that the question will not go away until the change takes place.

When we try to sort out who is representing God most truly we need to remember that Jesus said, 'By their fruits you will know them'. He said that firmly to his disciples who were trying to work out who were the real followers of Jesus and who were not. I look at the fruits of those who oppose us and see mostly exclusion and hate, and often abuse and even violence. I see people who seem not to notice the grace and gifts of the people they are denouncing, who have no respect for their loving relationships and who themselves seem often to be obsessed by sex. I have also experienced people who disagree with me and are yet quite loving— or try to be. The trouble is that when people speak of loving the sinner and hating the sin, it is hard to experience them as truly loving when the 'sin' is so completely linked with one's sense of being.

I have been told, 'You are just clinging to this lifestyle because it makes you happy, Dorothy.' What a strange thing to say. I suppose they mean that sinfulness sometimes seems to make people happy, but it is really a form of self-indulgence. I can only say to them that I think I am capable of seeing the difference between sinful self-indulgence and the deep peace and happiness which is a gift from God. I suspect that most people are. I am a serious, responsible person. I am a Christian minister who regards that calling as a grave and sacred trust. I can only say that I have no sense of indulging myself in sinful temptation in relation to my sexual orientation. Far from it.

I believe that I am being true to my creation before the God who made me and that I am now engaged in a responsible and loving relationship which deepens my experience of God and the life of the spirit. I also believe that a life lived in true relationship with God is profoundly joyful and we should expect it to be so. I do not believe in a God who mocks us by creating us differently and then saying to us that we should not express that difference. Nor do I believe in a God who mocks us by telling us that what we experience as beautiful and genuinely life-giving is a sin.

When I consider why God made us differently from some others, I just look at the creation itself and see its infinite imagination. Why should we all be the same? We are of differing races, languages, histories, cultures, appearances and abilities. Maybe God had an another idea about difference. Or maybe we simply evolved that way at some early stage. Why not? Who are we harming? Nobody that I can see. In some cultures, homosexual people have been regarded traditionally as the particularly creative members of the tribe, or the people with special gifts for healing. The idea that we are threatening families ignores the fact that we are all part of families and can be creative members of them with no more negative impact than any other diversities which lie there.

There are words for homosexual men and women in the old tribes of most cultures. Sometimes they are words of approval, sometimes not. Sometimes the disapproval stemmed from the need for the tribe to procreate—that was probably a factor in the Hebrew tradition. Well, in world terms, we are hardly short of children now. Sometimes people disapprove of particular sexual activity in which they believe we are engaged. I have never heard anything mentioned which is not also practised by heterosexual people.

The fact that the apostle Paul did not approve of homosexual activity in a particular context of time, place and culture is to be noted but not necessarily authoritative for Christians. After all, we do not follow his thoughts about it being best not to marry at all. We no longer affirm slavery as he did and most of us have real questions about some of his ideas for relationships between wives and husbands. In fact, Paul was not really too inspired about issues of human relationships in general—his strengths lay in other directions. He was very wise when he discussed the relationship with God, especially the free and gracious relationship with God, through Jesus Christ. The biblical witnesses were mostly stronger in that area. They did their best to interpret and order their own community and personal lives through their understanding of God, but they were very clearly people of their time and place, just as we are. In fact they had no word for 'homosexuality' as such and clearly no concept of homosexual orientation. It is strange that conservatives take advice from ancient peoples on this issue when we would simply assume that they had much to learn on many subjects which have become more developed over the centuries in the company of a living God.

The Uniting Network was set up around ten years ago for gay, lesbian, bisexual and transgender people and their friends to further justice in the Uniting Church and I am proud to be part of that. Our opponents have referred to us as the 'homosexual juggernaut' which is somewhat laughable considering the fragile people included and our lack of funds and minimal capacity to organise. However, we have achieved a good deal—much of it, in my view, because many people in the network are deeply respected by those around them in the church.

It is a strange thing to battle for your right to exist. In the women's movement we were on new ground because the struggle was for ourselves, rather than some cause, but it was never about our right to exist. As a lesbian, the fact that I am and live out my life in this way is in itself part of the struggle. I am also proud to be the patron of Twenty-Ten which is an agency which cares for young gay and lesbian people at risk.

I live with joy, not just because I am who I am and find delight in claiming that, but because I have found the love of my life. Sometimes I find this so overwhelmingly good that I wonder if I can ever deserve it. Then I realise that I waited almost 60 years for this relationship when most other people assume they will have this experience many decades earlier in their lives. Most of the time I don't think of my sexual orientation at all. I simply rejoice that I go home to the woman I love, the one who expands my life every day—the one who makes real the concept of being in love.

Thanks be to God for this gift, a gift which invites a flight of freedom towards the songs in the universe. It is, indeed, a life of joy.

# 14 Jen

In 1985 I met Jenny Chambers. I had been conducting a funeral of a very distinguished woman and there were around 300 women at the funeral, including Jenny who sang during the service. At the wake afterwards she came up to me and asked, 'Are you a lesbian?' I gulped, looked into her eyes and answered, 'I might be bisexual'. She said, 'Oh good. What's your name and address?' She later rang and asked me to join her in a 'non-pastoral' dinner, which I did. Then she went overseas for some time and it was not until the following year that we met again. During that period, I nervously reflected on the reality of my sexuality and what this might mean.

In relating to Jenny, I faced the fact that I was not heterosexual or bisexual, I was indeed a lesbian. I am grateful to her for many things. The first is that she was not the sort of person to participate in messing around with either my life her hers. She had the courage to demand that I make my choice to be in a relationship with her or stay in my marriage and nothing less than that. In my heartfelt agony around the whole situation, I may have been tempted to try to hold things together.

We never lived together during the seven years of our relationship. I suspect that, had we done so, we would have had a shorter time together, so different were we in a multitude of ways. We often said that we were an odd pair, but I have no doubt that Jen was a critical and significant part of my journey and I will never regret the time I spent with her. Jenny was a teacher specialising in English as a second language. She had worked her way to a university degree after being sent to work in a factory as a young person by her adoptive mother—a battler par excellence.

I will always remember her introducing me to marvellous groups of lesbian women and the wonder of knowing that I had found 'my tribe'. It is really hard to describe this sensation to others unless they have had a similar experience. It was as though everything in my person wheeled together in a way I had never known before. It was like having walked through all of life as a stranger and now no longer being one. I should qualify this by saying that, beyond Jen's immediate friends, I also found that there were many different cultures within the lesbian community. Some were not even feminists—that was a shock! There were as many different lifestyles as there are in the heterosexual community, and not all of them were mine. After the initial excitement, this bonding with the lesbian community didn't separate me from the heterosexual world. On the contrary, I simply felt more peaceful and whole as I went on with my life and work on the wider front.

What did Jen give to me, apart from identity and new friends? She made me take myself less seriously—she taught me to play. She would sit in the back row of Pitt Street Church and, after I had received the plaudits of some of the congregation for my sermon, would say, 'You put on that parsonical voice again today' and bring me back to earth. She never was a member of Pitt Street Church, but she would cheerfully drift in and out of there occasionally. There was a certain mad wildness about her that stirred up my previously rather serious existence. We did a lot of laughing.

She also introduced me to the world of dogs! I will always remember the stern dignity of Scrumpy who sat in his basket and surveyed the world as he pulled out virtually all his hair. The fact that he looked absurd in his nakedness was no matter to him. He was supervising the world regardless. Then there was Bonny the Cavalier King Charles spaniel who was so enthusiastic that she was impossible to train beyond the simplest commands.

Charlie, her friend of the same breed, was something else. He could extract a Mintie from the depths of my bag, unwrap it, leave the paper beside my bag and eat it. He once seized the lunch of a friend who popped in briefly. When we returned to the kitchen all that was left was one lettuce leaf placed in the centre of the plastic wrap from around the sandwiches. Charlie didn't like lettuce. He really excelled himself when we were having a surprise birthday celebration for Jen. I brought the large fruit cake in from the car and put it in the bedroom ready to carry in in style. Two minutes later, all that was left was a small pile of crumbs mixed in with candles and decorative paper. Charlie didn't last much beyond that day!

Sometimes there is a question which moves you on your life and Jen once asked me such a question. After I had, as usual, corrected her in something she had said, she asked, 'Do you always have to be right?' I thought for a moment and then said, 'Yes'. I reflected on that further and faced the fact that I was the sort of person who often went around correcting people or arguing them around to my point of view—usually in the nicest possible way, of course! I asked myself whether I wanted to be that sort of person and whether it mattered that people said things, often of little importance, which in my view were incorrect. I decided that I wanted to reflect on my tendency to think that I was right, and, as far as possible, only make a stand when something was significant. I think our family history had a fair bit of 'correcting' activity in it and that wasn't always a good feature.

Jen and I were probably at our best together when we were on holiday. Apart from being a teacher she had qualifications in archeology. She would go back to England for regular digs and showed me around many parts of Britain. I will always be glad that I was part of her search for her birth mother back in Grantham. She had not had a good relationship with her adoptive parents and had always longed to find her real mother. At long last she decided to take the plunge and really seek her out.

When she located her mother's address, Jen was in England by herself. Her mother didn't know she was looking for her; Jen had been following clues which her adoptive mother had given her before she died. Jen rang me from Grantham and said, 'I think I know my mother's address. What should I do now?' I replied that I didn't know what she should do. Jen then said, 'I think I'll go and buy a bunch of flowers and just knock on her door.' She landed up at her mother's door about forty years after they had parted company and said, 'Hello, I'm Marion (her original name). I think you might be my Mum.' Her mother replied, 'Oh my goodness! You'd better come in and have a cup of tea.' How English can you get?

I think that Jen tried to leave me several times before she eventually ended the relationship. We were very different—held together by many strands of need in each of us. When she said that she was going, I was full of grief, but it only took me a few months to recognise that she was right, and that I had known deep down for quite a while that we did not belong together. She is still my friend—a very endearing person. I will always admire her courage in walking what has been a very tough life, including that of facing me and the many truths about myself.

*Part* 5

# The Church and the World

# 15 The Church

After our uneasy beginnings together, the Eastwood church had given me various representative roles at regional levels which later led to roles at the state and national level. From my highly nervous beginnings, I was gradually gaining confidence in speaking and debating. I was a regular member of the state conference. If I was finding my place in the structures of the church it was partly because, as a feminist Christian, I believed that women did have a place there and I wanted to take my place if I could. As there were so few women in these roles, some of us became token women on many councils and committees. People assumed we spoke for all women, which we never claimed, and they gave us attention and critique which they never would have given to men doing the same thing.

One of the excellent things about being in New South Wales was that no-one knew my father—I was no longer Colin McRae's daughter of whom much was expected and, if delivered, taken for granted. I was myself. At one stage I was surprised to be asked to address the Victorian state conference of the Methodist Church. Each year they invited one person to do this and, on this occasion, I was the one. It was a sort of state-of-the-church address. I sat on the platform and looked over the several hundred members of the conference. The president rose to introduce me. He said, 'We are so happy today to have Colin McRae's daughter to speak to us . . .' For one moment, I thought to myself, even now I am not my own person. Then I saw my mother and father sitting glowing in the audience and I decided that I had grown past that and could be happy to be known as Beth and Colin McRae's daughter.

I was deeply involved in working with Presbyterian and Congregational people in the preparation for the formation of the Uniting Church in 1977, especially in the area of social justice structures. I remember in 1976 being a member of the last NSW state conference of the Methodist Church before it became absorbed into the Uniting Church. At that conference, as was the Methodist tradition, we had lined up before us a number of men who were coming before the conference for permission to be ordained after concluding their training. As usual, they were asked various formal questions, including whether they were prepared to abstain from alcoholic beverages.

While all but one replied 'no', I sat there and listened and reflected that, whatever the general desirability of refraining from drinking alcohol might be, the Methodist Church had become obsessed with this sin above all others—if it was a sin at all. The thought that anyone would break a relationship with other Christians because they differed on this issue, while staying with people who might be guilty of any other sin, was bizarre. It also smacked of a dreadful self-righteousness. I had just read that most alcoholics come from families which were either total abstainers or alcoholics, so we didn't seem to be on good ground anyway. I stood up and said all that in the debate, including the thought that we had created a monster in being so obsessed with this issue. I then went out for lunch with some others and decided that I would daringly have a drink and that it would be a glass of alcoholic apple cider. It sounded and tasted very innocent and refreshing and I drank it down rapidly. As I floated around in my head and my legs felt weak in my previously alcohol-free body, I learned that all is not what it seems!

I was one of the nine women out of about 250 delegates at the final general national conference of the Methodist Church which met in Melbourne in 1976. The members of the three churches proposing to unite had voted to go into union, but this vote needed to be ratified by votes of each of the three national bodies. The Congregational Union had voted by about 90 per cent to go into union a few days earlier. The Presbyterian and Methodist national bodies were meeting concurrently in Melbourne. After some discussion, we took our vote and it went through by 87 per cent. We sent a delegate to advise the Presbyterian Assembly of our decision while we waited for theirs. We sang hymns, said prayers, and just chatted with each other, growing more uneasy by the moment. Then, all of a sudden, the doors into the hall swept open and through them strode a man wearing knee-breeches and waving a three-cornered hat with tears streaming down his face. It was the moderator general of the Presbyterian Church and he had come to tell us that his assembly had voted for union. I hadn't seen a Presbyterian moderator in full regalia before. We all stood and cheered and cried as we waited for him to tell us more. The Uniting Church is taken for granted these days, but this was a momentous and historical time—the fruits of nearly 50 years of negotiation.

We had the huge inauguration service in the Sydney Town Hall, including the wonder of women moderators (state heads of church) for the first time for those of us who had come from the Methodist and Presbyterian tradition. It was all very inspiring and hopeful as a new combination of people opened themselves up to a new future. One of the best things about it was that the old power groupings in each denomination were not recognised by the people from the other two denominations. We genuinely didn't know that you should bow and scrape to certain people when they stood up and said something silly in the debates—this came as a great shock to some of them. I recommend a union of different institutions as an excellent way of shaking things up so that people have to earn their places as leaders rather than inheriting them—it might be a good idea to have some of our political parties do some uniting! Not that anything lasts for long, of course. In the end, power corrupts and we collude with all sorts of destructive forces in our own interests, whatever our efforts. I sometimes think that the human condition demands that there be breakaway groups from all institutions. Then they gradually institutionalise and we need another radical challenge. Such is life and the church is no different.

By 1975 I was being asked more and more to take services for churches all over New South Wales in my role with the Ecumenical Council. Without being ordained, the one thing I couldn't do was to preside at the Eucharist and I was beginning to realise that I had a sense that I longed for that responsibility. I think I have always had an attraction to ritual life and a sense of the 'magic' and power of it.

At our church in Eastwood we had a guest preacher, Dr Gordon Dicker, from the United Theological College. He preached on the Bible passage about Zaccheus, the corrupt tax collector, who climbed a tree to see Jesus as he passed by among crowds of people. Jesus saw him there and called for him to come down because he wanted to have dinner with him. He went to his house and challenged him to return to the people what rightly belonged to them—which Zaccheus did. For some reason, which was quite obscure to me then, I experienced this story as my profound call to ordination. After the service, I asked Gordon Dicker if I could begin studying theology part-time as I wanted to go on with my work for the Ecumenical Council and not put too much pressure on my family. He said he thought that would not be possible as people only studied full-time. However, when I approached the principal of the college later, he agreed to allow me to begin the course part-time. I began studying at the United Theological College in 1976 with a view to ordination.

My feelings as I began the course were interesting. I loved being a student again with the challenge to read, the vigorous discussion and even the part-time feeling of being somehow less responsible! I now and then felt truly angry as I learned so many things which the church had never passed on to me as a lay person. There I was, after 42 years in the church, learning some quite basic modern Biblical scholarship. I felt cheated and determined that I would do better when I was a minister. It was in some ways an odd relationship I had with the lecturers because I was sometimes their colleague on councils and committees and at other times their student. However, we seemed to work out the issues and boundaries quite well.

Over the four years part-time and two years full-time study I was often the only woman in the class, or one of only two women. The Methodist Church had just decided that it could ordain women and the Uniting

Church came into being 18 months later with ordination of women firmly in its constitution. The few women who were in training met on one occasion and compared notes. We agreed that our experience ran like this: when we were first in class, we would try to contribute to the discussion and we tended to get one of two responses. The men would either ignore us altogether and then sometimes actually give recognition to what we had said when a man said it later. Or they would respond with words like, 'Nobody thinks like that!' Then, after we had some exams or assignments where we women did well, the men would start to realise that we were there and that we might actually have something to say. Later they would begin to treat us like honorary men and tell us sexist jokes, sometimes about their wives. All of a sudden they realised that we were real live women. Some of them were fascinated by this and tried to get even closer to us, some ran a mile in case they were tempted and a few felt quite comfortable with their sexuality and ours. We decided to share these experiences with the men of the college and they were mostly open to hear us. Some of them said that they had never really had women friends, other than their wives, and weren't sure how to handle such relationships. I must say, we wondered how they thought they were going to relate to the mostly women members of the church! Later, more work was formally done by the college on these issues.

Soon after I started studying I began to have uneasy feelings about moving to ordination. I discussed these feelings with the dean of students and other staff on several occasions. They defended ordination, not really knowing what was going on for me. Of course, my feminist friends were not entirely supportive of my decision in the first place—they thought I was joining a patriarchal and hierarchical organisation, and to some extent this was true. Around that time the college invited a speaker from the United States to conduct workshops among us. All I recall of him is that he was rather opposed to the concept of the ordination of women and made a fairly convincing case for that view. I became even more anxious. Then some other incidents happened in rapid succession. The principal of the college, Dr Graeme Ferguson, introduced me to an overseas visitor as, 'one of the most powerful women in the Uniting Church'. I challenged him and he said, 'Well, Dorothy, I see you demolishing chairpersons of presbyteries in the synod and assembly all the time.' Then when I was at the yearly synod meeting two young ministers came up to me and said, 'Dorothy, we need a heavy to help us get this resolution through. Will you help us?' A 'heavy', I thought indignantly! I am an underdog fighting for justice. Nevertheless, I helped them and we did get the resolution through.

Finally, there was the occasion when I did something I had never done before. I was a member of a national commission of the church and we were about to form a rather important subcommittee to do a particular task and I felt that certain people should be on it. I was known on this commission and others as being a frank and determined debater, but I had never really done any lobbying before. On this occasion I went to another member of the committee and plotted how we could get up the subcommittee we wanted. He too was unaccustomed to plotting and when the commission meeting opened, together we made it very obvious that we had some sort of plan. I will always remember that moment. There was a pause as some of the more powerful members looked at us with dawning recognition. We had entered their territory. We were playing their game and you could see the look of satisfaction on their faces. It taught me instantly that even though it is a more vulnerable path to take, when you don't play any cunning games but take your place in honest encounter, you are much more formidable than when you try to manipulate things. We lost ground that day and not because we were sprung. As my co-plotter said afterwards, 'Those who live by the sword will die by the sword!' I do not reject the idea that people may need to strategise in order to achieve their goals, but there is a fine line between that and cunning manipulation.

Then I was asked to speak at a rally of women's groups in a suburb of Sydney. I sat with the minister of the parish and watched as the women prepared the lunch—carefully and lovingly arranging each table, even folding the paper serviettes into waterlilies. I confess that I was thinking that they might have better things to do when the minister said, 'Just look at that, Dorothy. How do you cope coming to speak to women like this? They would have very little in common with you.' I looked at the women again and saw them through the eyes of God, instead of through my own arrogant eyes. I saw their absolute faithfulness, their readiness to do boring things week after week because that was what the church asked them to do. I saw that they had none of the privileges of travel and opportunity I had been given. I saw their faces, with their hope and expectation and their support. I turned to the minister and said, totally unfairly, in tones of indignation, 'I am looking at these women and I see my sisters, the most faithful people in the church.' He said nothing more and I gave them everything I had to give.

These events made me stop and think very soberly about who I was becoming. I decided to place myself under spiritual direction and found an excellent mentor in Sister Betty Kennedy, a Mercy Sister in the Catholic Church. I talked with her and the first thing she asked me was, 'Have you ever done any reflection on your own power?' With her guidance I spent more than two years doing that. I realised that I had been receiving messages about who I was becoming from many directions. Women would say, 'It's easy for you, Dorothy, because you are special.' I had separated myself from them in ways which were destructive to both myself and them. I had, thank God, honest and brave friends who did not reassure me when I asked their views on myself, but helped me in my struggle to reclaim my humanness.

I remember apologising for one of my worst and somewhat ego-ridden outbursts and my friend said, 'You just joined the human race, Dorothy.' I thought about that deeply, too. Had I really been thinking that I was somehow outside ordinary humanity, in spite of my lack of confidence and self-esteem? Yes, I had. I was the special and virtuous minister's child, was I not? Was I really still the shy, lacking-in-confidence person I perceived myself to be, or was I someone far removed from that? Even as I face that question decades later, I realise that deep down within me, there is still a remnant of that nervous child in the woman who relatively casually fronts for radio and television interviews and is quite prepared to address gatherings of any size. The nervous child goes to sleep when I do these things, but comes to the front as I leave the microphone and have to relate to people personally. At that moment I feel genuinely anxious and inadequate and would cheerfully and with great relief slink out the back door. I often do just that after I have spoken at conferences! I am always being told that people have been looking for me.

I reflected on these things in the late seventies and early eighties as I began my downward-mobility track. I counted and found that I was a member of 17 bodies within the church—far too many for one person. I faced that when I had accepted invitations onto these bodies, I knew that the church was looking for women and subconsciously thought that I was best equipped to do the task, without facing the fact that I also had to learn when I started out and that others could do that too. Every time I refused such invitations and divested myself from more power, I felt a sense of lightness of being; a liberation.

Then I took the hardest step of all. I decided that I would complete my theological training, but not to be ordained. I advised the college and they were surprised. I told my friends, who were gratified, and my family, who simply accepted my decision. I did not feel a sense of liberation after this decision, but I decided that maybe this was because it was such a hard one for me to make. Not very long after, when I was still working in the city, I went to the lunchtime Eucharist at St James' Anglican Church in King Street. I went forward to kneel and receive the elements and, as the priest put the chalice in my hands, I saw a golden light around it. When he took the chalice from me, that light stayed in my hands. I knelt there in wonder and heard a voice inside me saying, 'I have called you. You may safely take the chalice in your hands for the people.'

I felt that my path to ordination had been restored and with joy and vulnerability I decided to keep walking towards it. Then I realised why the Bible passage about Zaccheus, the corrupt tax collector, had been associated with my sense of vocation four years before. I could not take up my vocation until I restored to others what rightly belonged to them—not in money but in power. All this is not to say that all power is wrong. It is to say that power over others and power which is gathered to yourself is destructive both to them and to you. Power which is simply exercised in courage, in honesty, in love and justice is good. However, it is perilously hard to tell the difference. I knew that had I not gone on that journey of facing myself, I would have been dangerous as an ordained minister—a profession which is filled with temptations to power. I know now that all my life I will struggle with this issue because, having once tasted power, it attracts as surely as a bee flying towards honey. I also know that the best protection is to be surrounded by an honest partner, family and friends, which I thankfully have.

On December 12, 1982, my father's hands were among those which were laid on my head as I was ordained. All my life I will remember that moment. Initially it was as if a weight of responsibility was descending on me—as though the hands on my head bore the load of the whole world and its struggles. But then, almost simultaneously, there came a serenity which I can never fully describe. It was as though being and doing had come together in some mystery of peace and joy. After the formal blessing I rose to my feet and assisted at my first Eucharist. I remember approaching the breaking of the bread with fear and trembling as though something might happen as I dared to do it. What I found was a profound sense that my ordinary human hands were only the vehicle for the body of Christ which had a life of its own. I still feel like that. When I fought to retain my ordination later in my life, it was because my ordination is one of the most precious gifts that the church, and I believe God, ever gave me. Even if recognition of it is ever taken from me, I would still assume the priestly life.

# 16  Pitt Street Church

You cannot be ordained into the ministry of the Uniting Church unless you have been 'called' to ministry by a particular parish. Ordinands cannot go out and search for the parish which may be willing to have them. There are special processes involved and you just have to wait respectfully and hopefully for something to happen. The Pitt Street parish in the centre of Sydney asked the Sydney Presbytery (the regional body) for permission to call me. That permission was refused. I don't ever recall such a thing happening before or since, except much later when openly gay or lesbian people were being proposed by a parish, and I still don't know the reasons for that refusal. There was a rumour that they thought it inappropriate to send a newly ordained woman into a central city parish and that Pitt Street had some very strong lay people whom I might find it hard to handle. This was a bit odd as I already had significant national and international experience—lay experience certainly, but you would think that would count for something. Pitt Street did indeed have some strong laypeople in its membership, but I had been a strong layperson myself and the whole congregation at that stage consisted of 16 adults and five children.

When the refusal came through the principal of the theological college intervened and asked the presbytery to think again. It was decided that my introductory interview with the Pitt Street representatives had to be conducted in the presence of the principal of the college, the general secretary of the synod and the chairperson of the presbytery. I recall thinking that I was more nervous of that lot than the people of Pitt Street! After the meeting took place and the Pitt Street people and myself buzzed along with great excitement as we imagined working together, the call was upheld and I began my ministry with them in January 1983.

When I first entered the Pitt Street Church, I stood in the centre of that nearly 150-year-old building and could hardly believe my good fortune. I swear that building breathes. I felt its life, its carrying of the soul of the city and the griefs and joys of the thousands of people who have entered its doors. I touched the beautiful Australian cedar of its pews and which frames its walls and galleries. Later I listened to the wonder of its beautiful pipe organ; one of the finest in the country. I looked with respect at the way its more recent members had shifted its pews and arranged them so that they could sit around the communion table in the centre rather than all facing the front—a reflection of the changes in Protestant theology of worship. I stood in its high pulpit and decided that I would definitely preach from the lectern on the floor unless the church was full for some reason. I looked with wonder at the high arch over the sanctuary with its text, 'Where the spirit of the Lord is there is liberty', which I decided was one of the finest texts one could have overarching the ministry of the church.

I read of its history and pondered its nooks and crannies, its small intimate spaces and its huge soaring ceiling. I studied its various plaques, including those relating to the Fairfax family and David Jones who had been early and influential members of what was then known as the Independent Church. My guess is that John Fairfax and David Jones were attracted by the opportunity for strong lay leadership and the minutes of the early deacon's meetings of the parish reveal how powerful they were in its life. The obituaries to both men occur in the same book of minutes. I was interested to see that John Fairfax was obviously deeply respected, but I think they loved David Jones. Part of his obituary remains in my head: 'We will always love his hoary head and his trembling knees'!

Every day of my ministry there I would arrive at the church and enter it with a deep feeling of the building itself being a gift. I would stand there and reflect on what it held for me and for the many people who, as it opened its doors, would come and sit in its pews and pray, or simply sit

My induction as the minister of Pitt Street Church with Reverend Dr Graeme Ferguson and Reverend Bill Adams, 1983

still in the quiet, or sometimes weep. I would look at its high galleries and imagine different banners which would grace it—something which we worked on in creative ways over the years. I would look at its corners which told the world what our parish stood for—its peace chapel, its community corner where the parish gathered to share their lives and morning tea after church, its amnesty corner with its candle which committed us to work and pray for freedom and justice for all people, and its children's corner with a cupboard of toys and a very large bear sitting on the floor. I would go up the gallery stairs and look down on its heart and think of all who had made it what it was over the decades. I fell in love with Pitt Street Church and, even though I now have my membership for the rest of my life with the South Sydney Uniting Church parish, I know that I will make

With BLF chief Jack Mundey in the church he helped save

my farewell to the world at my funeral at Pitt Street with the sounds of the great organ around me.

In the late sixties the minister of the parish, the Reverend John Bryant, had decided, in the face of an ageing and shrinking congregation, that the way forward was to pull down the old church and replace it with an office block with a chapel underneath. He arranged for a final service in the church which was attended by hundreds of Congregational people (the church was by then a Congregational Church). He offered the people present the opportunity to take anything they wanted away with them. They took the odd pew, the baptismal register and almost every-thing that moved from the kitchen. The church was closed and the small congregation then moved across the road to a 'shopfront church' in an attempt to start another sort of ministry in the city.

The Builders' Labourers Federation, led by Jack Mundey, was engaged at that time in the preservation of some of the old buildings in Sydney which they thought should be part of the national heritage. They put a green ban on Pitt Street Church and refused to pull it down. There was a cartoon at the time which depicted the minister carrying a placard saying, 'Pull the church down', and Jack, a card-carrying communist, saying, 'Keep the church' (or something to that effect). The BLF won the battle and the church became registered as a heritage building. A new minister came on the scene, a small group of marvellous people came to Pitt Street from the South Sydney parish to help begin the renewal of the congregation, the paid choir was invited to join the congregation as unpaid singers and the future of the church was assured.

When representatives of the NSW Organ Society came to inspect the organ which had been left to the rats, I am told that they cried with joy as it sprang to glorious life. The congregation later restored it and even added some of the missing stops which had been omitted in its original construction. I remember reflecting with others on the ethics of restoring an organ when the homeless people of the city lay at our door. One of the things my time at Pitt Street taught me was that while there is a need for an unceasing commitment to those who suffer, a tackling of every system and moment of injustice, so humankind needs its beauty and its music, its art and its poetry. It was this organ which contributed to my survival as I faced tough times later. It was the quiet beauty and healing atmosphere of that old church which gave strength and comfort to thousands of people as they tried to live another day. As Jack Mundey said when I asked him why he had saved the church, 'This is part of the soul of the city.'

The small congregation and I continued the commitment to rebuild the congregation. There was only one member left from the earlier congregation—an elderly woman, Marion Harris, who stayed with us until the time of her death. As we tried all sorts of new things over the years, I would sometimes ask her how she found things. She would say, 'Very interesting, dear.' On one occasion after she fell asleep during a service and had to be saved from falling from her pew, she apologised and said, 'I don't know what came over me, dear. I think I may have had a little turn.' We all loved Marion.

In the first year of my ministry there we celebrated the church's one-hundred-and-fiftieth anniversary. As a prelude to this, we decided to offer drinks to the people who gathered on the church steps to wait for the buses which stopped there. We put an urn out on the wide window ledge with an array of beverages around it, and some of us gathered there to serve people. As we approached people bearing our gifts, most looked nervously at us and refused our offer. Some actually ran away! I can still see John Floyd, one of our keenest members, with drink in hand, pursuing someone down the street in an effort to get him to receive our gift. It taught me very early that the church in Sydney is regarded with deep suspicion. People do not trust the church's gifts, almost certainly because we usually attach a price to them.

Just before the one-hundred-and-fiftieth anniversary, I also learned a good lesson from one of the members of Pitt Street. We had received a letter from a group of, I think, Turkish people, asking if they could conduct a hunger strike on our front steps. My heart sank as I thought of it and I took it to the little parish council for a decision. We had a very righteous discussion covering questions about whether it was ideologically sound to have hunger strikes, whether we knew enough about the situation and whether this particular group was of good reputation. Then Bob Chester, who was a foreman at Garden Island, said, 'Well, bloody hell! I don't want them dying on our steps when the Governor arrives for our anniversary!' We all laughed with relief. We had been thinking the same thing but weren't game to say it. Bob had even calculated that these people would start dying at around the time of the service! I learned from that moment that there are times when we can't respond to even the most worthy of requests, and sometimes we need to celebrate things and cherish ourselves instead. We told this to the congregation in the service that Sunday and were thankful for a God who we believed would understand and forgive that.

The people of Pitt Street were very good at celebrating. Each quarter they went out together for dinner and made toasts to any good things that happened over those three months. As we grew, we took over whole restaurants and later had celebrations in the parish hall.

We had a great one-hundred-and-fiftieth anniversary and it was quite an experience sitting with the president of our church in the high pulpit and speaking from there to crowds of people. During the service we unveiled a plaque in the foyer of the church to honour the Builders' Labourers Federation for their critical part in saving the church. Jack Mundey was present as we did this. Over the years I used to chuckle to myself as I saw big burly builders' labourers standing in the foyer proudly touching that plaque and leaving with a sense of importance.

In the early years, when the congregation was very small, I did about 18 months of industrial chaplaincy at the Fairfax newspaper company— just for four hours each week. This was a very challenging experience, to say the least. For a start, I found it very difficult to float around striking up conversations with people—industrial chaplains don't have offices, they are meant to mingle! Once one of the women said to me, 'You look like a shag on a rock, dear'. I told her that I was. After a while, I asked some of the staff how they saw the chaplaincy and they told me that you couldn't really tell things to chaplains because they wouldn't understand the life of ordinary people and might be shocked or make judgements. I thought this was a very significant comment on the relationship between the church and the community, perhaps especially in Sydney, and that understanding was very formative in all I tried to do in the church from then on. It took me about six months to convince the people there I wasn't dangerous to them.

Sometimes people would ask me how I could believe in a God of love. I learnt that this was a real question, not an attack, and I had to ask myself some hard questions in response. I learned to speak a different religious language because my cliches meant little to these people, and to explore how I could actually talk in any meaningful way about why I was a person of faith and what faith could be about. I have always been grateful to the hard-working staff of Fairfax, from the often industrially deaf older men on the presses in the basement who called me 'Love' and laughed at the idea that I would be their chaplain to the journalists madly trying to get their words on pages.

At Pitt Street things were changing as the congregation grew. Attracting the first 30 people was the hardest because often people would come in, look nervously at the empty pews, and say things like, 'Oh, I'm sorry. I was just looking for the cathedral', then beat a hasty retreat. We developed a style of worship which we hoped was contemporary, had dignity, but which would be accessible to people who had never been in a church before. There had always been a significant lay participation at Pitt Street and as we went on the services were prepared by groups of people and we learned to do that well.

I learned to work with the street people who slept under our windows, sat on our steps during the day and came in and out asking for various things. I came to love them and found that, because they had nothing to lose, they would sometimes tell me good raw truths about me and life in general. Of course this had nothing to do with the fact that some of them would nick my purse if possible and tell me the sob story of the month in order to try to get money from me. Occasionally I would by chance follow them out my door and hear the person say to the waiting others, 'Nah, didn't work on her.' I especially liked the story about the person being a really clean type but whose clean clothes were in a locker at Central Station and they didn't have enough money to get them out of the locker and have a shower. The dying grandmother who lived in Brisbane or somewhere equally far away was a perennial. I became pretty good at distinguishing who was the really needy person and who was the one doing the rounds—who was often still needy but had learned certain ways of surviving which possibly should not be encouraged.

I loved Craig who had tears tattooed under his eyes and who would just come in and say, 'Well, Reverend, I got pissed again last night and thrown out of my digs. Can you spare a couple of dollars for a coffee?' I couldn't resist him. One day he came in and offered me a donation of ten dollars. I asked him if he could really afford it and he said he wanted to give it and would I give him a receipt. I still sometimes hear his voice from some spot where he is camping out in the city as he shouts, 'Hello, Reverend. Remember me? I'm the one who gave you ten dollars!' Then there were the Polish ex-priest and the ex-doctor, both alcoholics, who sat daily on our steps and had earnest and learned discussions on theology and life in general. They were a treat and we had many conversations. The doctor died under my office window and I imagine the priest is now dead too. There was also the young woman who travelled everywhere with her dog. She barely had anything for herself, but the dog was always well cared for. Pitt Street had virtually no money to give away—it never was a wealthy parish. I suspect that, for this reason, we had a different relationship with the street people of Sydney who seemed to believe it when we said we had no cash to give them.

You never knew who would knock on the door. Many people were mentally ill and were out on the streets after the deinstitutionalising that took place following the Richmond Report. Some of them lived in boarding houses with no supervision or trained staff to care for them. They were set adrift and at risk because the government didn't provide the resources required to go through with such a big shift in policy with responsibility and care. I remember a paranoid man curled in a foetal position under one of our desks. We phoned hospitals and doctors and no-one wanted to know about him. The only way to get help was to call the police and watch his terrified response as he was picked up. If in doubt, I learned to detect whether someone was spaced out on drugs or mentally ill by asking them in authoritative tones, 'What is your name? Have you had your medication today?' If they had been in an institution they immediately responded obediently. To this day, we haven't worked out how to gather mentally ill people into our community in ways which respect their needs and yet give them as much freedom as possible. I guess we just don't want to know about it as they may cost too much or strike fear into our hearts as we see before us the way illness of the mind can distort human life.

I very rarely felt afraid, even when I was alone in the building with my office door open. Some of this security was related to the fact that I was within a couple of metres of Pitt Street. But mostly it was because I found over the years that, if you have a sort of inner authority and calmness, it prevails in many situations, even if someone is much bigger and stronger than you and disturbed. That is not to say that we took needless risks and I always knew that my theories on this were not infallible. It was the same sort of trust with which I learned to walk the streets of the city and Darlinghurst by myself at all sorts of times and in all sorts of places. When you work with people they get to know you and the word goes around that you are okay and are to be received as part of their community. I once had lunch with a prostitute who told me that sometimes her work was a bit like mine—giving confidence and care to people who felt ugly or rejected. I spluttered a bit over that one!

My partner in all this was our administrator, Reverend Ron Denham. Ron and I are very different and that was part of the strength of our relationship. Before he retired, he had been a Presbyterian minister in the inner city around Redfern and Waterloo. He was one of the congregation who came across from South Sydney to help Pitt Street. He taught me many things—the beauty of Presbyterian order which the Uniting Church has never quite learnt. He taught me to value honesty in relationships—daring to tell the other exactly what you think and receiving that without affecting the relationship, other than adding to it. If I tended to inflate the figures of new members coming into Pitt Street by rounding them off or to pump up my prestige, he would say, 'Why do you need to do that, Dorothy? You are all right. You don't need to prove anything.' On the other hand, if I said to him, 'That's sixties stuff, Ron. We are into spirituality now,' he would take that in good humour. He taught me to try to never to create dependencies or to affirm people in their victim response to life, but to treat them with the greatest respect which you can offer another and the conviction that they are able to make real choices towards life and maturity. We knew that some people needed more support in doing this and that people did not start out equal in any sense, but freedom and growing up was always the commitment in any relationship. That was the way he saw God dealt with humankind and I liked his God.

It was also an absolutely gracious God who left failings behind and invited a new day.

The other thing he taught me was a deep love of the city itself; its landscape and its people. I developed a spirituality which can find its renewal forever within the city and all it holds. I found that there is infinite renewal in a weed growing in a crack in the concrete, the sun on the face of a tall building, the humming life of crowded streets and the little spaces beside a piece of sandstone. I learned to create worship and rituals which celebrate the city. Once we had a service for the city workers—the garbage collectors and cleaners and other city council staff who added to the life of the city in so many unseen ways.

Perhaps the centre of my ministry with the people of Pitt Street was between 1986 and 1988. In 1986 John Howard, now Australia's Prime Minister, made a statement about Asian immigration. After this there was a rise in the level of attacks on Asian children in school grounds and Asian people in the streets. In the inner city, there were numerous bits of racist graffiti including the much-repeated, 'Kill an Asian a day'. Some of us at Pitt Street began a campaign to wipe out this graffiti as we felt to leave it there was to collude with racists. We had small teams of people who would go and paint over the offensive words. A very keen member of most of these teams was Dr Elizabeth Ramage. Liz was known for her artistic covering of words with flowers and fishes. One night when she and a few others were out she called out to her teammates to shine the torch so she could see what she was doing. A light shone on the wall and when she expressed her gratitude, she turned around and it was from the headlights of a police car! It was actually an offence to paint out the graffiti as that was regarded as another form of graffitiing.

At one stage we discovered a huge piece of graffiti aimed at Aboriginal people which stretched along the pedestrian tunnel at Stanmore railway station. This was such a big job that we decided to approach State Rail for permission to wipe it out. We were refused permission and told that the railway graffiti removal staff would get rid of it when they came around about six months later. We decided to proceed with an act of civil disobedience. Four of us formed the team and went along in daylight to do the job. In spite of our commitment, we decided that we would prefer not to be caught, so we asked James, one of our team, to keep watch for us. After a while I looked up and there were the railway staff observing our efforts with interest. I hissed to James, 'I thought we said to keep watch!' He said, 'I didn't think you meant the railway staff'! We were hauled up to the stationmaster's office and the railway police were called. When they arrived they went through their routine of 'name, address and occupation'. They found they had a student from the conservatorium of music, a preschool teacher, a doctor from the Health Commission and a member of the clergy. We agreed that we were a somewhat unusual graffiti team and they asked us why we were doing it. After a long discussion they cautioned us and let us go. The next morning at six o'clock the media were at my door and our story was splashed across the daily papers—I have always assumed that the railway staff notified the media because we certainly didn't. After this, State Rail changed its policy—it wiped out the graffiti there and other offensive graffiti as soon as possible after it appeared.

Shortly after this, we invited Archbishop Desmond Tutu to speak at a rally in our church. The Anglican diocese of Sydney had refused to allow such a rally in the cathedral and we believed that he should be heard in a church in Sydney. It was a marvellous night and the church was full, with almost 2,000 people and several hundred waiting outside. It was very special to get to know Desmond Tutu a little; to meet a man who, although absolutely committed to the freedom of his people and the ending of apartheid, was still a man of joy and gentleness.

We never knew which provoked what followed, the graffiti event or the rally with Tutu—maybe it was both. Soon after, a group of men wearing swastikas on their arms and carrying the Eureka flag (to my great offence!) marched down the aisle of our church during Sunday worship and placed on the lectern a scurrilous pamphlet headed 'Sodomy and Gonorrhea in the Uniting Church'. They were members of National Action, a neo-Nazi group which was active in Sydney at that time. The pamphlet included personal attacks on me, including a quote from a letter purporting to be me writing to a woman with whom I was in a relationship—in fact it was a page from a pastoral letter which I had handwritten for our typist to type up. There was stuff which was supposed to be about my marriage alongside all sorts of racist material related to the parish. We learned later that anything they had about individuals or the parish came from the rubbish bag which we put out for collection. One of the bits of information taken was also a page from our members and friends list which had addresses and phone numbers on it—including mine.

This was the beginning of two years of attacks on me, some members of the parish, my house and the church. The pamphlet was sent widely to the press and across the Uniting Church. I had some very special letters from major journalists assuring me that they would never print any of the material. The church authorities asked me to meet with the synod lawyers to see if I wanted to press charges against National Action. They asked me if any of the statements in the pamphlet were true and I told them that, even though the sources quoted in the leaflet were false, my sexual orientation was in fact homosexual. They received this information with respect and understood that I did not want to press charges.

I started to receive death threats by phone in the middle of the night and a series of attacks began on my house. I stayed with my phone number for some time as Melissa was overseas and I wanted her to be able to contact me at a time when I couldn't always track her down to give her a new number. I stubbornly wanted to stay readily available to people, especially members of the parish. However, it was frightening to receive the calls and, in the end, I decided to have a silent number, which I have sustained ever since. It was interesting (in a bizarre sort of way!) to find that ordinary language without any swear words can be so abusive. The level of hate in a person's voice can be chilling indeed. On occasions they played the Nazi anthem into my ear—which was, of course, set to the tune of 'Austria' which is a great hymn. Every time they played it in the night, we sang it in strength and determination the following Sunday. We sang it to the words 'Once to every one and nation comes the moment to decide, in the strife of truth with falsehood for the good or evil side'. We sang that hymn many times over those years.

My front fence was grafittied with the words: 'Poofter lover, Jew lover and nigger lover'. While I agreed with all those sentiments, I didn't like the names given, so washed it off after a bit. My gate was then painted with 'Lesbian slut'. Sometimes, in the dead of night, there would be a knock on the door. If I looked over my balcony, I would see two men who would then walk silently and slowly away. Somehow this was more scary than if they had shouted or run. Then other members of the group would stuff vomit and faeces into my letterbox or throw them over the front door and down the side of the house. I wondered where they got so much of such things and then later realised that some of the letters which we were sent from the group to us were in Children's Hospital envelopes with the printed address crossed out. Sometimes I would see one of their leaders stalking me by sitting opposite my house in his car and watching.

At the church, week after week, there would be all sorts of things dumped across the doorway which had to be cleaned up before anyone could enter. An Aboriginal family who were members of the congregation had a brick thrown through the window of their house and some others had threatening phone calls which told them that the caller knew their address and their children and they had better watch out. In spite of this, through the two years of this period, no-one left the congregation. In fact, it grew and grew.

Initially we decided to simply remain silent about the attacks because we didn't want to give National Action the satisfaction of publicity. However, in the end, we decided that the community had the right to know what was lying in its midst and what was the extreme result of racist activities and attitudes. We wrote an open letter to National Action in the *Sydney Morning Herald* after which two things happened. The attacks were stepped up a bit, and dozens of people emerged from all over Sydney who had also been attacked by National Action—mainly with bricks through windows or smashed car windscreens. We formed a group called Coalition Against Racism and met to plan what we would do together.

In the middle of it all, I learned a very important lesson which has determined my life ever since. I had been taught to be heroic and stoic. I learned in that period that I would be far stronger if I was prepared to admit my vulnerability. There was a point where my whole day would be focused on preparing to go home—would I go early and feel secure because I was locked in there, or would I go late so that there was less of the night to get through? My attackers had taken charge of my life. I found that when I shared with other people how scared I was, my life was returned to me. People offered to come around as soon as an attack took place and have a coffee and clean up if necessary, even if it was three o'clock in the morning. We all somehow reclaimed the initiative and I began to go home cheerfully. Of course, I was scared when anything happened. But there is a world of difference between living your life with dread and being justifiably scared when something happens.

We lived this out as a congregation by continuing to wipe out racist graffiti, writing letters to newspapers about racism and generally taking our place in community action for justice. At one stage we invited people to a rally to 'Celebrate the Unity of Humankind'. A large crowd of people came. We invited a number of well-known Australians to share their most significant experiences of human unity, which they did most movingly. Then we invited people of different ethnic origins to come forward and offer their gifts into the Australian community. Sixty-one people came forward. We then closed that part of the gathering with an Aboriginal woman coming forward and saying that when justice is done to her people, they will be able to fully offer their gifts into the Australian community. It was deeply moving for everyone present, especially when we sang over and over the song from the musical *Les Miserables* which had become our theme song as a congregation: 'Do You Hear the People Sing?'

At this time, National Action sent most of the Uniting Church parish secretaries across New South Wales a letter containing soft-porn pictures of two women engaged in sexual activity and said that I was part of this. It wasn't a very smart move as most of the secretaries did not trust people who sent them such pictures and the synod authorities told them to put them in the bin.

We also formed a special relationship with the local members of the African National Congress in Sydney and they held special memorial services at Pitt Street when leaders died in South Africa. I will never forget the sound of the unofficial African national anthem, 'E Afrika' (God Bless Africa) being sung as we grieved another death and determined to keep the struggle going.

And what were the police doing through all this? From the first attacks we contacted the police and Special Branch was assigned the case. In relation to the attacks on the church building, all they needed to do was have a stake-out in the police union building directly opposite for a few hours on a couple of nights one week and they would have got the perpetrators. Instead, they visited every now and then, usually in response to another complaint from us, and suggested what I thought were inane ideas for catching those involved—like the officer who sat in my office, flexed his muscles and told me that he was once a footballer and he would get the offenders. Then he suggested that we allow him to hold a stake-out in my office so he could look out the window and catch them. I pointed out that you couldn't possibly see the front door from my window as there was a huge column in the way, so he did nothing.

On the home front, I decided I would visit the officer in charge of the Leichhardt police station, which was about five minutes from my house, and suggest that all officers from his station be briefed about the case so that when I rang in the middle of the night I didn't have to start from scratch, and so that they wouldn't treat me like some paranoid old woman. The officer in charge said this was quite impossible as this never happened and that each situation must be dealt with as it arose. Indeed, it was quite clear that the police force as a whole did not see any connection with these attacks going on in many parts of the city, even though National Action had been referred to Special Branch for observation.

After almost two years of this, some of us from the Coalition Against Racism decided to seek a meeting with the Minister for Police, Ted

Pickering. The delegation was Adele Horin, a journalist from the *Sydney Morning Herald*, a representative from the Jewish Board of Deputies, a staff member from Community Aid Abroad and myself. A few hours before we were due to meet the minister, his secretary rang to say that he had decided he would only meet with me. I thought quickly and said that the Jewish Board of Deputies would be very disappointed to hear that. In five minutes she was back to say he had changed his mind and would meet with us all—thank you to the Jews!

We went through all the security checks to meet with him (envying his protection) and then began to tell of our experiences. He was flanked by several staff who took notes. He did not seem very interested and appeared to think our stories of bricks through windows and smashed windscreens were perhaps part of living in a free and democratic society where people have differing opinions. We were astounded. We left his office and sat in a coffee shop to work out what we should do. We decided to wait a little and think about it. The next day the minister issued a press statement to the effect that he was very concerned about the degree of violence in our situation etc etc. Much later, when something else arose about Ted Pickering, Adele Horin did relate his conversation with us on that day via her column.

The media in general were very supportive of us through these two years. One day we came out of our morning service and there across the steps of the church were dozens of journalists holding placards saying, 'If the police won't defend this church, we will'.

A few weeks after our meeting, I had a call from a very senior officer in Special Branch. He said, 'Reverend McMahon, I suggest that you give no more information to the officers of Special Branch.' I asked why and he said that he could not say but that was his advice.

Around this time, the members of National Action made their most serious attack. They donned balaclavas and set fire to a life-size fibreglass effigy of a woman on my front doorstep, also setting alight the fence which I shared with my neighbour. They took a photo of themselves doing this which they sent to the *Sydney Morning Herald* together with an open letter to me saying that they would bring down my ministry. Fortunately, Jenny

Chambers was waiting at home for me and she rang the fire brigade and the police and dragged a hose from the back garden through to the front to try to put out the fire. I arrived home from a parish meeting to find the local fire brigade in front of the house and the blackened figure of the effigy lying on the footpath. I must say I had a gleeful moment when, some time later, a police patrol car arrived and two young police officers swaggered out. The first thing they saw was what appeared to be the burnt body of a woman lying on the footpath and I watched them do an alarmed double take. Then they hastily brought out their notebooks and asked me my name and whether anything like this had happened before.

After that, with a new officer in charge of the case, Special Branch moved fast and arrested a number of people. We were told that one of the main perpetrators, Wayne Smith, was later murdered by one of the other members of National Action. Another was caught up in a case for insurance fraud (for which he spent some time in prison) and was connected with the attempt to shoot Eddie Funde, the leader of the African National Congress in Sydney.

Many years later when Special Branch was disbanded, we were informed that we could claim our dossiers related to their work, which I did. It was very thick and as I read through the bits that were not blacked out it became absolutely apparent to me that the officers on our case had been spending their time following me around to meetings I attended, taking the names of those who were at the meetings and recording their car numberplates. The last thing they had been doing was tracking the activities of National Action.

When I originally asked if National Action had been responsible for all the attacks, the police were evasive. They said it was 'complicated'. About ten years later, I was travelling home on the bus from work and sat in the second-back row. I couldn't help overhearing a conversation between two people behind me who mentioned that they had been on a television program representing a certain group. I knew of the group and I looked around to see who they were. As soon as they saw my face there was a pause in the conversation, then they started saying very loudly, 'What was the name of that lesbian slut who was the minister of the Pitt Street Church?' and other comments which reminded me of some of the threatening phone calls I had had in the middle of the night—the words of which are engraved in my memory. After this went on for some time, engaging the interest of the other passengers, I turned to them and said, 'Let me introduce myself. My name is Dorothy McRae-McMahon.' At that, they rose to get off and shouted abuse at me all the way down the bus. This incident set me thinking and I suspect that there were at least two groups engaged in the attacks on us and that a group other than National Action was responsible for those on the church. The lovely ending to this event was that, as I sat on the bus literally shaking, the man sitting next to me turned around, took my hand and said, 'I know who you are. I am a gay man and I want to thank you for what you did. I will sit with you on the bus until you get off at your stop.'

A few months before the end of the racist attacks, I visited Scotland. I had always known of my Scottish heritage, but it hadn't been at the forefront of my consciousness. It was my sister Carmyl who had the clan book which had belonged to our father. Just before I left for the airport, I rang Carmyl and asked her where exactly the McRaes had come from. She told me that our family had lived at Portree on the Isle of Skye and I decided that Jen and I would go there when we visited Scotland.

I was quite unprepared for the impact of entering the light on the west coast of Scotland—it gave me a profound sense of somehow coming home. I looked in awe at Skye's harsh and beautiful landscape. I picked a sprig of heather which I still have framed on my wall. I immediately recognised the culture within which I had been raised through my father—restrained, dignified, direct but courteous.

The experience which will stay with me forever happened when, quite by chance, we came across the old McRae clan graveyard. It was on the side of a hill just south of Inverinate. I walked into the graveyard, stood in the ruin of the tiny sixth-century chapel and read the inscriptions on the gravestones. I looked around at the bare Scottish mountains and asked myself, 'How did they survive here?' Immediately I felt a rush of energy from the ground into my body and an inner voice which said, 'We survived and you will too'. The mountains around me became joined with the tower blocks of Pitt Street and then all was peaceful and silent again. I wondered whether it had even happened, but I felt stronger and full of determination. I felt quite sure that my ancestors had given me courage and strength from their life and I had a tiny glimpse of what their land must mean to Aboriginal people back home.

When I came back, I contemplated resuming my family name, but I also wanted to hold the name of my children and two 'Mc's' seemed too complicated. Then someone gave me a CD of Scottish music. I put it on and as the pipes played 'Scotland the Brave' my whole soul stirred and I knew that I did want to carry the McRae name, even if it was cumbersome. I assumed my double-barrelled name from then on and have never regretted it.


In 1988 I was awarded the Australian Human Rights Medal and I accepted it with a deep sense of pride on behalf of all those who were part of the struggle against racism, knowing that I was just one person in the midst of all that. As for the people of Pitt Street, our worship had become raw and real, arising out of pain and vulnerability and determined courage and a commitment to be part of the history of removing racism from the face of the Earth forever. We also lived as those for whom the usual little issues about who did or did not do the flowers or wash up after morning tea disappeared.

Some years later, when the battle against apartheid was won and Nelson Mandela released, I was asked to prepare the liturgy for his welcome to Australia which was held in St Mary's Catholic Cathedral. It was interesting to see that bodies like the Salvation Army, which had ended its membership of the National Council of Churches, and parts of the Anglican communion who had been highly critical of the council during the struggle because of its support of the African National Congress were among those who wanted to be in the front seats of the cathedral to shake the hand of Mandela. However, I was proud to be among the 'comrades' invited to be in the crypt after the service and to hear that the first body which he thanked for support was the Uniting Church in Australia.

One of the gifts of my time at Pitt Street was learning to walk with people towards their death. It was a period when many gay men in the prime of life were dying of AIDS and some of them invited me into their lives as they moved towards death. In spite of the grief of these journeys, I saw through them that life in the end is about depth rather than length. I witnessed their dignified and brave journeying, their honest questions and their pain. I saw many different ways of dying and sat with them as they reflected on the meaning of death and of life itself. It was in this period that I developed the funeral liturgy which is possibly the most widely used of any of my liturgies. I will always remember those people and will carry their gifts with me for the rest of my life.

At the end of 1992, I knew that I would have to leave Pitt Street Church as in those days we had fixed terms for parish churches. I felt sad to leave my special friends there, but at the same time I knew that it was time to go. I had offered all that I had to that work and I felt that fresh ideas and leadership were necessary. The people of Pitt Street taught me to offer all that I am and have, and not to be afraid or offended if some of that is rejected. They affirmed my humanness and that of others as simply part of the good journey with each other and our God. They taught me the beginnings of being able to experience conflict without assuming that I must sort it out instantly—something which I needed to learn for my next work.

# 17 Director for Mission and Beyond

As I prepared to leave Pitt Street, I was asked by several presbyteries to stand for the position of National President of the Uniting Church. I agreed to stand, with some misgivings, because I had the sense that it was time to spread my life outwards in some new way. I lost the vote and I was glad to do so in retrospect. Dr Jill Tabart, who was elected, made a much better president than I would ever have done. Not long after, I was approached to offer myself for consideration for the position of National Director for Mission and I believed that this was the spreading out which was far more right for me. I was given this role, beginning in 1993.

The task of the National Director for Mission was to oversee the Uniting Church's work nationally in the areas of relationships with overseas churches, evangelism, social responsibility and justice, multicultural relationships and frontier services (remote and outback work in hospitals and patrol ministries) and initially, until it was given autonomy, work with Aboriginal people.

I was saved from my almost non-existent gifts for organisation by two marvellous personal assistants—Margaret Tasker for the first four years and Gwenda Davies for my last year in the job. Each had my measure very rapidly and would come into my office and say things like, 'I notice that you are doing ever so many little things on your desk, Dorothy. So, what is the big one we are avoiding today?' Marg worked out a sort of filing system which I would actually use, which is still mine today. They cared for me, often said 'no' for me (something I still find hard to do) and generally saved me from things over and over again.

I think I didn't do the job too badly but as I look back, and even while I was doing it, I think I knew that my occasional lack of discretion was not always appropriate for senior management. If I began again, I would do try to do that differently. I did have to face my anxiety about conflict as I sometimes had to make hard decisions or needed to face staff with things. All my instincts were to smooth the path, to rapidly stop the pain for me and for them, but I knew this was not healthy or helpful to anyone. I did learn that to sit someone down and say, 'Have you noticed how people are reacting to you? Have you thought whether there is a better way of working?' in a direct and honest encounter is far kinder than freezing people out and talking about them behind their backs.

All through my time in that role, I was still drawn to the sacramental life of the church, which was less open to me in a position outside a parish. I found myself expanding the ritual life of our national staff. I started adding ritual life to some of the international meetings which I attended as Director for Mission and eventually this flowed on into the leadership role I was given in the World Council of Churches Worship Committee.

For several years, while I was Director for Mission, the church was discussing the whole area of human sexuality. In 1982 I had been a member of the National Assembly Standing Committee which responded to the first critical question which arose formally within the Uniting Church about homosexuality and ordination. It was a question from a Victorian presbytery about whether a lesbian woman could be ordained. The committee stated in reply that sexual orientation was not a bar to ordination, but that the way that sexuality was expressed could be taken into account. Some people took this to mean that the homosexual person concerned must be celibate. As the person who seconded that resolution, I do not believe that was the intended meaning—I believe that it was referring to the more general sexual ethics required by the church for clergy, whether heterosexual or homosexual. However, my memory of this is that it was not fully discussed.

When that statement was made there was some concern within the church and a task group was set up. Chaired by the Reverend Dr Gordon Dicker, this produced a book called *Homosexuality and the Church* which invited the church to be open to further exploration of the issues. This led to another task group which was asked to take all sorts of issues about human relationships and sexuality to the wider church for discussion over a period of years. At the Perth National Assembly in 1997, the results of the work of this Sexuality Task Group was put in front of the church for decision.

Even though I had never really hidden my sexual orientation and had certainly never lied about it to anyone who asked me, I had not at that time made any public declaration. I have never believed that anybody needs to collude with those who would bring them down due to anti-homosexual positions or homophobia (and there is a difference). I was also not prepared to offer to my opponents the chance to end my ministry while I was at Pitt Street or on the national staff of the church. I believe that all of us are owed the dignity and self-respect of choosing our own time for 'coming out'. However, I decided that since the church was deliberately focused on issues about sexuality, this was the time for me to advise it that I was a lesbian and in a committed relationship.

The journey towards the Perth Assembly was very tough. I remember preaching at St James' Anglican Church in Sydney at Easter, weeks before the assembly, and thinking what an irony it would be that I might be preaching for the last time as an ordained person in the very church where I had first experienced the affirmation of my vocation. I told the Uniting Church staff working with me what I was planning to do. One of those staff was the incoming president of the church, the Reverend John Mavor. He came to me and asked me to be one of the selected group of people who would present him to the assembly for installation as president. I asked him to go away and think what it might mean to have me do that, knowing what was to follow. He came back the next day and asked me to be one of his presenters which I was very moved by. Last year I watched, with great gratitude, as he led the debates on sexuality which took place at the assembly in Melbourne. John is a Queenslander and appropriately known as an evangelical leader in our church, so this is a brave stand to take.

I remember boarding the plane to Perth with a sense of foreboding, but also with a quiet in my being, as I knew that I could do no other than be true to myself at this point. I had been advised that I had only one minute to say what I needed to say as the business committee had planned to allow as many people as possible to speak. Foremost in my heart and soul was a knowledge that the church had the power to wound me deeply, because it was like family to me. When the time came for the debate I sat beside a friend and decided that I would go to the microphone as early as possible to get my speech over. I had written down what I would say as I could not trust myself to get through it in any other way. This is what I said:

> I wish to advise the assembly that, as we debate the issue of homo-sexuality and ordination, my own ordination is in question. I am a lesbian and in a loving and committed relationship. Some of us carry within our own beings the question which faces us as a church today. Are we indeed, by our very nature, people who cannot be the bearers of word and sacrament? Or are we perhaps those who the early disciples would have said are 'not following us' but are casting out demons in the name of Jesus, those of whom Jesus said, 'If they are not against us, they are for us'?

> Are we the true or false prophets? Jesus knew it would not be easy to answer that question, not as easy as quoting laws or texts, not as easy as identifying those who say 'Lord, Lord'. 'By their fruits you will know them,' he said. So all we can do is to ask you, my sisters and brothers, to make your judgement by looking at the fruits of ministry, of life and of faith.

> An elder in Terrigal prayed recently, 'Dear God, may we only find each other as Jesus has already found us.' That is my prayer for us all.

I sat down shaking and feeling that every ounce of energy had gone out of my body, but that what was left was a stillness and calm, even a quiet joy.

I watched as the assembly went on with the debate, as Aboriginal people with whom I had worked opposed me and then came up with tears and told me they were sorry. They knew that I had fought for them and their justice, but that they could not support me in my struggle. They were more divided than they appeared to be on this, as I discovered later. They told the church to go on without them and I knew they meant that, in true Aboriginal style, they would sit with it and would come to talk about it later—they didn't mean that they would leave. The assembly, with its sense of responsibility for Aboriginal suffering and for the way people of other ethnicities experienced racism and prejudice, felt it could not move to a decision. I understood all that and I still do. I knew how hard it is for some people to fight on many fronts at once when their people are so vulnerable, and that our missionaries over the centuries had given Aboriginal, Pacific and Asian peoples a very conservative form of the faith. In saying all this, I am not for a moment suggesting that some people do not genuinely oppose my point of view on sexuality and do not have the right to do that.

At the end of the assembly, the general secretary thanked me for my contribution to the work of the gathering and the members gave me a standing ovation, with only a handful of people dissenting. At the Perth Assembly many decisions were made, but those which focused on the ordination of homosexual clergy were deferred. This meant that the 1982 resolution about sexual orientation being no bar to ordination stood. I believe that, had we gone to the vote, we would have won with a huge majority, but the Uniting Church rightly tries hard to achieve consensus decision making. My view of that time was borne out when the matter was reintroduced in Melbourne last year—precipitated by a move from the conservative forces in the church. When it came to living with diversity on the issue of homosexual people being ordained, we had around 90 per cent of the vote with us.

On both occasions, while the media focus was relentless and exhausting, it was respectful and kindly to me. The truth is that the church is lagging behind the community when it looks at homosexuality. I believe that when the church is less inclusive and less loving than the community, it should pause and think very gravely about its life.

We returned to Sydney and I took up my work in the assembly office. The attacks on my continuing to hold my position began—both to me directly, to other staff and to the president. People threatened to withdraw funds from programs which I was supervising, something I regarded as highly unethical given that it meant betraying vulnerable people who had nothing to do with me personally. In the end, I began to think that I couldn't bear to see this going on. Nor, I began to believe, did I really want to spend my daily life defending myself.

Weeks later when the new Assembly Standing Committee met, and as I listened to the discussion from around the country and heard the reports from the synod general secretaries who were also struggling under demands for me to resign, I decided to offer to retire a few years early. The standing committee discussed the issue for nearly two hours and then, I was told, reluctantly agreed to accept my resignation. I remember ringing my partner, Ali, from the meeting and telling her that I no longer had a job. Even though it was in some measure my own decision, it was still devastating. One of the things I had learned in this struggle over the years was that, if you defend yourself against attack and pain, you shut part of yourself down so that you feel less of the joy and love also. I had decided not to shut myself down like that, leaving myself open to feel the pain in its raw truth. The many letters I had from supportive people in the church and the community and the loyalty of my colleagues helped me with that.

There were also two formal complaints made against me in efforts to have recognition of my ordination withdrawn, but both failed. The church's disciplinary committees decided that I was in breach of no regulation of the Uniting Church. It was interesting to watch the complainants bring the cases against me (in a grim sort of way!). It was clear that they looked at many more gay and lesbian publications and websites than I had ever done. I had never even heard of most of the ones to which they referred. I am sure that they were genuine in their concern, but I still wonder why they were so passionate about the issue and what it is they fear. I had never knowingly done any damage to the church and had been recognised as one of its leaders. I don't believe that anyone will be condemned in the end by believing in a God who can cope with all sorts of diversity.

After that, I drifted around the church, carefully keeping to the safe edges. It took me years to heal from the wounding. I know that some people think that I am foolish not to shake the dust off and leave the church and I well understand that point of view. I would never suggest that anyone stay to be destroyed, but I guess I am stubborn and I still have a deep love for the church, especially the Uniting Church which honestly struggles with such issues and does its best.

One of the things I experienced was the community in general rushing towards me, asking me to speak to all sorts of groups and in many situations. I wrote almost 150 papers in six years, quite apart from other things. I found all sorts of people wanting to discuss theology with me and to receive my skills in ritual life. I must say that I felt as though the community was subconsciously trying to comfort and heal me from the attacks of the church, as though they themselves found the church wounding in their human journeys, and some people said as much.

I still contribute my skills in writing liturgy to the church in general, in books which are largely published in Britain and in subscription series in Australia, New Zealand and the United States. I love creating rituals and the poetic prose imagery in the prayers seems to flow from my fingers as I sit at my computer and focus on some theme of life and faith. I have read that the McRae clan in the highlands of Scotland produced many priests and poets and I like to think that, in some humble way, I am part of that.

If I am still an active member of the church, it is because the church came alive for me in the little parish of South Sydney in Waterloo. There the struggling people couldn't care less about my sexuality. They have significant things with which to deal and they trust those who are genuine, respectful and loving. Our little congregation is perhaps the richest experience of the church I have ever had. Its life is raw, real and full of tears and laughter. I often think that if you can place the gospel on the ground among us and make it live, it will live anywhere. I will always remember our most recent Pentecost service. We were, as usual, seated around our communion table with its cross and the flowers that Juliette always collects for us. Alongside the cross was the candle which Fred lights for us each week, and the small candles waiting for our lighting when we bring our prayers of intercession. Vladimir Korotkov, our minister, was, with his usual earnestness, exploring ideas about the absence and presence of God in his sermon.

As we listened, we suddenly realised that what we were seeing in front of us was an amazing ray of light coming from above the gallery and slowly moving down onto the cross and Juliette's flowers. We stopped Valdimir's preaching and pointed it out in wonder as we received a sense of the gift of the Spirit of God among us. Then Vladimir continued and mentioned the dove of peace which descended on the disciples long ago and, as we watched in amazement, we all saw a tiny feather slowly spiralling from the high roof of the church and landing on the table in front of the cross. We all laughed and cried. We knew, of course, that we have some pigeons living in the church roof, but all agreed that the timing and placement was a little miracle for we struggling humble people in South Sydney.

From this little congregation miraculously comes *The South Sydney Herald*. It is the main local community paper in the South Sydney area— a 16-page tabloid which we distribute to 16,000 households every month. Our minister is the managing editor, Trevor Davies is our news editor and networker and I am the features editor. Even though she is not a member of the parish, my partner Ali is our photographer. We all work on the paper voluntarily and we and volunteers, some from outside the parish, do the paper rounds to get it distributed. It doesn't break even with advertising, so the parish covers the extra cost from its very slender budget as a community service. Sometimes distinguished journalists give us their writing free of charge, and lots of other people contribute articles. We feel as if the local community regards it as their own paper and, as we sit and plan our issues in coffee shops, they often come up and give us ideas. Our intention, apart from sharing local news and information, is to affirm good things and good people in an area of Australia which is often referred to as 'notorious' and presented as a place without hope.

When the gospel comes to people whose lives offer the hardest questions for life and God, it is hard won and it is either relevant or it dies. Worship becomes full of both greater pain and greater joy as people survive their next moments and laugh with delight at small victories for life and faith. We are the oddest collection of people and the life which we share is full of gifts. Our services are often interrupted by people coming and going for all sorts of reasons and we receive those interruptions as special opportunities. We can hardly wait to tell each other when things go well or to hold each other when they don't.

This is the true church, and as far as I am concerned, the one with which I will stay.

# 18 Moving Wider

When I joined the staff of the NSW Ecumenical Council in 1972, my world widened out on many fronts. It set me among staff and inter-church councils from all the mainstream churches around the country and beyond. This challenged my neat little Methodist views of what the church could be like for a start. I had always seen myself as open to other styles of church, but I didn't have much direct experience of these. Methodism really came from the working-class section of society and, although that had shifted over the centuries, it still had a good deal of that culture and flavour. It also carried within it puritan attitudes to life, especially in the areas of drinking, swearing and gambling. Its worship was quite homely with the minister making up the prayers as he went (it was 'he' in those days), giving long sermons interspersed with enthusiastic and loud hymn singing by the people, and bits of Eucharistic liturgy tacked onto the end of services once a month. Indeed, those who needed to go home to attend to the Sunday roast didn't stay for that bit.

As I moved into this wider sphere, I found myself blown away by the beauty and grandeur of different ways of worshipping. I saw the mystery and majesty in their choreography and use of imagery, silence, colour, and links with ancient tradition. I loved my new friends who had the odd glass of wine, who knew their way around pubs (which I had never entered), and who sometimes said, 'Damn!' I think I grew up and put some things into perspective in ways which I had not done before. These people taught me to be open to all sorts of diversity, and to see a universe which might embrace creativity beyond my imagining.

One person who stands out for me in this journey is the Reverend Murray Johnston. We were colleagues in the international aid scene—he in Victoria and I in New South Wales. He pushed my life outwards in many ways, especially in my understanding of the great traditions of the Anglican Church and its Eucharistic life. However, the greatest gift he gave to me was the gift of music. Until Murray came along, I had never really entered the depths of classical music and the world of jazz. I had just had the tiny taste of Bach in my childhood. The big music of the great composers is now central to my spirituality and, indeed, to my survival. I put it on and my heart and soul lift. I play it as I write and it seeps into me as a sort of underlying inspiration to keep going. I even stand in the middle of the room and raise my arms as though the music flows through my body as strength and courage. It was a gift which I will carry with me all my life.

Because my work was primarily related to international aid, I was confronted daily with poverty, oppression and need. This context wheeled all things into a new order of importance. It didn't mean that small personal decisions about one's lifestyle had no significance, but it did put them into perspective. This was a period when aid agencies were engaged in feverish discussions about how they could bring change in effective ways, as against handing out charity. We knew that charity in the hand-out sense was often necessary in emergencies, but we also knew that in doing that, we often created dependent people. We also recognised that the giver holds the power and the receiver tends to be the mendicant. We explored ways in which the future could be changed for each and how power could be transferred. We rejected the starving child image as a means of raising money for the poor as the people receiving help told us it was demeaning. We were relating to people who sometimes suggested that all aid should stop for a while to allow their people to recover their self-respect and fight for some form of independence. While this was mostly too drastic, there were compromise ideas.

We knew even then, from hard figures and experience, that the trickle-down theory did not work and never would. (The theory that if you put in funds at the top of the structures of societies—in business, government or non-government—it would inevitably trickle down to those at the bottom.) I find it interesting that the Australian Government of the day researched which international agencies managed to get real aid into the hands of those most in need. The Australian Council of Churches and the Catholic aid agencies, plus a couple of secular agencies, were given the highest rating and thus deserving of receiving government grants for their work. Thirty years later, capitalist governments which are subject to the forces of economic rationalism act as though the trickle-down theory is valid in the sharing of wealth at home and abroad.

Sometimes the attitude of those who gave was odd to say the least. I mean, what sort of person is so demeaning of another human being that they think the other will be deeply grateful for a gift of their used tooth-brushes? I kid you not. I actually received such a gift from a church member to send to the poor. Quite apart from the insult, this person obviously hadn't stopped to think that the cost of sending the toothbrushes would far outweigh their value—which was non-existent in the first place!

In my indignation, and as part of my work, I began going around the churches and harassing people for money by making them feel guilty. I told them in no uncertain terms about poverty and need and despair. I gave them figures to back up my descriptions. They sat quailing before me as I thundered out their responsibility before God to respond! I did get some money by doing this, of course—mostly in one-off gifts rather than ongoing commitment. I grew up a little, faced my own fears as I looked at a struggling world, and was overwhelmed by the task of moving towards justice. I learned that even I could stay with this confronting picture if I acknowledged my fear, my guilt and my own incapacity to respond in many ways. I shared this journey with people. I told them that I too wanted to turn off the news because I could not bear to hear anymore and I didn't know what to do. Together we forgave ourselves and found small ways to make a difference.

The experiences given to me by the church in the Middle East, Africa, the United States and Asia changed my life. They profoundly affected the way I saw the world in general and my place in it, and I feel immensely privileged to have been given these opportunities. While they were all provided by the church, they carried me beyond the environment of the church in each place. As a relatively radical person and one who had worked in the area of international aid, I had read about the lives of people in other places, but nothing prepared me for actually seeing those lives lived out. Nothing prepared me for meeting women and men who cared so much for their people that they would risk their lives for the cause of justice. I met people who are undoubtedly the saints and martyrs of our day.

# 19　Into the Middle East

I boarded the Olympic Airlines plane headed for Cyprus. It was 1972 and this was the first time I had ever been overseas. I had been chosen to attend a conference in Nicosia organised by the World Council of Churches and the Vatican on 'A Woman's Role in Peace Education'. I remember being scared to go to sleep on the long flight just in case the plane landed in Nicosia before heading on to Athens and I didn't wake up. Obviously an inexperienced traveller!

Of course, I did land and disembark safely and anxiously took my place in the conference, hoping I would be able to participate adequately. Many of the women were older than me and most seemed to be experienced in international events. On the first night a number of us went to a Greek-Cypriot tavern for dinner. There I sat entranced as I watched Greeks in their own environment. They really did dance and sing *Zorba the Greek* and throw plates to break between the dancers. We joined them in the dance and they laughed and welcomed our attempts and threw the plates for us too. I thought with regret then, as I did later when I entered Arab cultures, that once people have migrated to Australia, we rarely get to see them singing and dancing and laughing and crying as they do when they are in their home country, unworried by prejudice and criticism. I grieved for that loss of passionate life.

The conference was an eye-opener. In Australia at that point, people who worked for peace were often labelled 'communists', whereas in this company, it was perfectly responsible and acceptable to be a peace activist. There was a great deal of information shared as we worked together in cross-cultural groups. I learned much about the analysis of political situations and the underlying injustices in many environments around the world.

I worked with a black South African leader who on one level was far more confident than me, but then revealed the profound damage done when you live all your life surrounded by racism. Each small working group had been asked to present a report on their work to the plenary session of the conference and our group decided to make our point by reversing race roles in the presentation—those of us who were white would take black roles and vice versa. This black South African woman said that she couldn't possibly play a white woman. When we pressed her for her reasons she said that all her life she had been taught that she was inferior to white people and so would find it impossible to act as though she was white. I saw that the depths of the human spirit can be so wounded by racism that it sometimes never recovers.

I became friends with a white South African woman who was a leader in the Black Sash movement—a woman who was taking considerable personal risks to make her stand against apartheid. Later on she and her husband and children paid a visit to Sydney and they stayed in our home for a few days. They were exploring whether to migrate to Australia. As a guest in our home, she didn't lift a finger to help me as I coped with caring for my own husband and children as well as four extras. She graciously sat around and thanked me for all my efforts on their behalf and occasionally directed me kindly towards making life more comfortable for her and her family. I felt like her housekeeper. As they left, they said they had decided not to migrate as they knew they couldn't cope without servants and our houses were far too small. I thought to myself that none of us can afford to feel that we ever encompass the whole spectrum of justice, because even those of us who are radical may never realise what aspects of our own lives betray our convictions.

When we visited the modern history museum there, I was shocked. Deep within me had been the conviction that British soldiers were somehow more civilised than the armed forces of other countries and cultures. They were 'gentlemen soldiers'. That museum contained the history and documentation of the British occupation of Cyprus, not so many years before, and I was faced with the fact that all wars brutalise some members of all armed forces. I also realised that, when given clear evidence of atrocities, even the British Government will turn its eyes away and take no action.

Another person I met at the conference was Shulamit Aloni who was a member of the Israeli Parliament. After Cyprus I had been asked to visit some of the Palestinian refugee and community development projects which the Australian churches had been supporting, and I travelled with Shulamit into Israel. I was very impressed by her sense of justice and she shared with me much about the longings of the Jewish people for a safe and recognised homeland. We swept into Tel Aviv in grand style with diplomatic status and farewelled each other as my business was with the staff of the Middle East Conference of Churches from then on and they were Palestinians.

I don't know what I expected it to be like in Jerusalem. I suppose I had excitedly anticipated how it might feel to walk on the ground where the founder of my faith had once walked. I also knew that I was entering a tragic battleground where two great Semitic peoples struggled for justice. In relation to the first, I was not disappointed. I was amazed to find how small it all was and then remembered that the distances were mostly walked. I stood on the Mount of Olives and looked across at Jerusalem (after duly paying the old Palestinian to move his camel from in front of the view!). There below me was the Garden of Gethsemane with its old olive trees, the graves of Jews, Muslims and Christians between us, and the gate to Jerusalem which both groups thought might be the entry point for the archangel Gabriel at the day of judgement. There was the huge golden dome of the mosque reminding me that three great faiths hold the ground of Jerusalem sacred to their tradition.

My host, a Christian Palestinian, took me to the Church of the Holy Sepulchre. I remember standing inside watching hundreds of tourists queuing to look into the alleged tomb of Jesus and reverently kissing bits of wood and stone. I felt like standing in the middle and shouting, 'He's not here, he's risen!' I felt that if Jesus is anywhere, he is out there with the Israelis and Palestinians in the pain and joys of their lives, not captured in that memorial. We went to a quiet place beside the Lake of Galilee and it was there that I felt as though I was really on sacred ground because it felt ordinary, a place where fisherpeople and other people might work or walk.

My Palestinian friend took me to the refugee camps at Ramullah and then down to Jericho. I had not visited a refugee camp before, let alone one in which the inhabitants lived in exile in their own country, sometimes within sight of the homes which had been theirs. Many of them told me through my interpreter that their families had been there for more than 20 years and that they daily prayed to Allah asking what they had done to deserve their life.

As we went down to Jericho it was interesting to see the buses full of gullible tourists pulling into the inn where the Good Samaritan had taken the man attacked by robbers on the road to Jericho! A quick read of the story would have told them that it was just that—a story, a parable. I was also amused by the many places where you could buy bits of the original cross. It surely must have been a giant cross!

I was taken to visit some of the small villages near Hebron where our churches had been supporting development projects. The idea was that as one village got a project running and earned money, they would pass what was left of the original grant on to the next village. Many were craft projects such as for the Palestinian women who made beautifully embroidered clothes but had no money for sewing machines so had been sewing them up by hand, which did not sell well. We were aiding them to buy some sewing machines which then gave them a chance to be competitive in the export market.

One of the features of poor village life was that people had very large families in the hope that at least some of their children would survive. When we could lift the level of income, women were coming to the project leaders asking for help with birth control because they could see a future for their children. This began to diminish the cycle of poverty. In one village, a leader asked if I could help with advice about a gift which had come from a church in the United States. She led me to a room which was entirely filled with little packets of biscuits. I suppose the donors meant well, but it was somewhat embarrassing to inform the woman that they were in fact weight-reducing biscuits!

After our travels, my host invited me to dinner with his family. We sat in his modest house at a round table with his family. There was a large bowl in the centre and he told me that the family had been carefully saving for this occasion so that they could give me their greatest delicacy for dinner. It was spleen. As one for whom any offal is a problem, I gulped and selected a very tiny bit with lots of vegetables so that it wouldn't look ungrateful. I was relieved to see the family joyfully take advantage of the rest!

I was interested to observe that, contrary to my prejudiced expectations, the opinions of the women at the table were given with confidence and received with respect. In fact, it seemed to me that they received more respect than I was accustomed to receiving in Australia. This taught me not to make assumptions about other cultures by looking at external appearances such as veils and other modest coverings. Again, I was reminded of how little we really know of each other in a multicultural environment and the riches which we fail to share.


When I arrived at the Tel Aviv airport to fly to Lebanon, I no longer had diplomatic status with my friend Shulamit. My whole suitcase was upended and the tape on which I had been recording my visit was confiscated. I often wondered what they made of it because it had been a last-minute idea as I left Australia to save my having to write a diary. The only person in the house who had a spare tape was my 13-year-old son, Robert who had been pretending to be a disc jockey with his friends and their efforts were still on one side of my tape!

As I was driven into Beirut from the airport, I thought it might well be my last journey. I imagined dying in this foreign country as the taxi driver made his extraordinarily dangerous way into the city with horn blaring every few seconds. Mind you, this was also the style of every other driver on the road. They would tear into intersections and play a game of bluff trying to get through. I asked the driver how anyone knew who had right of way. He said that it belonged to the first driver to make eye contact with the other.

I was in Lebanon to look at refugee projects and this time my host was an American Methodist. The first thing we did was to go to a Maronite wedding which was quite special and I was very touched that those concerned would have me there. By this time, I was beginning to think that we Australians are not as hospitable as we like to believe. After that, I visited the Palestinian refugee area. This was very different from the poor but stable refugee camps within Israel. It was a huge area where people lived in bits of tin and cardboard tied together, or anything they could find to create a primitive shelter.

We went on to visit the headquarters of the Palestine Liberation Organisation. There I met young men who had been born in the refugee camps and could see no future for themselves. They could not go back to Palestine, there were few places for them anywhere else, and some were determined to refuse to go anywhere but back to their homeland. There was little or no work for them in Lebanon as most of the refugees were poor farmers with few skills and no land to farm. As well, the economic and social fabric of Lebanon was being threatened by the huge influx of refugees. I realised that these were young men who had virtually nothing to lose. They were, indeed, the fertile ground for terrorists; people of deep and abiding anger who had nowhere to go and little to do.

One day my host took me to the coast of Lebanon for lunch with a friend. I saw the beauty of the countryside, its ancient villages and its famous cedars. As we sat in the cafe, his friend offered me a drink. I said that I didn't drink alcohol as I was a Methodist. My American Methodist host was very surprised as he had not heard of this! His Lebanese friend felt that no meal could be complete without a glass of something and pressed a drink which smelt like aniseed and looked harmlessly like milk upon me. As my alcohol-free system was deeply shocked I was profoundly grateful that we had the meal ahead of us before I had to stand up and walk. I might add that in my later years, I have discovered that a gin and tonic is far superior!

# 20 Into Asia

In 1977 I was contacted by the staff of the Christian Conference of Asia to see if I would co-chair the first Asia Women's Forum to be held in Manila in the Philippines. This forum was a departure from the usual women's activities connected with the CCA which had largely been meetings of representatives of women's organisations in the churches of Asia. This time it was to be a meeting of, for want of a better term, women activists in the Asian region.

The planning group for the conference met in Manila to do its work at the height of the struggle against the Marcos regime. To be honest, I can hardly recall our meetings because the impact of the struggle taking place was so much greater. As we met with the women who lived there, the stories of danger and courage, of torture and death were always with us. There were marches and vigils of protest and all manner of conversation.

I found myself becoming engaged on the periphery of this struggle and was ultimately invited to be a member of the Resource Centre for Philippine Concerns—a group of about ten people from outside the Philippines who later met in various places to be given information about what was going on to take back to their countries. This was an attempt to get past the extreme censorship which was instituted by Marcos and a safer way than trying to get information out via Filipinos. The people involved in this struggle had a profound impact on my life—one which always reminds me that my little struggles for justice in a country like Australia are as nothing compared with the life-and-death commitments to justice required of so many others around the world.

It was during the preparation for the Women's Forum that I first met Sister Christine Tan. Our paths were to cross several times and every time we met I was inspired and challenged by her life. Christine was a tiny woman but huge in stature. She was head of her order and at one point the mother provincial for the Philippines. Her order had as its major focus the rehabilitation of prostitutes in the slums of Manila, in the Tondo. Christine came from a wealthy family and was a woman of some confidence. As she and her nuns worked with the prostitutes they saw that the underlying problem was poverty. They decided to sell off almost all their convents and the valuable land surrounding them and go and live with the women in the Tondo. They did this quickly and decisively before the church authorities could intervene. In response to this, Christine was demoted from her role as mother provincial and sent to Rome for a period of 'reflection'! When she returned to the Philippines she became deeply engaged in the people's struggle against President Marcos. I shared a room with her on several occasions and she told stories of nuns lending their habits for the successful disguise of men in the rebel forces as they tried to cross the military traps set for them. What moved me about her was that, in relating to me and others, she was so absolutely ordinary and unassuming as if what she was doing was matter-of-fact and insignificant.

We would sit in a room planning, knowing that there were soldiers with guns sitting outside the door watching what we were doing and where we were going next. They were there to menace the women within, to remind them that Marcos was not fooled, that he knew they were part of the struggle against him. We would come out and get into a car and the soldiers would follow for a while. When they dropped off or we managed to get rid of them by adroit driving, the women would look around carefully and then say, 'Hey, let's sing our song!' They would all laugh and sing a song about freedom that Marcos had banned. They did so much laughing and singing, so much writing of poems and producing of art. It was as though the deathly journey could only be lived in the company of the highest forms of joy and creativity. It was so different from the rather grim and serious life of the activists at home, including myself, and yet there was so much more at stake.

As the Women's Forum approached, it was decided to move it to Penang as things were getting difficult and possibly dangerous in the Philippines and some people who were going to attend might not have been able to get entry visas. Penang, with its strongly Buddhist culture, was so different. At that stage there was an Australian army base nearby and the soldiers spent quite a bit of their time off on Penang. As we travelled the roads, I observed them walking around the place, often carrying large supplies of liquor. I also saw them in one of the big hotels choosing the woman they wanted as they sat holding numbers in a glass viewing room.

About 60 women from 17 Asian countries attended the forum. We quickly found that most of them had been warned by the male leaders in their churches to be suspicious of the western feminists from Australia and New Zealand. They were told that we were militant, anti-male, anti-family and generally immoral. This idea was rapidly challenged when we began to share together the stories of the things which concerned us as women. We discovered that although there were indeed differences in focus according to our cultures and political situations, there were also many issues which we had in common. They were issues like domestic violence, rape in war and peace, sexual abuse, our longing to have more participation in the life of both church and society and freedom from inequities and exploitation in the workplace.

Our eyes filled with tears as we listened to Sister Christine Tan tell of a female leader in the Philippines who at that moment was lying in a coma in hospital due to torture by the military. Christine looked at us and said, 'I don't want your tears, or even your prayers. I want your anger!' She went on to discuss how she believed that part of being truly human, and truly Christian, was to react with indignation and anger when people suffered injustice. This involved far more than passing resolutions and making statements, it needed to arise from some deep sense of offence when humankind was betrayed in this way. We saw in her a woman whose very soul sang with the power of her commitment to active love and costly justice.

I was also learning the hard way how to handle cross-cultural relationships, especially from a position of leadership. Had I known what I know now, I would never have accepted the invitation to co-chair the Asian conference. I learned that while people on one level may want the skills you have, or even the power that you bring, they don't necessarily love you for giving it. Deep down I felt I was still seen as a representative of colonisation and privilege, an alien Westerner.

I was invited to prepare the report from the forum which was to go to the assembly of the Christian Conference of Asia a few days later. When I was asked to do this, I accepted the invitation with relief as I felt I could do something useful and clear and I knew I was quite competent at writing and presenting such reports. After all, they had said, 'Would you write the report, Dorothy? Seeing English is your first language you will find it so much easier than the rest of us.' I wrote the report and at the final meeting of the forum gave everyone the draft. They took a quick look at it and said it was not very good and not Asian enough. In all honesty, I was angry. I felt used and abused.


Over the next four years, when I represented the Australian churches on the general committee of the Christian Conference of Asia, I began to see things more clearly. I learned to stand well back and offer what I had in ways which elevated others rather than led them or represented them, or even to do nothing more than being there.

When I attended the assembly of the Christian Conference of Asia, I met a young woman from the Philippines named Jessica Sales. We often sat together in the plenary sessions of the assembly. She was about 22 years old, a recent graduate in social work, and conducted a workshop on her work of supporting the families of political prisoners in Manila. After the workshop she sat down beside me and said, 'Dorothy, I think those words may cost me my life and I don't really want to die.' I just looked at her speechlessly and wondered what on Earth to say. She paused and thought for a moment, and then said, 'But I have to live.' I knew she was speaking of living vividly and fully; of not restricting her life. At the time, although part of me wondered if she was being a trifle dramatic, I had some sense that I was in the presence of someone who may well pay a heavy price for her choices. When I returned home I made enquiries about her through my contacts in Manila and was informed that she was indeed arrested by the military on her return to Manila. Later I heard that her body was found in a mass grave with evidence that she had suffered horrific torture. I knew that I would never have to face the choices which lay in her life, nor did I think that I would ever have the courage to choose as she did. What this did confirm for me was the recognition that life is not fundamentally about length, but about depth—that some people can live to be 100 and not live as much as Jessica Sales did in her 22 years.

Later on I had the privilege of meeting Father Ed De la Torre, a priest working for justice and freedom in the Philippines. As I met him, and when I met Nelson Mandela, I believe I saw something of the beauty which people may have seen in Jesus. That is not to say that either of those two men were Jesus. It was just that each of them radiated a special life which evidenced itself in a paradox. On the one hand they were more humble and human than most of us choose to be, so they felt eminently approachable. On the other hand there was something about their presence which made you want to either just touch them as an encounter with holiness or keep your distance in awe. When Nelson Mandela walked down the aisle of St Mary's Cathedral in Sydney after his release from prison, people reached out to touch him as he passed and I understood that impulse.

Like Mandela, Ed De la Torre had spent years in solitary confinement. After several years in prison and a wide international campaign, he had been released and Cardinal Sin of the Philippines had sent him to Rome to be reoriented in some way. He came back and resumed his activities in opposition to President Marcos and was sent to prison again for several more years until the regime fell. In prison he used to design various images of little doves with words about freedom on the back and these were reproduced as pendants for sale to aid the work in support of the families of political prisoners. We used to sell them in Australia and I still hold one as a reminder of Father Ed. His special work was on behalf of the hill tribes of the Philippines and he used to tell marvellous stories about their life and culture and the way they inspired him.

Some years after I met Father Ed I to attended a conference on the Philippines in New York. Someone had invited a man from the hill tribes to address us. On reflection, it was a rather strange thing to do. This man had never been away from his hill country before. He had never been on a bus, let alone a plane, and there he was in New York at a conference. No-one seemed to speak his language to any extent and his way of coping appeared to be to sit under a tree by himself, looking meditatively into space.

When his turn came to contribute to the conference of about 100 people from around the world, he came onto the platform, sat on the floor and began to sing. It is impossible to describe the sound of that song. All I can say is that we all listened transfixed to a cry of longing, of sadness and pleading, for the return of the land to his people. Even though we didn't understand one word, the message came through to our hearts and challenged us more than any fine speeches might have done. He sang for quite a long time, then stood in dignified silence for a while and walked away. I knew that his song belonged to all displaced and oppressed indigenous people whose life is dependent on their land in ways which most of us will never really understand. I knew that I was part of that displacement and the grief and pain which follows for indigenous people.


As a member of the general committee of the Christian Conference of Asia I attended meetings in several parts of Asia, including India. This was a mixed experience. In Bangalore we attended a large gathering of

Christians from around Asia. The local church leaders had arranged a special dinner for us and we were seated at the tables talking after we had been served. I was near one of the bishops from Bangalore when he was approached by a small, very thin man. The man bowed to the bishop and said, 'Please, sir, our people have been working for the feast since five o'clock this morning without a break for food. Would it be all right if we eat now?' The bishop literally turned on him and said in a loud voice, 'How dare you ask such a thing. Can't you see that our guests are still here and may want more service! Go away!' The man slunk away in humiliation and we sat there in shocked silence. The bishop resumed his cheerful conversation as though nothing had happened. Such is the sinful side of the church.

Another experience offered other possibilities. I had been working for some time with a man from the Cathedral of the Church of South India in Bangalore, Alex Devasunderam. We had been sending regular funding from Australian churches for a particular aid program that he was running. Alex believed that it was damaging to people to simply hand out aid. Instead, he would use the gifts of overseas churches to work with the poorest people to help them start money-earning projects. Alex would go into their area, get to know the people and their natural leaders, and train those people to plan their own projects. When they had their plan, they would be invited to go to the bank concerned and negotiate an interest-free loan to use as their starting capital. After the loan had been paid back over time, it would be available for someone else's project. In this way, those in need never became mendicants and they learned life-changing skills.

When I met Alex in Bangalore, he invited me to meet some of the people with whom he was working at that time. We went to a huge dump where people were living in holes burrowed out at the bottom of the compressed rubbish. It not only gave them a measure of shelter, but some warmth because of the rotting material above. There was no water in the area and no sewerage. The women walked some kilometres to bring back washing and drinking water on their heads and there was an area assigned as the sewerage area, to put it politely. The women usually waited until the night to go there for reasons of modesty.

As we entered the area, the children initially ran away because they had never seen a white person before, especially one wearing a big hat. Alex took me to meet some of the women and they acted as though they were showing me into a normal home as they displayed the holes where they lived. They were welcoming and smiling as though I was an honoured guest. Unlike the other parts of India I had been to, there was not a single incident of begging. One of the women gestured to me to follow her to her home and then indicated that she wanted to show me something inside. I bent down and entered and there she proudly showed me a thin dog suckling four little puppies. She smiled with joy as she stroked them.

I talked about this with Alex as we left and said that, had it been me, I think I would have eaten the dog, given that I was virtually starving. He said that maybe I could learn from that woman that when life is so desperate and fragile, sometimes people hold everything as sacred and simply share their vital and meagre resources with each other, including with other creatures. He reminded me that those who are poor are not necessarily less enjoying of pets than those of us who are rich; that there are greater values which can be sustained than survival itself.

My last visit to Asia was to Sri Lanka in 1994. This time I was attending the Christian Conference of Asia as a keynote speaker. I had already attended the pre-conference women's meeting and played a very different role than that which I played in my first trip into Asia—well in the background! It was interesting to see how far things had moved in the confidence of women in the two decades. They were far more assertive in the life of the conference itself and there was no more talk of 'beware the western feminists'!

We were intensely conscious that we were in something like a war-zone with military roadblocks and threats of 'terrorist' activities. If I put terrorist in quotes it is because by this stage, after witnessing the struggles for justice in many different places around the world, I was very wary of giving particular names to activities in any conflict. It would be very interesting to calculate the number of innocent civilians killed by official armed forces against those killed by people named as terrorists. It would also be interesting to reflect on which type of violence came from the powerful and which from the weak, which from the poor and which from the rich. In the twenty-first-century climate of terrorist activities this comparison may be a little harder to make, but I am still loath to make such clear distinctions between different forms of violence and struggle. If there was one thing my travels in Asia had taught me it was to be rigorous in analysis of any situation rather than falling for political statements from those in power.

At this assembly I had been invited to reflect on the future issues for the church. A friend who was there representing the United Church of Canada said she would shout me dinner if I was game to say the word homosexuality in my keynote address. I decided that I would do this, if only because the word is largely absent from the church's discussions in Asia, and yet I knew it was a real issue. I put it in lightly as something which was being discussed by many churches around the world. The response was amazing. Many people came up to me and thanked me for saying up front what their Asian speakers felt unable to say and to confirm that issues of sexuality are indeed simmering along underneath the silences in the culture. And I won my free dinner!

One of the best experiences I had in Sri Lanka was during the final worship service held in the Anglican Cathedral in Colombo. Included in the service was what appeared to be Hindu dancing as a way of illustrating a Bible reading. It was as though a joining of life, culture and faith had broken through old boundaries and found common ground for good and celebration. There were some protests from members of the conference after this event, but I found it quite inspiring.

# 21 The Nairobi Assembly

My first direct experience of the World Council of Churches was when I was suddenly and surprisingly chosen to be one of the then Australasian Methodist delegates to its Nairobi Assembly in 1975. The WCC is a body made up of delegates from over 300 national churches across the whole spectrum of mainstream churches, from Orthodox to Pentecostal, apart from the Catholic Church which participates as an observer church. Every seven years these churches gather in a great assembly of about 3,000 people plus about 2,000 observers, for more than two weeks of discussion and worship. There were 12 people who represented the Australian Churches at the Nairobi Assembly.

I will always remember the impact of entering Africa—its marvellous rhythms of dance and drums and singing, alongside the feeling of walking through streets among people who sometimes gave evidence of feeling hostile towards a white minority in a country which had suffered much from their rule.

I had my most profound experience of white racism in its destructive subtlety when I was invited to visit a friend of a family member who had lived in Nairobi for many years. She lived in a grand mansion on the outskirts of the city, set in what appeared to be a park surrounded by high walls and with armed black guards at the gate. She was a kindly, older white woman from England who was active in her local church and who told stories of how she loved the Kenyan children and taught them in Sunday school.

As we ate, a middle-aged Kenyan servant stood impassively behind her, waiting for any orders for service. My hostess described over dinner how she, unlike some others, provided comfortable accommodation for her black servants in cottages at the back of her house. Then she half-turned towards the servant and said, 'They are very nice-looking people, aren't they? They have such good strong bodies and I quite like the colour of their skins now I am used to it. I find them to be very good servants.' I sat there transfixed as she talked further in this vein and then returned to discuss other things. I watched the expressionless face of the man who was being discussed as though he was some favourite dog. I found myself thinking, 'If I were this man, I think I would kill this woman come the revolution.' And I knew she would never understand why I would do that. I vowed to myself to work for the rest of my life to end racism and to try to discern it in myself.

At the assembly, I had been invited to speak during a plenary session on the theme of 'Women in a changing world'. I can't remember what I said, but I will always recall what happened at the end of the session. As I moved to join the queue for morning tea, I was confronted by a very angry African man. He waved his hands and shouted that I had betrayed the faith and the Bible in asserting that women should not be submissive to men and said that I would destroy families and the church. I stood there shaking in the face of his rage but, before I could say a word, an African-American man came up beside us. He put his arm around me and said gently to the African man, 'Brother, haven't you heard the good news about women? In my church at home, women have taught us a different way of relating in mutual love and respect. Our women have been freed to be strong and we men have been freed to be gentle and vulnerable. Let me tell you all about it.' He took the African man by the hand and led him away talking earnestly. As I watched in wonder, I thought to myself that this was the dream I had for relationships between women and men.

During the assembly, all the delegates were invited to attend a Kenyan church for Sunday worship and were assigned to different congregations. We boarded a bus to go to the African Brotherhood Church. We seemed to travel for hours to get there, winding around mountains and out into villages where people came to look at the unusual sight of a bus.

We finally arrived at a little church and were ushered into our reserved seats. The church was packed and people were hanging through the windows. After the welcome to us, amazing singing and drumming began. This was followed by the minister reading from the Bible before he turned to us and said in English, 'Now, who will be giving the sermon?' A brave European woman who spoke some Swahili volunteered and the minister said, 'Now, you must all listen very carefully because we will have the questions afterwards to see if you heard.' Sure enough, when the sermon ended, he asked questions of the congregation like an examiner to ensure they had listened!

Next thing he announced the offering and we watched as people came forward with all sorts of farm goods—little bunches of vegetables, live chooks, sticks tied in bundles and other produce, which they placed in the sanctuary. A few placed small amounts of money in a bowl on a stand. Then the minister said, 'Now, we will have our auction!' He proceeded to auction off all the produce which had been brought forward, complete with gavel to count down the last bid. Then we had more songs and drumming. The service took more than two hours and then we were invited into the hall for lunch. We observed that we were the only ones eating and were told that, when we finished, the adults would eat and then the children would have anything which was left. The children sang to us outside the window while we ate. We surely ate sparingly and talked all the way home about the hospitality and joy of a people who had little by any standards.

One of the most significant events at any WCC assembly is the Eucharist. In Nairobi, there was a service of preparation for it where many different people, men and women, old and young, participated and then the African churches had been asked to preside over the Eucharist itself. Because of the then dominant culture within churches in Africa, there was not one woman present—not even a reader or a server, let alone anyone presiding. As a feminist in the church, I was not unaccustomed to this experience but, for some reason, this time it disturbed me in a way which was far more personal. I sat there with tears of grief running down my face and debated whether I could participate. In the end I did, but something new had stirred within me which went beyond the principle involved. I realised that my feelings were predominantly of grief rather than anger—grief that the church was incomplete without full female participation.

# 22 The Canberra Assembly

For the Canberra Assembly of the World Council of Churches in 1991 I had been asked to be part of the Assembly Worship Committee, which I regarded as a high honour. I was now ordained and the minister of the Pitt Street Uniting Church. In my role as a member of the Worship Committee, I met with about a dozen people from churches around the world to plan the 13 major worship services for the assembly. We worked together on this for about five years, mostly meeting in Geneva.

Although the members of the committee were very experienced in producing many different forms of worship and had wonderful ideas, virtually none of them were writers of liturgy, so it became my task to listen and gather up ideas and try to form them into words for each service. While this was both a challenge and an honour for me, it reminded the WCC Planning Committee to seek more diversity in this respect for the next assembly as, no matter how hard you try, there is a distinctive style which belongs to each liturgical writer and it is better to have variety.

At the assembly, it had been decided that one of the main services would begin with a procession from the main conference centre to the worship tent. It was a walk for justice, or something of that sort. Some members of the Worship Committee, including myself, had to help get it started and then we had to race ahead of the procession and arrive at the worship tent before everyone else. By this stage of the assembly, I might say, we were almost walking in our sleep and running on adrenaline alone for survival in our huge task.

A group of Canberra children of many ethnic backgrounds had been chosen to lead the procession and they were excitedly lining up at the head when along came a group of Aboriginal people who had been present at the assembly who took their place in front of the children. By this time, the members of the assembly were coming out of their session to take their place in the procession. I rushed up to the Aboriginal people and, I was told later, proceeded to signal to the group to come in behind the children instead of in the front and used 'a voice with which white people order Aboriginal people around'. I didn't wait to see what happened but rushed on to get to the worship tent ahead of the procession. What did happen was that the Aboriginal group moved to the side of the procession and then went back to their own tent rather than to the service.

I was pulled out of the service and asked to go to the Aboriginal tent. When I arrived they were all seated in a circle and I was asked to listen to them give an account of how they experienced my behaviour. This they proceeded to do for about an hour as I cried with regret. I apologised and expressed my profound sadness that I had added to their pain. They then asked if I would make a public apology to them at the great Eucharistic service the next day. After a sleepless night and much anxiety, I did this and my apology rang around the world as the media of many nations picked up the service. In talking with my Aboriginal friends later, I realised that, although they had been given a good deal of space at the assembly to tell their story, there had been no apology from the Australian churches in response. They desperately needed a formal apology from someone and I unwittingly gave them the entry into that possibility, even though it was but a personal apology. It was a memorable and heavy-hearted moment.

# $\mathcal{23}$  The Harare Assembly

In 1993 I was asked to be the moderator (chairperson) of the World Council of Churches Assembly Worship Committee. I was to lead an international committee in the preparation of the worship for the Harare Assembly in 1998.

When the request to assume this responsibility came by phone from a WCC meeting in Johannesburg, I was so honoured I agreed on the spot to do it. Afterwards, I remembered that being simply a member of an Assembly Worship Committee for the Canberra assembly had involved the hardest month of work in my whole life. Still, given that no woman had been a moderator before, I couldn't resist.

When it came to taking up my task as moderator of the Worship Committee, I recall preparing for our first meeting in Geneva. I knew I would be facing 17 church leaders from 17 different national churches around the globe. Some of them would be bishops or archbishops. I decided that we would start by sharing a bit about our lives so we could get to know each other. I planned in my head a sort of CV to share which I hoped would convince them that I was qualified to do the task. When the day came, I was jet-lagged, unlike most of the delegates, after 28 hours of flying.

When I looked around the circle of people, I felt truly daunted. I suggested that we begin the sharing and asked a man from the Pacific to start for us. Rather than outlining an impressive personal CV, the dear man thought that we were to share our life struggles and pray for each other. He set the scene. Before we knew it we were all quite vulnerably sharing some of the tough things we were facing in our churches and countries of origin, and in our personal lives. We found ourselves with tears in our eyes and with an entirely different view of our task and who we could be together. That is not to say that we didn't have our moments, but somehow we never really moved past the gift of that first trusting sharing which had been created for us by that good man from the Cook Islands.

From the first building up of trust we found that each of us had particular gifts to offer. I can still see an Indian leader and musician saying in the middle of some earnest discussion, 'I feel a hallelujah coming on!' As we paused, he proceeded to take from his bag a smallish box which when he opened and closed the lid made a sort of droning sound. This was to be the background for his 'hallelujah' which he would teach us to sing. On the first Sunday of our meeting we went to a service at a church in downtown Geneva which we decided was a bit proper so we proceeded to walk down the street together singing our hallelujah and laughing as we went.

It was no easy thing to bring together worship which was acceptable to parts of the church as disparate as African Methodist and Armenian Orthodox and everything in between. If we really hit a wall, we would stop and ask those concerned to try and tell everyone else what was at stake for them and then share what was at stake for those who did not want the change made. We nearly always found some way through and by the time we got to Harare, we were a committed team.

A year before the assembly we met in Harare to soak up the environment and to meet some local people. Since our previous meeting, I had 'come out' to my church in a public manner as a lesbian and I knew that this news had rocketed around the world on the ecumenical news services. My own church had affirmed its confidence in my holding the position with the Worship Committee and there had been formal affirmations from the WCC staff. But what would my committee do with me? I walked in to chair the first meeting and was aware of virtually every eye being on me in a new way. I looked at the faces of my friends and proceeded. I could see them deciding that I was still the person they knew and felt them making their commitment to me. Some of them did that in words when we broke for morning tea, but I will never forget the opening of that meeting and their gift to me.

We were committed to employing local people to produce as many of our resources as possible and needed a symbolic gift to give to each person present at the final service of the assembly. One day some of our members were walking along the road and, as usual, casually perusing the bits and pieces of craft for sale spread out on blankets. One young man had a whole lot of small objects made of wire. There were bicycles and birds and in among them, a little wire cross. 'That's it!' they thought. They picked it up and said, 'We will have 5,000 of these, thank you.' The face of the young man was a study of disbelief and trembling hope. He and his family lived off the order for the year which led to the assembly and he delivered the 5,000 crosses about two hours before the service.

We went to a church in one of the poorer areas of Harare on the Sunday we were there. We sat with the local people on blocks of concrete in the bare hall and listened to their choirs sing and their drummers drum—choirs which would do anyone proud anywhere. When I remarked on this to a young person's choir member afterwards, he asked if I would send him a tape of some Australian church youth choirs. I said that I didn't think we had very many and he said, with surprise, 'But what do they do?' For the first part of the service, we sat among the people. I sat next to a young mother with a little boy on her knee. As the service progressed, the little boy climbed off his mother's knee and moved in beside me. He took my hand and looked up into my face. Then he moved closer and studied my every feature as if he were committing them to memory. As he did this his mother leant over and said, 'He hasn't seen a white person before.'

We were invited to sit out the front during the sermon and, as I watched the anxiety and awe on the faces of the people during the long and impassioned delivery, I asked the church leader next to me which Bible passage was the subject of the sermon. He handed me an English version of the Bible and pointed out the passage. With amazement, I read a passage that was mostly unfamiliar to me. Some verses were indeed in the Bible, such as Paul's thoughts on the need for children to honour parents and wives to honour husbands. However, the verses in between which threatened hellish punishment for those who did not and some added thoughts about obedience to church leaders were sheer inventions of the English translators. Such was some of the missionary activity in Africa.

During our meeting time in Harare, we were hosted by the Zimbabwean Council of Churches and they provided a small bus and a driver to take us anywhere we needed to go. The driver was a very gracious man who patiently carried us around, coping with sudden changes of plans, waiting while we did or saw various things, giving us helpful directions and generally caring for us. When the time came for us to leave Harare, we decided we should give him a tip—throwing in a minimum of ten Zimbabwean dollars each. Most of us gave a bit more than that as Zimbabwean dollars are worth very little in other currencies. We purchased a nice little wallet, put the dollars inside and then presented it to him on our final trip. He was very grateful for our speech of thanks and, as we watched, opened the wallet and looked inside. His face registered a mixture of shock and unbelieving wonder. We felt gratified that we had apparently done the right thing. Later on, one of the Zimbabwean staff told us that we had given him more than the equivalent of one year's salary! We were glad that we had been so easily able to be generous but were challenged by the fact that this man had to live on so little.


When we returned to Harare in 1998 for the assembly, we were required to arrive before the delegates and visitors to get our bearings and begin preparations. Buses took us from the airport to the University of Harare on the outskirts of the city which was to be our home and working place for the next four weeks. We were housed in the student residences and the activities of the assembly were spread around various parts of the campus. The first thing that became clear was that we would get very fit walking and carrying as we had no access to a car. Because the Worship

Committee was based over near the worship tent now rising impressively on the university oval, we found ourselves walking at least two hours every day just to get from our accommodation to our meals and to our workplace. Very good for body and soul—well sort of!

One memorable experience occurred when I went to dinner in the student dining hall and sat with a man from Harare. He sat with his meal before him on the table, not a greedy meal, even though he had served himself from the buffet. I sat opposite with my dinner before me, thoughtlessly gathered from the supply on the side tables, and opened my mouth to begin a conversation with him. Then I saw that his eyes were fixed with wonder on his plate as he looked reverently at the food which was there. After some moments, he lifted his fork and slowly, carefully took a mouthful of food. He raised his eyes and gazed thoughtfully into the distance as he chewed—with a deep and solemn joy, a fleeting smile passing across his face at intervals as he savoured each taste, each fragment of food, as though he was storing it up for the future. After each mouthful was finished he surveyed his plate in wonder again and made a careful selection until the food was gone. He sat before his empty plate in meditative silence and then respectfully left the table. I knew I was seeing a man eating a meal as though it was a Sacrament. He was eating as one who had never seen such food before and knew that, after the assembly of the World Council of Churches, he might never do so again. I looked at my meal. It looked different. The world looked different.

For the assembly the student residences in which we stayed were to be cleaned by the previously unemployed women of the Widows' Association of Harare. Night and day they cleaned the corridors, the rooms and the bathrooms, working long hours for very little pay. They were welcoming women; kindly to the delegates as visitors to their city. Each day most people went off to their meals and the WCC meetings and left them to do the cleaning. One morning I returned to get something from my room. As I approached the bathroom nearby, I heard unusual noises—ecstatic noises, sounds of happiness, with much laughter and some singing. I looked in the door and there were the cleaning women, clutching tiny fragments of soap, bathing and showering in joy and delight. They were lifting up their arms to feel the water flowing over their bodies, almost dancing under the showers and lying back in the full bath in bliss, encouraging each other in this wondrous moment of access to hot running water. When they saw me, the sounds suddenly stopped and then we all laughed together, celebrating the moment and my recognition that they had 'seized the day'. One of my colleagues on the Worship Committee also had this experience, so they must have taken the opportunity more than once. The Widows of Harare live in my memory and have given me a new joy and thankfulness for water.

Once our little group, the Worship Committee, looked at our task in earnest we realised that we had a huge circular tent in the middle of a muddy oval with around 4,000 chairs arranged in rows before a large platform. Thankfully some pot plants had been placed before the platform which softened things a bit. We had to transform this into a worship space, find people to lead the worship, let them rehearse and then cue everyone when the worship started. Television cameras from around the world were already being set up to film the opening worship.

We decided to hang some African cloth around the back of the stage to make a sort of sanctuary area and made contact with some Zimbabwean women who gathered some for us. About ten hours before they were to be delivered, we were told they had been stolen so we had to leap into a taxi, find some shops and buy up anything we could find. We then triumphantly hung them over the railing at the back of the stage and cleverly attached them with velcrose which we had found in a shop. After that, we had to clean the 4,000 chairs which were covered with dust and bits of mud, and try to find some straw or something to put in the aisles to cover the mud.

At last all was ready. The great crowd from around the world was gathering. The procession of church leaders was lining up. The camera crews were in place. Suddenly we realised that all the cloth at the back of the sanctuary was beginning to descend to the ground! The velcrose had melted under the heat of the tent and the television lights. Never have so many mending kits and stray safety pins been found so fast. The WCC was duly opened with its worship and we breathed a sigh of relief.

After this we were told that people in wheelchairs were having trouble getting to the tent in the mud. So, a Swiss nun, an English woman who had recently had a hip replacement and I 'borrowed' some shovels from around the campus and made a sort of bridge across a muddy trench with rocks and stray bits of straw and grass. The people in wheelchairs were duly grateful and we felt very strong and clever, while admitting that digging was not what we had anticipated as part of our task as the Worship Committee!

Early in the piece, we had planned a night vigil which included a sort of Easter journey for the delegates and decided that we needed flaming torches to mark a meditation point. We found some big sticks, wound the rags we had cleaned the seats with around the tops of the sticks and dipped them in baby oil. They made quite impressive flaming torches. This being so successful, we decided to use the idea in one of the later services for a symbolic moment. The men in the committee felt that the flame was less than grand, so they scrounged some paraffin oil from some-where and soaked the rags for some hours. The flame was to be lit at a high point in the service and carried by a young Indian woman. We didn't feel we could rehearse it as we would use up our rags. However, Gwen, the English woman, and I felt just a tad anxious about this torch so we decided minutes before the service began to go behind the tent and see if we could try it out just for a second. We put a match to the torch and the whole thing went woomph! as the flame shot into the air and ran right down the stick following the oil. We hastily extinguished it in a muddy pool and found ourselves a large candle to use as a substitute!

I managed to attend only one business session. That session was the one when Nelson Mandela addressed the assembly. I had met him when he visited Sydney shortly after his release from prison and I wanted to hear what he had to say to this gathering of church leaders. He literally danced down the aisle onto the platform with people singing and dancing around him. He thanked the WCC for its loyalty to and support of the African

National Congress throughout the struggle against apartheid, and the church in South Africa which made it possible for him to be one of the few non-whites to be given an education.

Then he said, 'I am looking at your faces to see eternity there' and stood in silence and looked at the delegates carefully. I don't think anyone knew exactly what he meant. I sat in a side gallery and looked at the members of the assembly as they reacted to him—the primates, archbishops, patriarchs and presidents and other church leaders. Some appeared quite peaceful, others seemed offput by him looking at them. Other people looked embarrassed or innocently enquiring. I pondered what a face with eternity written on it would look like. I believed that it would be a face which showed love and compassion, humanness and openness. Nelson Mandela said nothing about what he had seen but I expect that many people decided that they did, indeed, see eternity on his face.

Finally we arrived at the service to celebrate the jubilee of the modern ecumenical movement. This service was not one we had created—it was the work of the WCC staff and the heads of the various sections of the churches. As often happens in such a process, it was a fairly complex and wordy liturgy, far removed from the style we had developed for our own services which rested less on words and more on imagery and action. However, it was handed over to us to facilitate. It had been decided to use mostly young people as leaders as they were the church of the future. We had to find what seemed like multitudes of people to lead various sections of the service and rehearse them just hours before it happened. We hadn't seen the text before so we were somewhat flying blind. We knew it was a very significant historical moment and took the leaders through the whole service, showed them when to mount the platform, where to stand and so on.

I was in the congregation, anxiously following each section, reading ahead and overseeing the cueing of leaders. Quite suddenly I saw what we had missed—a heading which simply said 'Prayer'. The WCC staff had also missed it in their preparations. We had missed it because there were no words underneath the heading, but I knew it was meant to be a key moment of prayer. I signalled to one of the staff and mouthed 'What will we do?' He just looked helplessly at me. The leaders of that section of the service were about to mount the platform and I knew that when they came to the heading, they would wait respectfully for someone to pray. With a thudding heart, I simply joined them in the line, mounted the platform with them and knew that I would have to think of something as we walked across to our places. Even as I approached the microphone, I couldn't think what to do and then, inspiration! 'Let us pray together in silence,' I said, then felt extremely clever as I remembered the word for silence in each of the languages being used—German, English, French and Spanish. There was a hush and finally I announced, 'In the name of the Christ, Amen.' 'Amen!' said everyone.

I laughed later when some of the Australian delegates told me how they had watched me mount the platform and had felt so proud because at last I was visible as the moderator of the Worship Committee and an Australian. Numbers of people said how wise it was to have a time of silence among all the words. Little did they know!

When we came to the last worship service of the assembly, it was close to Christmas so we had candles and sang 'Adeste Fidelus' ('O Come All Ye Faithful') as our final hymn. I will never forget the sound of that carol and the representatives of the world churches walking out into the darkness with their candles to return to virtually every part of the Earth and its struggles.

However, even before the sounds had died away, dozens of trucks appeared on the oval and within what seemed like minutes all the seats were on the trucks and the great tent was being dismantled. The centre-piece of our worship had been a magnificent wooden cross carved by one of Zimbabwe's finest artists. It was so large that it was mounted on a huge stand. So, here we were, with the tent coming down around us and this valuable cross needing to be safely moved and deposited somewhere. We managed to convince some workmen to help us take it out of the stand and to put the stand on a truck for delivery somewhere, but we were still left with the massive cross. We decided it should go to the administrative office of the WCC. In the dark and mud, about eight people lifted the cross and trundled off with it. When they arrived at the administration building it was locked so they decided to try another spot. When they arrived there, the guard wouldn't let them in. Talk about 'no room at the inn' as this little band of people earnestly carried a huge cross around the Harare campus in the dark and were refused entry at each place. Finally they convinced the student union to let them leave it on the pool table in their bar room. A very suitable *Life of Brian*-type ending to the sagas of the Worship Committee!

*Part 6*

# Movements for Change

# $\mathcal{24}$ The Peace Movement

In Sydney, in the seventies, the Women's International League for Peace and Freedom was made up of a very impressive group of mainly middle-aged, mostly university-educated women. As the name suggests, this is an international movement for women interested in peace and it has, for many decades, had observer status at the United Nations. I was among the youngest there in those days. We met in Mosman in the house of a woman whose husband was a distinguished medical practitioner and had the most interesting and informative discussions. The members of the group were better read than anyone I had ever met—they really researched the topics that interested them and gathered their information from overseas as well as in Australia. They were very fussy indeed about seeking the truth. I sat at their feet and listened and learnt as they explored things together.

If they believed that they had information which needed to be considered by the wider public or government or some other institution, they would write letters to newspaper editors or politicians or other leaders— sharp, clear letters, founded on the best information they could get. Letter writing was not something I had done much of before that point, but the WILPF women set me on a path which I have followed ever since. They never gave up if their letters were not published and I realised that, for every letter you see printed, there have probably been three or more refused. I also learnt that if you care about something, absolute faithfulness and perseverance is required.

Our most memorable effort was at a point when the Vietnam War had been going for a while and Robert Menzies was Prime Minister of

Australia. It was rumoured that he was going to announce the bringing in of conscription at a senate election rally in Hornsby. So we decided to go along and planned what we would do. We arrived at the rally early and sat right in the centre of the hall, which rapidly filled and overflowed with Liberal supporters. It was the first time I had seen Menzies in person and I could not help but be amazed by the power which he exuded and his charisma. I felt that if he asked everybody to prostrate themselves before him, they would have done so—the excited support was both palpable and frightening.

In the middle of his speech, he did indeed announce that the government would be bringing in conscription. At this point the six of us from WILPF stood up from our seats in silence and placed black veils over our heads. Barrie, listening on the radio at home, said that he had never before heard Menzies momentarily at a loss for words. We then filed out of the hall with our black veils over our heads. People actually spat at us as we left and followed us out shaking their fists. It was really quite frightening. The media picked it up and our photos appeared in the next day's papers.

This was one of the best protests in which I have participated. It was typical of the WILPF women—well thought out, non-violent and effective. It didn't stop Menzies bringing in conscription, of course, but people did notice what we had done and the struggle against conscription continued.


Around this time Barrie was directly connected with the Coalition for Peace and I took part in their activities and protests as well, but was more directly related to a group which some us started and called Mothers and Others for Peace. We modelled our approach on the US movement called Another Mother for Peace which had as its logo a flower and the words 'War is not healthy for children and other living things'. We changed the name to be inclusive of all women, but we still targeted our monthly newsletter at women who were at home. We gave them information about the Vietnam War and ideas for letter writing—an activity which could be conducted from home. As well as writing articles, I was the Letraset expert, spending much time laboriously creating the newsletter's headings. In fact a good deal of life seemed to revolve around the arduous production of various little publications and flyers—one-finger typing of stencils with pink corrections all over them, turning handles of duplicators, walking around tables collating and stapling, and addressing and stuffing envelopes. People don't know they are alive in these days of computers and photocopiers!

Not long after putting my name to a whole page ad against conscription in the *Sydney Morning Herald*, there was a knock on the front door and standing there were two men, I kid you not, dressed in raincoats with hats pulled down over their eyes. They flashed ID which indicated they were from the federal police and asked to come in. I sat them down in our lounge room and they pulled out the ad from the *Herald* and showed it to me. They pointed out the name and asked if it was mine. I agreed that it was. Then they took out their notebooks and one asked solemnly, 'Did you intend anyone to see this?' I looked at them with amazement and pointed out that I had paid a good deal to ensure exactly that. They looked very serious and busily took notes. Then they said that was all and left! I pondered that if this was the level of security we had in the federal police, we could not have too much confidence in them. I was already familiar with such men, who we thought were from ASIO and the police, standing among us at demonstrations and picking up a stone and saying, 'Why don't we throw stones?' in encouraging, agent-provocateur voices.

By this stage, we were also pretty sure that our phone was tapped. A senior Justice, who was a close friend, told us the formula for checking this by dialling certain numbers and so we were in little doubt that we were being monitored. You could sometimes even hear the click and the sound on the line changing as you spoke. When my brother John applied to join the public service in Canberra he was faced with a dossier on his sister when he went through the security check. It wasn't like we were doing anything especially nefarious or secret, other than being part of the organisation of the peace movement—which was enough to make you notorious at that time.

*

The peace movement of the sixties and seventies was made up of a very mixed bunch of people. There were varieties of Christians and varieties of communists. There were unionists, Labor Party people and people who normally voted conservative. There were thousands of people who had never had any connection with radical movements or organisations before. There were students and young people who were directly affected by conscription, their families who were worried for them and older people who could remember other wars. The Save Our Sons movement came into being as mothers protested at the wastage of life possible for their sons in a conscripted army. Women probably played a stronger role than ever before in a protest movement and of course, at that stage, we were often the ones who had the time to do a lot of the organising and hack work which underpinned the movement—many of us hadn't yet embraced working motherhood. As time went on, there were hippie types alongside grim and doctrinaire activists. We always sat uneasily together, especially in the planning of our strategies. Because the movement was so large and diverse there were initiatives taken by various groups and sections as well as huge combined efforts in bringing together the major rallies.

I recall a meeting of about 200 people putting up ideas for our next strategies as a movement. I have a vivid memory of the then Churches of Christ minister, now ABC radio presenter, Terry Lane getting up and suggesting that we might stand on street corners and in railway stations and hand out flowers with messages of peace to people passing by. There was a shocked silence and no-one knew what to say. Hand out flowers? We, the tough and radical organisers of major demonstrations who were on about a dreadful war? What was he thinking? I recall recognising that he was trying to break down this tough, grim image and to surprise people with something gentle and beautiful and I agreed with him, but didn't have the courage to say so. Needless to say, his idea didn't get up.

In my involvement in all the protests, I found that I could produce pretty professional-looking banners. We had been taught to paint large notices as preschool teachers and now I was turning this skill into making posters and banners to carry. There was obviously some point to my vocational training after all! Sometimes I added a flower to a banner with respect to Terry Lane's idea. I became expert at finding the right sort of cloth and paint to make huge banners that would last in rain, hail or sun and using my sewing skills to mount them onto poles. On one occasion, I had the satisfying experience of marching under one of these banners when I looked around the crowd and saw five more being carried by other groups with whom I had connected over the years.

At the height of the women's movement, a group of us who were by now feminists went to the leaders of the coalition against the war and made a case for more women to be in the leadership of the movement. These were the men of the left; the radical edge of social change. They looked at us and said that we had a cheek in thinking that our cause was other than trivial in the face of the issue of war and that we should wait until the war was over before we bothered about such things. We felt betrayed. The men of the left were just as oppressive as any other men. They were also unable to see that there is no hierarchy of injustice—that if you are genuinely fighting to end one injustice, you give credibility to your cause by standing against all oppression and injustice. As the war moved to its end, we began to separate ourselves more clearly into our own movement and to place a distance between ourselves and those anti-war leaders.

All these experiences in the struggle for human freedom, equity and rights rocked some of us in the peace movement who had thought the issues were much simpler. So it was with relief that we resumed our marching and protesting for an end to nuclear testing in the Pacific and a reduction in the world's nuclear armories. In Sydney, tens of thousands of us spent each Palm Sunday for years marching in the sun and cheering our speakers as they called for change.

Then came the Gulf War. We were simply not prepared. We watched in near silence as the United States assured us that this would be a quick and painless war. Its targets would not be innocent people, we were told, as the missiles flew and the bombs rained down again. 'Ah,' we said, 'this will be another Vietnam'. It wasn't. It unrolled before us like the media event it was organised to be and then stopped. We believed that it was really about oil. We knew that many innocent people in Iraq had died, but somehow it was over almost before it began. Very soon the truth about the inaccuracy of the missiles began to emerge, but we were still unable to discover the whole truth. There were few casualties among the attacking forces, nothing to build a campaign on. The peace movement did very little.

The wars in between had often been in Africa and Asia, civil wars usually, and with little at stake for Western powers. Here and there humanitarian aid was offered and some people grieved the loss of life which would have been regarded as catastrophic had it taken place in Europe or North America. But we were mostly silent again.

Kosovo seemed like a rerun of the Gulf War with somewhat different things at stake in terms of power, but at the centre another ruthless dictator and a war which cost few lives of the countries who intervened. 'We only hit military targets', they said as they bombed the whole infrastructure of a poor country and accelerated the destruction of the lives and homes of those they claimed to be defending as the tyrant acted in revenge. They held press conferences with overhead computerised projections of their targets, like slide shows. 'Sorry!' they said as they bombed the wrong targets. A few of us made protest and then it all stopped and we moved into relieved silence and contributed to the efforts to rehabilitate the lives and villages of those who had been affected. We congratulated our governments as they took a few hundred refugees from the million or so homeless.

And East Timor. What can we say? We watched the systematic terrorising of a people for 25 years. There were a small number of people who kept this before us. Then we saw a chance for the East Timorese to decide their own future. Everything we had seen should have prepared us for what would follow their trusting vote. The international community, all of us, betrayed them. There were no ground rules in place for their protection,

Receiving an Australian Government Peace Award from Prime Minister Bob Hawke, 1986

nothing that could happen before huge numbers of people were massacred almost before our horrified eyes, their villages destroyed. We, the people who had always marched for peace, then marched and called on our governments to send troops into East Timor. Our long-time critics called us hypocrites and asked us where we would be if disarmament had taken place when we called for it long ago? It was a question which was only partly justified. We had always tried to hold justice and peace together because we knew that without justice there is no peace. We were not calling for our armies to bomb the Indonesian army out of existence from safe havens in the air, nor were we asking for them to go in on the ground and gun them down. We were, nevertheless, asking for something which required armed soldiers who had been trained to kill to be our representatives in keeping the peace in East Timor.

Then came September 11, the move against the United States on its own territory, followed by its response in Afghanistan. Of course there had been terrorist attacks in countries in many places, but not within the US by people from outside its borders. The peace movement was virtually silent again.

It found its voice when the so-called Coalition of the Willing violated international agreements by initiating a pre-emptive strike against Iraq. I will never forget the huge Rally for Peace held in Sydney just after the Iraq War began. As a very experienced demonstrator, I have no doubt that this was the largest protest march ever held in Sydney with probably more than 600,000 people involved. What an amazing achievement! I found it deeply moving to be there among so many thousands of people who had never marched for peace or anything else before. We failed to build on that, again I suspect because of the clever media coverage of the war and the ambiguities involved in the removal of an obviously terrible tyrant. A split developed in the group organising such events and I think we haven't yet really worked out how to deal with wars that appear to end relatively quickly.

# 25  The Women's Movement

My participation in the women's movement was not exclusively focused on the struggle for justice within the Christian Church, but it began there and was largely played out in that environment. I guess that we who formed the women's movement in Australia mostly chose to live out its struggles in the environments in which we had most influence or spent most of our time.

In 1968, 12 women from six different Christian denominations—Catholic, Anglican, Presbyterian, Methodist, Congregational and Quaker—came together and formed a group called Christian Women Concerned. We were of varying ages and numbers of us were mothers of small children. I can always remember the year it happened because I was pregnant with my last child—so I must have been 34 years old. We were brought together by Dottie Pope, an American Methodist who was in Sydney because her husband was working for the Central Methodist Mission. She had been surprised and concerned by the lack of participation by Australian women in both society and the church, which was very different to the situation in the United States where women had always taken a stronger role and the women's movement had already gained some ground. She saw Australian women as lacking in confidence and assertiveness—which we undoubtedly were at that time.

It sounds very odd indeed now, but we decided that our first effort would be to invite women to a gathering in the Sydney YWCA hall where women would speak on the topic of Easter. This needs to be seen in the context of the time when there were, I think, only a couple of ordained women in the whole country—Congregational ministers. The idea that women could speak publicly about their own views on a central theme of the faith was quite radical. We advertised the meeting and hundreds of women came—confirming that this was exciting and new.

Dottie told us about how groups of women in the States had trained themselves to be speakers. They formed themselves into panels, chose their most important concern and prepared a five-minute talk about it. They then offered themselves to other women's groups as a panel of speakers. After each speaking event they evaluated how they had gone, critiqued each other's efforts and made creative suggestions. We began this process and found, to our surprise, that most of us could do it quite well. All we needed was the genuine support of the others and a bit of passion about something.

When we were invited to speak to other women's groups, we observed that the women to whom we spoke were impressed by our efforts, and surprised by the fact we were speaking about social issues. For this reason, very early on, we decided that every time we went out as a panel, one of us would speak on being a woman in today's world. The speaker would also reflect on the idea of women's liberation and of connecting with the worldwide women's movement. In the meantime, Dottie had introduced us to the idea of consciousness-raising groups where we began to share often painfully and honestly how we experienced life as women. We read endless books, mostly from the US, alongside a few like Germaine Greer's *The Female Eunuch*. We began to attend women's 'speak outs' and participate in marches and demonstrations, all the while keeping our eye on the church.

Some of us began to be the token women on various church bodies. Because we were gaining confidence in speaking and demanding that women be given a place, that place was often given to us, and I say 'place' advisedly. One or maybe two women would be put on a committee or council and people would feel that they had fulfilled all obligations. Even though we mostly refused to be put off by this, it was daunting. Very unhelpful dynamics took place and some women became fed up with the process. As one who was often the token woman in the early days, I experienced it over and over again.

I recall being on a Methodist standing committee where there were around 50 men and two women. The other woman, Jean Skuse, was often absent as she had major responsibilities as General Secretary of the Australian Council of Churches and also with the World Council of Churches. When I spoke in committee debate it was obvious the men assumed I was speaking for all women. If I said nothing in a meeting, they would say things like, 'Nothing to say tonight, Dorothy?'—this was not something they would say to the majority of men who rarely said anything. If I spoke more than once, they would murmur about women always being on their feet and taking over meetings, ignoring the fact that leading men on the committee always spoke several times.

Having said that, I had a much easier ride than Jean who was a single woman. If she made a speech which they didn't like, you would hear things said like, 'You know what she needs' and worse. (All very Christian, I might say!) They gave me a little more respect because I was married—presumably I had the mark of male acceptance upon me. On the other hand, when Jean and I walked into meetings together, we would hear things like, 'Here they come. Watch out, everyone!' On one occasion, I was at a gathering with my husband and a male minister walked up to us and said, 'So, which is Mr McMahon?' If we ever tackled people on these remarks they always replied, 'Can't you take a joke?' Sometimes Jean would be attributed with something I had said and vice versa. It was as though we were a single voice and faceless—we were the generic woman.

We learnt the hard way, and have no doubt that it was hard. The jokes weren't funny because the malevolence behind them was quite apparent. We hated being told that we were not real women and certainly not at all feminine, whatever that meant. They obviously thought we were tough and could take anything, but this was not so. It was painful and cost us dearly. The measure of that is how strongly I still feel about it decades later! We recognised that, if we wanted to make changes, we would need to bring women onto decision-making bodies in groups rather than in ones and twos. It was not as though we wanted to take over, just to have our fair share of the decision making which formed the present and future of the church. If every woman had left the church or stopped money-raising, providing meals, visiting the sick and generally running things, it would certainly have collapsed. I used to say that the church was not built on the rock, it was actually built on lamingtons!

The men took little notice of the fact that Jean Skuse had worked for the United Methodist Church in the States and been an observer at the United Nations. She was the first woman to be General Secretary of the Australian Council of Churches, and a very distinguished one at that. She chaired the very major and difficult world conference on the program to combat racism for the World Council of Churches and later was elected as a moderator of the World Council of Churches. Most of the men on the committees on which she served for her own church had no international experience and no significant reputation anywhere outside their own locality. I learned a huge amount from Jean and always believed that she took much of the weight for us all in those early days. The time in which she did this and the fact that she was a woman and a layperson meant that her contribution was never fully recognised.

The men seemed to fit into fairly consistent groups. There were the men who simply hated us and those who were sort of fascinated but still didn't like us. Then there were the flirtatious ones who pretended to be our friends but were not, like the 'radical' minister who came up behind me, put his hands on my breasts and when I pulled away in offence said, 'Don't you like to be touched?' I told him very sharply that I liked to choose who touched me. Today, I would make a formal complaint of sexual harassment, but we had not yet reached that stage in the 1970s. There were also the men who would come up to us after a tough debate and say enthusiastically, 'Good on you! I quite agreed with what you were saying!' We were glad of their vote but wished they had the guts to get to their feet in the debate rather than leaving it all to us. Finally, there was a small but significant group of men who were not threatened by us, who unswervingly gave us encouragement and support and openly took their stand beside us. They were sometimes viewed as lesser men for doing that. The hardest to take were the women who opposed us, even though we knew that this was part of the process of change.

In 1973 we persuaded the Australian Council of Churches to set up its first Commission on the Status of Women in the Church. In 1974 we published a book to give the results of our work greater publicity—given that the figures were truly damning. These included the fact that at this time the Anglican diocese of Sydney had three women among some 600 clerical and lay representatives; the 1973 general conference of the Methodist Church had 33 women out of 520 delegates, and the general assembly of the Presbyterian Church included eight women and 530 men.

The Congregational Church, the Quakers and the Salvation Army did better, although if a woman officer in the Salvation Army married, she had to take the rank of her husband if it was lower than her own.

The general consensus by women in the church was that their major roles were 'supportive and fundraising, keeping the buildings in order, and carrying out a wide range of community services'. Many women at the time told us that they were quite satisfied with this role.

When submissions were invited to an enquiry by the Commission on the Status of Women in the Church one submission said:

> I think that I was a popular nomination [to a particular church board] because I am a widow.
>
> (a) It would have been an embarrassment if a woman were on and not her husband.
>
> (b) It was expressed at the time that there is no point in having husband and wife on the board at the same time, as you only get one point of view from two people.

I was one of the women delegates at the last general conference of the Methodist Church (apart from that constituted to carry out the vote for union) and by this stage we were pressing for the use of inclusive language in documents, worship and debates. In response the president made a joke about 'all women embracing all men'. I remember rising to my feet in rage, seizing the microphone and telling him that this was not a joke and that his remark was unworthy of his office. I sat down, shaking, and there was a long shocked silence, after which he apologised.

In 1973 we held a national conference on Women's Liberation and the Church in Sydney. It was a landmark conference with women from all the mainstream churches giving papers and networking on many issues. The energy for change was palpable and some of the alliances which were formed there last to this day. At this time, as we approached the formation of the Uniting Church, we were beginning to think that we needed to make an effort to ensure that the lack of participation in decision making by women in the Methodist and Presbyterian churches would not be carried into the new church. We were also concerned about the lack of inclusive language in the foundation document for the new church—the Basis of Union—but agreed that it would be advisable to focus on one main issue rather than two. We decided that the representation of women in decision making was the more important. I was delighted many years later to be one of the committee which, at the request of the Uniting Church Assembly Standing Committee, rewrote the Basis of Union in inclusive language.

We decided to push for a regulation which ensured for the first six years of the life of the new church at least one third of all committee and council members should be women. We didn't ask for more than this as we knew that most bodies were constituted to have about half clergy members and at that stage there were not enough ordained women to make any other proposal practicable. We were convinced that the major task was to break the pattern so that both women and men could see another model. We believed that, by making this a regulation, women would feel that they were not taking places from men as we suspected they might feel otherwise.

The Joint Constitution Commission which was forming up the recommendations for the constitution and regulations for the new church was made up of 21 men and seemed impenetrable when it came to offering ideas. We decided to approach the Joint Constitution Council which had some women members and which would eventually receive the work done by the commission. We were shocked to find that we were refused permission to formally access the council with our written submission and were not able to get the names and addresses of its members to send them personal letters. However, we refused to be defeated on this one and, bit by bit, through friendly members, gained the names and addresses of those concerned and sent them our proposals without permission.

When the conservative recommendations came through from the Constitution Commission to the Constitution Council, they were challenged by those people who had read our proposal and agreed with us. We didn't quite win as our ideas were amended to read that for the first six years of the life of the Uniting Church, one third of the lay representatives of all committees and councils should as far as possible be women— rather than one third of the whole. However, we regarded this as a significant victory and a breakthrough in the history of our churches. People like Jean Skuse, Marie Tulip, Betty Marshall, Keelah Dey and Marjorie Spence were critical players in this struggle and should be honoured for their absolutely tireless efforts. The late Justice John Dey was always our friend as a leader from within the commission and council.

While all this was going on, we were approaching International Women's Year in 1975. The Australian Government invited submissions for the granting of funds to projects for women, and our little group, Christian Women Concerned, decided that we would have a go. We thought we would put up a number of suggestions in the hope of getting a grant for one or two. We asked for money to fund an international conference of women in the church, a national conference, a lecture series to be held at Sydney University, a series of pamphlets on women's issues and a book on the history of women in the Australian church. We requested $45,000 to carry this out. We were astounded when we were the first grant given and we got the lot! We then had to carry all these things out in one year with a team of about 15 women. We did it, apart from a few months' delay on the publication of the book. We nearly killed ourselves achieving our goals but it set us up financially for some years as we made a profit on most of our projects.

We were by this stage also publishing a regular paper called *Magdalene* in which we printed articles, stories, poems and reports on Christian feminism. We chose the name Magdalene because we knew that Mary Magdalene had been falsely named as a prostitute in Christian tradition when we believed that she was actually a strong woman who was a close friend of Jesus'. We went through the usual arduous process of getting this into print with typing, Letraset headings and running off, but later managed to get professional help with the printing and collating. In all these things, you would have to say that we were nothing if not keen!

In 1978, when we explored with other women what was happening in the Uniting Church after our efforts with the regulations, it became evident that some women who had been 'quite satisfied' with the lack of participation in decision making before union, changed their minds when there were regulations in place. It didn't feel like pushing men out in the way it had done for some women before that. Especially at the local level, things changed quite rapidly. In the years which followed, the Uniting Church gradually moved towards the benchmark of 50 per cent women on all its decision-making bodies.

However, after this initial shift, there was a slight decline in enthusiasm from women and we realised that it was not a matter of simply getting the numbers, it was a matter of changing the culture and process of decision making. We also found that to create any sort of equity in participation for women was far more complex than most people had imagined. In 1980 I was chairing a national commission of the Uniting Church and observed that, after being enthusiastic members of the commission, some of our best women members were dropping off. I asked them why and was told that they hated the style of meetings and decision making. I felt very concerned and then suddenly faced the fact that I was in the chair and had the power to bring in some changes. I realised I had been priding myself on learning the established processes and being as smart as the men in using them in the chair—how we delude ourselves!

After some reflection, I decided to exercise my responsibility as the chairperson and announced that I would lead the commission into a more consensus style of decision making. I suggested that we might open each meeting at the commission by sharing a bit about our own lives so that others could be supportive if necessary. I mentioned that I had noted that when people were feeling angry or anxious or tired, this indirectly influenced the formal debates. There was a stunned silence and some men said they thought this would take valuable time from our meetings. I stood my ground and we proceeded.

In the end, people found it actually saved time in meetings because it gave us a way of forming a community with each other and so the debates changed character and were easier to resolve. After I left the chair, it was still the tradition to begin meetings like that in our commission and others sometimes envied us as we raced through our work in good spirits. We also kept our women members after that. Later on, under the guidance of its first woman president, Dr Jill Tabart, the Uniting Church brought in a process of consensus decision making for all its committees and councils. Also, meetings which men had often previously set for times like six o'clock on weeknights were moved to accommodate women who often had family responsibilities at that time.

As Christian feminists, we were also part of the wider women's movement. When I went to rallies and meetings and marches I found myself challenged to think more radically about life and to find the common ground on which all women stood.

At this time I imagined that one day I might like to return to some sort of paid career, so I began to rehearse what changes that would mean at home. Should I teach Barrie to cook? Should I train our children to iron their own clothes earlier than I had planned to? How much time should I devote to cleaning the house and baking cakes? Barrie was quite cooperative in exploring these issues, although his cooking was pretty rudimentary!

I told our children that I did not want to celebrate Mother's Day. I said I wanted justice for mothers every day of the year instead of a cup of tea in bed and a gift on one day of the year. They saw me writing letters to editors of papers and speaking at many engagements. I doubt that they and their peers had any idea how significant the changes at this time were. They would not have believed that their grandmother could not let her friends see her husband pouring a cup of tea for himself at a church gathering. They would have found it very hard to believe that, when young, I could not have imagined that my destiny was other than marriage and parenthood for the rest of my life—with a modicum of training and work while I waited for that.

Most of the women's movement was involved in trying to remove the idea that women were the sexual objects of men and that our bodies were not our own. I wore long, mostly Asian-made, skirts and very little make-up—which probably made me look like a hippie. I saw this as defining me as a woman who could wear what she liked and outfits which didn't include high heels.

I remember going into various types of church and community women's groups and suggesting that we each think of one thing around us that we would like to change and then deciding the first move we would take towards that. It was a way of revealing to women that they did actually have power. It was also about supporting each other in having a go at something.

I had a profound moment when a leading Christian feminist from overseas used the term Mother God. Although inclusive language was important to us, I was offended and told my friends this. They asked me to go away and think about why I was offended. I felt this address was disrespectful to God. Then I had to ask why was this so. Was the image of God as a mother to be less respected than the image of God as a father? I faced that deep down, I felt that the divine life was less connected with women than men—a salutary realisation!

This was a period when violence and abuse in the home were kept hidden. In the early 1980s, as members of the Commission on the Status of Women in the Church we prepared a slide show for church leaders who gathered for a meeting of the Australian Council of Churches. The faces on the slides and the voices on the tape were of women who had suffered domestic violence and abuse. At the end of the presentation there was silence and no discussion. The church leaders pressed on with their business. Later on there was talk about the Commission on the Status of Women being in the hands of militant Sydney feminists and that it should be moved to Perth. As chairperson of the Council on Violence against Women for the NSW Government I can say that we still have a long way to go on this issue, but that we have come some distance in 20 years.

My choice of career was not too enthusiastically affirmed by my sisters in the women's movement. They thought I was joining the patriarchy and the hierarchy of the church. I did some soul-searching about this and recognised that I never was a revolutionary, but a reformer from the inside of institutions. I knew that I had a genuine and strong sense of vocation and so, with many doubts, I felt I should follow my heart. I became somewhat separated from the main Christian feminist group at that point—partly because I felt silently criticised and partly because I was so stretched in combining work, study and parenting.

I was gratified to hear the principal of our theological college, Reverend Dr Graeme Ferguson, say that within a decade of women being ordained, they had already had an influence on the style of ministry. I think that we did demystify the role of clergy to some extent and we grappled with the nature of the authority which is normally associated with such roles. The very fact that we were there meant that the clergy role could no longer be associated with the perceived right of men to dominate women. Of course, we had to resist joining the boys' club and conforming to their patterns of behaviour. I think we only partly succeeded in that.

When I talk with my daughters, I see them just firmly and quietly defining through their lives the role and status of women today. I suspect we still have a long way to go on the fundamental right of women to equal pay for equal work, and on leadership roles—political and corporate. Whatever the future, I will be there cheering on the next generations of women in their efforts.

# 26 The Republican Movement

I have been a republican for at least 30 years and can recall sitting down for the then national anthem at a function in 1975. I realise this is a little at odds with accepting a Jubilee Medal from the Queen in 1977 for my work with women in New South Wales. At the time I wrestled with giving it back, but noticed that those who took that sort of stance received much publicity which drew great attention to their being offered the award. I felt that I would just receive it quietly and wear it to protest marches for fun— something I felt would annoy the Queen should she ever know. I think now that I should have simply returned the medal. I didn't, so maybe the truth is that I wanted it!

Why do I feel so strongly about this issue? It is not because I have anything against the Queen personally. Indeed I often think about the whole concept of royalty and ask why, for many of us, there is a certain fascination about having a royal family in palaces and coaches and crowns. I know that I cannot resist watching programs about such people and looking at their palaces when I am overseas. I even read articles about them in magazines in waiting rooms! I suspect this is about connecting with magic things from our childhood fantasy life. It links in with the romance of imaginary chivalry, with knights and maidens, dragons and dungeons. Yet there is nothing logical or appropriate in the idea of one really ordinary family receiving such adulation and living in multiple palaces set in parks of beautiful gardens with priceless treasures around them and masses of servants recognised and paid for by the people. And yet, I still sense the magic that we long for and the pomp and circumstance which lifts our pedestrian lives.

Having said all that, I am still a firm republican because this queen and her family really do not belong to us. If the British hold to their present royalty, we can continue to watch the 'magic' from afar if we choose. Some of us can even celebrate this part of our ancestral heritage. However, I fail to see why we think we need this head of state of another country as our own.

My mind was absolutely made up after being invited to be present when the Queen visited the Sydney Town Hall in 1992 for the one-hundred-and-fiftieth anniversary of the city of Sydney. I was invited as one of the city clergy and decided to go out of curiosity and also because I was the only woman member of the clergy and didn't want the men to have it all to themselves. Several hundred of us gathered in the Town Hall and waited about an hour for the Queen and Prince Philip to arrive. After they walked between the gathered people down one side of the Town Hall on a red carpet to the stage, the lord mayor made a speech about the city of Sydney and presented the Queen with what appeared to be an urn. She handed it to one of her attendants who put it on a pedestal on the edge of the stage. The Queen and Prince Philip then walked off the stage and down a carpet on the other side of the Town Hall, briefly shaking hands with a few people on the way, and then went off in their procession of cars. We couldn't believe it. She had said not one word to us—not even thanks and good luck! This was our head of state and she had nothing to say to us. I thought that this queen doesn't know us and doesn't want to know us. We are just another formal occasion.

I watched Prince Harry and Princess Anne at the Rugby World Cup. Do we really think they would ever support another team than England? Of course not, and neither should they, although they may have to answer to the Scots, the Welsh and the Irish! These insignificant issues are signs of the separation which really exists and which makes it absurd that we hold to our colonial history in our head of state.

In 1999 I formally joined the republican movement as a member of a group called The Just Republic which in the 2000 referendum wanted a president elected through some method which involves participation by the people, a full rewrite of the constitution into an inspiring document with an appropriate preamble and a bill of rights to follow. Having said that, we were prepared to cooperate at the time of the referendum, vote 'yes' to bring in any sort of republic and trust that we could all work on it to make further changes.

The bringing in of an Australian bill of rights is a critical issue for me, which grows in significance almost day by day as we watch all sorts of rights falling before the fear of terrorism. It is also important to me because, when you read a bill of rights, you have some image of what sort of nation that country hopes to be. A bill of rights takes hold of the fundamental values which that country recognises and describes what the people believe are the ground rules for their society. Every democratic country in the world has a bill of rights or its equivalent, apart from Australia.

I see the discussion on a bill of rights as one way of moving the Australian people from a cynicism and a sense of powerlessness. Imagine if we could genuinely engage in a widespread discussion about what values we want to sustain and what rights are essential in the forming of our life together. This is especially important at a time when many people are less trusting of the parliamentary process and of the politicians who make decisions on our behalf. While all situations may not be covered by a bill of rights, it could be that in discussing such a document we assert our expectations more clearly and might work together in defining a more ethical public life.

After the referendum in 2000 was lost, the split republican movement re-formed itself into what is a basically unified group under the name of the Australian Republican Movement. Although that was not a new name, the whole organisation genuinely changed after 2000. To signal the significance of that change I, as a direct-electionist, was elected as convenor of the NSW committee of the Australian Republican Movement. This committee listened to ideas from the organisation's membership, established and visited local forums, arranged conferences and generated ideas for the national movement. We also addressed and stuffed envelopes with news-letters. Such is life in all good movements for change! As convenor, I sat on the national committee and participated in its evolution towards something more participatory and with a more diverse approach to the bringing in of the republic. This was not always easy as some people felt very strongly that they had the correct model and that it was just a matter of educating people about their ideas. I have always believed that any republic for Australia has to arise from the dreams of the people, even if mistakes are made along the way.

There is now a quite different Australian Republican Movement with the capacity to think more laterally on the issues and to engage with people on a wider front. Direct-electionists and non-direct-electionists came together and began to work on various models for the election of a head of state for people to consider. Greg Barns and then Professor John Warhurst took the national chair of the movement. Richard Fidler, now playing a national leading role, invited several distinguished Australian writers to create their own versions of a possible preamble to the constitution.

Unless there is a change of prime minister, we are unlikely to get a chance to move towards a new opportunity for the Australian people to think again about being a republic, but that day will come. In the mean-time, I always hope that we can find ways of encouraging a deep and wide reflection on who we are as a people, what we hold dear and who we long to be.

*Part* 7

# What Became of the Family

# 27 The Death of My Mother

In 1992, I stood before the chancellor of Macquarie University in Sydney and received an Honorary Doctorate of Letters. 'There,' I said, 'I can do it, Mother!' 'No,' she said in my head, 'I am very proud of you, dear, but of course it is not a real degree.'

In 1997, I stood in the Great Hall of Sydney University, clad in my hood and gown, clutching my precious Bachelor of Theology degree with the widest smile on my face. I was 63 years old and I had my first academic degree. 'There you are, Mother. I can do it!' I said. At last she was silent.

For the majority of us the most powerful voice inside us is that of our mother. My father still speaks *with* me sometimes, but my mother's voice speaks *to* me, deep within, and reminds me of who she thinks I should be.

My mother was a good woman, maybe even a remarkable woman. She died suddenly in 1977 at the age of 70. I well recall the day as I was in Sydney, helping to organise the annual general meeting of the NSW Ecumenical Council. My brother John had just rung and told me that our mother had been rushed to hospital and was given, at the most, an hour and a half to live. I knew there was no point in leaping on a plane to try to get to Victoria in time to make my farewells to her, so I just numbly kept on working. There I was, weeping to myself, and going up and down in the small lift taking things to the meeting room floor from our office, accompanied by the leaders of the NSW churches. Naturally they asked me what was wrong and I told them my mother was dying.

I recall one bishop telling me that I could have confidence that my mother would soon be a saint in heaven. I thought to myself indignantly,

'What a stupid thing to say. You don't even know my mother and the fact that she may be a saint in heaven soon is absolutely no comfort at all!' Most of them treated me in a helpless, embarrassed way and were obviously very relieved to get away. Finally, the head of my own church arrived and said firmly, 'Don't be silly, Dorothy. What are you doing here? Go home at once and cry properly and get ready to fly to Victoria.' So I did. The fact that it took me so long may well have been connected with the teachings of my mother—a sacrificial stayer if ever there was one!

The next day I flew to Victoria to comfort my father and join the rest of my family in preparations for the funeral. I was told that our mother had died wondering how Father would cope without her because she had been so sure that he would die first and he had never really learned to cook or to iron his shirts. At the same time she was earnestly witnessing to her joyful faith to all the nurses around her, as was her habit in many situations. She died in peace.

That night my father invited me to walk with him around the garden, as he would have done with my mother. She liked to do that each day to admire all the plants which he was growing for her. As we walked and stopped to look at each bud and flower in the quite large garden, we were astounded to discover that every single flower in the garden that she had admired and commented upon before she went into hospital had died overnight. The plants were still alive, but every flower was dead. Even her garden grieved for my mother and honoured her going. She certainly would have believed it, not because she was due for that honour, but because she believed that things like that happened and was well accustomed to various sorts of phenomena happening in her life.

My mother's death did not go unnoticed in the community where she lived. When she died, the daily paper of Shepparton in Victoria carried a banner headline, 'BETH MCRAE, EVERYBODY'S FRIEND, DIES'. When I saw the headline, I asked myself whether 'everybody's friend' had really been my friend. I decided that she had been my very loving mother, but not exactly or always my friend. People came from many parts of Australia to attend her funeral and there were more than 600 people present.

\*

The life of a Methodist minister had required that our family move every three to five years. My mother hated this. She would just get every house as she wanted it, make friends and establish herself and we would move on. However, she loved the status and traditional role of being the wife of a minister in the country towns and provincial cities in which we lived. She took it very seriously, led many women's groups, ran prayer meetings, attended functions at the side of my father, protected him from too many callers or persistent ones, gave talks and generally led a busy and responsible life. Everywhere we went as my father moved around Tasmania and Victoria she had a powerful impact on the lives of many people. They still speak respectfully and lovingly about her friendship with them. She also took very seriously her role as the mother of the minister's children, children who were to model the life of Christian children.

She had a simple faith which determined her every move in life. Her God was a friend and she consulted this friend daily about everything that she had to do or was worried about. Her main concern was that, although she found it a bit overwhelming when we outstripped her in education, we would all have a chance to have what she never had. It didn't worry her much that our school uniforms were homemade or hand-me-downs or that our dresses for school dances were out of date. 'You do look beautiful!' she would say, no matter what.

While she liked our father to be proud of her, she was not unduly worried about things like clothes and didn't bother wearing make-up for most of her life. For many years I thought this was a principled stance and felt guilty when I dared to apply a small amount to my teenage face. Then, in her late fifties, she came to me and said, 'Dorothy, could you advise me about a lipstick colour for myself? As I am getting older, my lips look a bit pale.' I said, 'I thought you didn't approve of make-up.' And she said with surprise, 'Oh no. I just couldn't be bothered with it!'

Apart from trusting in the power of the God she loved, it seems to me now that my mother had two main ways of dealing with unpleasant realities in life. The first way was to count your blessings and turn a negative into a positive. She encouraged herself and us to do this. Just recently I was being driven through a beautiful part of New Zealand. My partner Ali, who is a Kiwi, wanted to show me this scenery with the sun on it so that the waters and mountains of the Marlborough Sound sparkled at their best. However, it was a cloudy day. 'Don't worry,' I said. 'The fact that the sun is not shining will probably mean that we can see it much more clearly and without glare.' All of a sudden, I knew that this was the voice of my mother speaking. Ali rightly replied, 'What rubbish! Of course it's more beautiful in the sunlight and I wanted you to see it.' I laughed and said, 'That was my mother speaking,' and I was encouraged to tell my mother to go away and be quiet!

My mother's other strategy was to pretend to herself that the reality in front of her was not true. It is odd that small things are remembered so long but I recall going to her as an anguished teenager and asking for something to stop the pimples on my chin. She looked at me and said, 'You look beautiful, dear. I can't even see the pimples.' When she died I wanted to say, 'There really was a pimple on my chin, Mother! And you know full well that you could see it as clearly as I did.' That moment was echoed much later when my own daughter came to me and said the same thing in the presence of her grandmother. Quick as a flash, my mother gave the same response to my daughter as she had given me. With fierce determination I said, 'Well, I can see the pimples very clearly, Lindy, and we will have to get something for them!'

I recently asked my daughter Melissa how she remembered her grandmother and she said, 'She was loving, but stern.' It was a relief to finally put the right words to my mother. I pictured her very straight back and heard her voice. There it was, coming to me again in all its sternness. Lack of commitment to tasks and to others was not permitted. Sacrifice of oneself was the way. If you felt pain, you had an early night and pulled yourself together. I recall, as a young married women, asking her for an aspirin. She hunted through a cupboard and finally found a packet, its faded design indicating its great age, and offered it to me. Even aspirin was something you only took if things were grim indeed.

This stoic approach to life did not mean that she was not a warm person. Early on I think she decided that I was the most vulnerable of her children, which may have been true at the time. It was only after she died that I associated her loving voice with her stern voice and saw that the voices were often really the same. Because she loved me dearly, when she sternly directed my life I often felt that it would be a betrayal of that love to disagree with her perceptions of the way I should go. Often her eyes would fill with tears if I, or others, challenged her. It took me many decades to see just how powerful and somewhat manipulative this was.

In some ways, I felt as though I was her mother, caring for a vulnerable person who was often emotional and seemingly very needy. At the same time, I always felt as though she would consume me with her love. In spite of this combination, or maybe because of it, she absolutely determined my life in very significant ways and at critical moments. She formed the view I had of myself and which contained my being for the first 30 years of my life and had a strong influence on me for at least another decade after that.

Once a wise friend asked me, 'Who was more powerful—you or your mother?' I was just about to say that I was more powerful when I realised that my mother had determined my life in so many ways, sometimes against my will. I faced the fact that my mother had a great hold over my life.

My siblings were not nearly as disempowered by their relationship with our mother, possibly because I was the eldest. They challenged her often, especially Carmyl and David. Over the years, I observed that she still loved them. I especially recall watching fearfully as Carmyl, when small, lay on the floor and screamed her anger and even kicked our mother. A therapist once asked me what happened after that and I couldn't remember. I thought I must have blotted it out. I asked my sister and she said that nothing happened—our mother just ignored her until she stopped.

For most of my life I lived hundreds of kilometres away from her. Each time we met, which was about once a year, I would think, 'This time I understand my mother and the history which formed her. This time I am an adult of wide experience. This time we will be two women together being mutual friends.' She would come and clean my windows (the only time they were ever cleaned!). She would catch up on the ironing and muse that the things at the bottom of the basket smelt musty—how could that be? I felt relaxed about all that—she really liked giving her love to me in that way and I was happy to receive it from her.

'I am a feminist, Mother. It has changed my whole life,' I said to her in 1975. 'Oh no, you're not, dear,' she said firmly. 'You'll never be one of those women. You love your husband and children.' End of discussion. Once when she was staying we went and did some shopping in suburban Sydney. At the greengrocer's my mother said, 'You probably know my daughter. She does marvellous things for the community, you know.' The greengrocer looked mystified as I hustled my mother out. By the time she left for home, she had introduced herself to all the shopkeepers and had established herself as the mother of a famous daughter who they should know! They seemed quite fond of her and offered her their best service. My mother was very good at seeing people as she wanted to see them. If we didn't live up to that image, she often pretended that we did. When she died, I hoped that in the moment of total awareness of truth which I believe comes at the time of death, she would really see me as myself, not as she wished I would be.

When Mother died many things were revealed more clearly for what and who they were, including our father. The often rather remote, scholarly and seemingly wise father was now seen as one who had been far more dependent on our mother than we had ever imagined. His later life confirmed this in startling ways. Maybe the voice of our father which I thought was periodically relayed through our mother was really sometimes her own strong voice. And was it her voice or his which indicated concern for my wellbeing when I advised him that I was about to retrain for ordination? He wrote that when my mother held her first son in her arms she felt that one day he would end up a minister, but she had not thought about me in that way. He asked what would happen to my children and did I realise that a minister's life would be tough. My mother died before I was ordained and he was still saying things like that on the day of my ordination.

I am glad that, by then, I could sometimes address my mother just as sternly as she had addressed me. One of the things I said to my mother after her death was, 'I really was one of those feminists, Mother, in spite of your telling me otherwise.' And now I am who I am; a woman who has a female partner. What would you have thought of that? It would have been a hard one to pretend about and cover over with something more acceptable, I think. I like to believe that you accept who I am now, in your state of greater wisdom.

You wanted me to be someone of your own creation sometimes. I can do that to people too, but less often now, dear Mother, because I found that was dangerous for them and for me. I believe that you don't need to do that anymore, wherever you are alongside your close friend God. I don't even need to try to have your kind of God anymore because I have found my own whose face and voice is a trifle more distant than yours, but still as gracious, and perhaps more allowing of rest and recreation and fun.

On the other hand, mother of mine, I wish I had said to you that I celebrate the childlike delight in small things which I find in myself and which reminds me that I am truly your daughter. I love being a person who, like you, laughs at small ridiculous things and who sees lots of tiny gifts along the way for appreciation. You would have laughed with me at the sight of the traffic witch's hat which someone had put on top of the ball on a fence post in Rozelle. You would have followed with me the dancing line of paint on the footpath which someone had trailed round posts, up over seats and in little circles of joy—we would have laughed with delight at the fun of it. And the sign on the bins at the entry to some of the old Sydney buses which read, 'Please dispose of your ticket thoughtfully at the end of your journey. Please do not use this bin if the tickets fall through.' You would have really loved that one!

We both always took ages to see the point of a witty joke, due to our innocent, simple minds. As the family used to say, 'Don't tell them a joke on Saturday because they will laugh in church on Sunday'! We both never had any sense of direction, never noticing where we are going when other people drive us because we are so busy talking or looking out the window.

I am now the age you were when you died and I find myself smiling and talking to all sorts of strangers, especially children, just as you used to do. I saw a woman walking towards me in the street just before Christmas and she looked absolutely beautiful in a stunning, flowing dress. Without thinking, I smiled at her in appreciation, then after she had passed I thought I had better explain. I turned around to see her standing anxiously by her car looking at me. I went back and, it was just as well that I did, because she had assumed that I was laughing at her because she was over the top in her party dress. She was deciding whether she should go home and change! Smiling at strangers can be complicated.

I also find you, my friend, when I am the tough survivor and purveyor of hope in the face of forces which would stop most people in their tracks. You were very good at that, dear Mother. My way of doing that is not to count my blessings, but to be hurt and angry, as is my right as a self-respecting human being, and to share that with others. My God is not threatened by that, dear Mother, and nor am I. After I have had that honest response, I rise up and confront the toughness of life, moving with the optimism which I am sure comes from your determined genes. You could be formidable and so, I am told, can I.

I am really saying to you, Mother, that I am now free to let live in me some things which were part of you, or which you gave to me, and to claim them with gratitude and deep respect. I am also saying that, whether you like it or not, or understand it or not, there is a whole part of my life which now dances free to be itself. I am a strong woman, Mother, maybe even stronger than you were. Some of this strength is hard won, because of my own fear of claiming it and probably because I created voices for you which you never had. That is life, dear Mother, and my own children could tell you about the voices with which I will leave them—loving but fallible human voices. If we ever meet again, maybe we can talk honestly at last, compare our notes as strong women, mothers and grandmothers and offer each other grace. And then we will laugh at some small ordinary thing which we alone see as very funny.

Rest in peace, dear Mother.

# 28 The Death of My Father

After his time as separated chairman (the equivalent of a bishop) for the north-west of Victoria in the Methodist Church, my father decided that he wanted to finish his career as a minister back in a parish. He was sent to Shepparton and was delighted to spend his last professional years near the Murray River of his childhood. He and Mother loved their time at Shepparton which was a warm and lively place. On his retirement, they bought a small, old weatherboard house in Mooroopna, just across the Goulburn River from Shepparton—observing the professional protocol of not staying in a parish in which you have been a minister, but close enough to sustain friendships.

He and Mother set themselves up in the first home they had ever owned. Dad, as usual, organised the compost pits, dug the earth ready for his vegetables, organised the chook yard and planned his garden. He arranged all his tools neatly in the large garage so that he had a suitable workshop for all his projects. He and Mother made friends with the neighbours and linked up with the little church at Mooroopna. For a time he even filled in as minister when the parish was waiting for another minister to arrive.

When Mother died, he was devastated. They had still been two people in love who walked around hand in hand and Dad had been very dependent on Mother's strength and many other things. Just before I left after Mother's funeral, Dad asked if I would help him with three things. He asked if I could tell him where Mother kept the towels, then suggested that I might iron a shirt in front of him so that he could see how to do it. After that, he said he had worked out that his favourite meal was a chop, mashed potato and peas. He thought that, if I could show him how to cook it, he would be all right. He could boil an egg which he thought would be useful on other occasions. Mother was excellent at teaching all her children, including her sons, to cook and be useful around the house but she had certain fixed ideas about what was appropriate for my father. I remember once, not long before she died, being at a church function with them and Dad wanted a cup of tea. I suggested that he might get it himself but Mother stepped in very firmly and said that she couldn't let other people see Dad getting his own cup of tea! Of course, he regularly did so at home as well as helping with household chores in general.

Dad was 73 when Mother died and as the years went on, he spent more and more time reminiscing about her and their early life, telling stories and writing things down. I don't think he ever really recovered from her death. Because he was reserved and distant at times, I think I equated that with him being strong. After Mother's death, I was less sure of that. I think he was far more dependent on Mother's strength than I ever realised. He was certainly very dependent on her love and support and her protection of his space. He didn't need to worry too much about learning to cook because the local people were almost always asking him to dinner. He said he had never had so much fancy food in all his life. He was dearly loved by many people as a pastor and friend. I remember talking with a woman who worked at the local hospital and she said that there were lots of women who would love to marry him, including herself.

Our Auntie Chris, who had moved away from Melbourne on her retirement, came and lived with him and we all felt reassured by that. They were rather alike in many ways and would be good company for each other, we thought. Then he broke the news that he was going to marry a local woman who was much younger than him. We were all stunned. He had said nothing to us about any relationship. Who could it be? She turned out to be a woman my age who lived in the local caravan park and had made contact with Dad, and previously Mother, when she had frequently come to the house asking for help. She was known to be rather disturbed, indeed she had a mental illness which we found later was resistant to medication.

She was also a virtuoso pianist who had trained with some of the most distinguished teachers in Australia but had found it hard to pursue this career because of her health difficulties.

Shortly after this news, it was Dad's eightieth birthday and we were all invited down to Mooroopna for the celebrations. The whole family came. His children and grandchildren each contributed a page to a special book to give to him. After we had almost finished the party, Dad introduced us to his fiancée. We found it extremely difficult to know what to say and how to welcome her into the family. We were all outside in the garden and I remember taking her inside the house on a pretext and trying to have a friendly chat with her.

I later told Dad that we would be delighted to have him marry because we knew he was very lonely without Mother. Then I asked him to help us understand why he was marrying this particular woman. He said that he was marrying her to save her, especially to save her music. I said, 'Put your professional hat on, Dad. Is that the right reason for marrying someone?' I pointed out that it may not be fair to marry her if it was other than a matter of mutual and respectful love. Nothing would dissuade him and a few months later they married. We were not all present at the wedding and the local people were obviously concerned for him and for his wife. Auntie Chris moved into a retirement village and they were on their own.

If I am not calling my father's wife by her name, it is because of what follows. I do it because I want to protect her. A few months after their marriage, she stabbed Dad in the back with a pair of scissors. He managed to crawl to the phone and get help from a friend. His wife was arrested, charged by the police with assault and severely reprimanded by the magistrate. No conviction was recorded because Dad refused the police request to support the charge against her. I visited them not long after and felt the chaos in the house. So many things had gone and there was evidence of damage. Dad insisted on staying in the marriage. Then they sold the house and moved down to Philip Island, far from any family members, and we were told that we were not welcome to visit. Some of us did, however, get requests for money.

The next thing we knew was that Dad was in hospital in Melbourne with a severed artery in his arm due to a stabbing and had lost the use of that arm. I was contacted by one of the doctors in the hospital who said that he felt our father had lost the will to live. I went down to visit Dad and asked him if that was true. He said that it was; that he was afraid of his wife and would rather die than go home. I persuaded him to come back to Sydney with me. His wife did not know where I lived. He stayed there for several weeks, gradually growing stronger, although he was in many ways a broken and sometimes bitter old man.

We had long talks about his future. I pointed out that his wife had no record of violence before their marriage and he might reflect on whether there was not a dynamic in the relationship which drew her to violence—not laying any blame for that, but facing that it had not helped her to marry him. In fact it had put them both in peril. He talked of his marriage vows but was finally persuaded that it might be in both their interests if he ended the marriage and went back to Shepparton and into the retirement village for which he had once been the chaplain. His brother Ken and sister Chris were happy to organise this. We all breathed a sigh of relief as he prepared to travel back.

The day before he was due to leave, his wife found where he was and rang us. She told him that she had 'found Jesus' and pleaded for him to come back to Philip Island. He went. In 1986, weeks later, he was dead. He had been rushed to hospital, the staff told us, with evidence of having been bashed. There was a coroner's inquest and the coroner ruled that he had died of a ruptured spleen, the cause of which could not be determined. We were not unhappy with this verdict as we had no desire for his wife to be brought before the courts. It would solve nothing and in many ways, we could not hold her responsible. Our father had made his decisions all the way through and had refused many chances to save himself and his wife.

We all went down to Philip Island for his funeral, as arranged by his wife. I imagined myself taking that funeral and how hard it would be to do it well, but the Uniting Church ministers there did a great job. Dad's grandchildren, both girls and boys, carried his coffin from the church and we accompanied it to a beautiful peaceful graveyard on the island near trees and the sea. We all knew he would be at rest there. We imagined our mother waiting to meet him in universal life and we could almost hear her say chidingly, as she used to do, 'Oh, Colin!' then holding him close and him bowing his head to her.

His colleagues and friends gave him a huge memorial service in Melbourne and we listened to his voice on tape, sounding as it had some years before. He was spoken of as one of the saints of the church. I doubt he was a saint. However, he was a good and gentle man. As I write this, I find myself weeping again as I remember that hard farewell. I weep for him, for his ending and for the woman he had married, who probably gained nothing from all of it. On the other hand, maybe she did. Maybe there were things in their marriage which she cherishes and I hope that is so. We lost many things beside our father. We lost all our childhood photos and all the things which were in the house which had belonged to our mother and father. When Mother died, we had each chosen a couple of small things to remind us of her and left the rest for Dad.

We, his children, still sometimes try to understand the last years of his life. I suspect he really always wanted to 'save' people and our mother used to firmly put a boundary on that on his behalf. I think, too, that he was very lonely in ways which friends could never enter. He had lived in total engagement with Mother—apart from when he was in the war, they were virtually never separated.

So, how will I remember him in the end? I will remember a man who typified the best of Methodist ministers of that time—a person with a radical commitment to social justice and a mature and deep understanding of theology. Like many of that era, he was conservative on issues of personal morality and he and I would probably argue about some of that today. To do him justice, he knew that some of his children did not remain total abstainers and he never gave any evidence of being other than respectful of that. I wonder how he would respond to having a lesbian daughter? He died weeks before I was going to tell him about that and I think he would have been deeply troubled to hear it. In the state of mind he was in at that time, he may have decided that for once he could not understand a decision of mine. In earlier days, I am confident that he would have wrestled with me until we worked out something together.

I loved his dignity—the reserved and courteous way of relating which I instantly recognised when I went to Scotland. There was a certain vulnerability in him, perhaps more than we ever knew, but there was also that steely stoicism which I am sure was borne in his genes and carried here from the harsh mountains of the Scottish highlands. Life was a matter of pulling yourself together and getting on with it without fuss. You looked things in the face and moved towards them.

I will remember a father who once told me I was his friend as well as his daughter. I will carry with me almost all that he ever taught me about faith and the world. If I meet him when I die, I will have some big questions to ask him and maybe we will sit in a peaceful place in the universe and grapple with the choices each of us made for our life.

# 29 My Siblings

My life and the lives of my siblings separated out not long after my marriage. None of us had cars at that stage which inhibited lots of visiting and we mostly met once a year at the home of our parents in Shepparton and later in Mooroopna. This was always a great gathering, but with all the children to be watched over, we really didn't have much time for deep and meaningful conversations! Mother wrote to us all almost every week and gave us news of each other as we were not very good correspondents.

When I first married, I saw most of Thaïs as she and her boyfriend, John Worner, used to come out to us at Oak Park when they were students living in residential colleges at Melbourne University. The food in the colleges was not wonderful in those days and they often came to our place for the weekend roast and other goodies. When they married, they settled in a suburb of Melbourne and we kept in touch until their early deaths.

After Carmyl graduated as a physicist and worked at the Peter McCallum Institute in Melbourne, she and her husband, Don Winkler, lived in Melbourne while he finished his training as a teacher. They spent time in Indonesia, followed by life in various country towns in Victoria including Merbein and Cobram where Don taught at local high schools. They finally settled with their four children—Bronwyn, Michael, Stephen and Tim—in Tallangatta, a small town not far from Albury.

For many years, our families shared camping holidays at the caravan park at Pambula Beach on the south coast of NSW. It was interesting to

John, Carmyl, David and me, 1992

see how our city bred children would cautiously explore the area around the caravan park, venturing only a few metres into the bush, while their country cousins would take off fearlessly, anywhere and everywhere. Our children became close friends which was special as our kids missed having any family in NSW.

Carmyl devoted herself to the life of each place they lived. While in Tallangatta, she wrote a cookery book for children and gathered stories from the local area into a book. She began Indonesian cookery classes for local people, ran a weekly children's music group with a friend for many years and helped initiate and run a shop for local people to sell their craft work. She also spent six years as a local youth worker and ran parenting courses in the surrounding area. When Don retired, he and Carmyl began teaching Indonesian in the local primary schools. Carmyl designed special resources for teaching Indonesian in schools and this has been well received by teachers across the country.

When I stayed with Carmyl and Don recently and reflected on the different journeys our lives had taken, I felt that Carmyl had chosen to live deeply while I had lived widely. What struck me as we walked around Tallangatta together was that Carmyl and Don have become pivotal citizens in the place they live. They have influenced the life of a whole town. This intensity of life and relationships; the sticking with others through thick and thin, is something which I have never really done. Carmyl's fine mind has given gifts over and over again to the people with whom she lives and moves, expanding both their lives and hers in ways which may never be recognised. She has a generosity of spirit which moves me beyond words—a strength interwoven with kindness, and a joy in life which is not based on ego or obvious rewards, but deeper things than that.

Carmyl is fiercely loyal and generous in the extreme. She looks like our grandmother, has the fine and precise mind of our father and the determined cheerfulness and strength of our mother.

John has been hard to keep in touch with at times as the predominant theme of his life has been moving! After he graduated in applied science at Melbourne University, he married Josie Waddell and worked in Canberra as a public servant. He then decided to train as a teacher and taught science and maths before retraining and following his heart into music teaching. He taught music in the state system in Victoria for a while before he and Josie moved to northern Victoria where they taught at an alternative Christian school and lived in a caravan with their young family of four children—Simon, twins Sally and Cameron, and Martin.

During this time both he and Josie became involved in the charismatic movement in the church and both had powerful experiences relating to the presence of the Holy Spirit within their lives. This movement is largely connected with the conservative streams in the church, and they initially followed this direction. At this stage I wondered whether we would part ways in terms of our understanding of life and faith. I had some interesting conversations with John, especially about whether or not we had prayed hard enough for the healing of our son Christopher. John had discovered that he had a gift of healing like our mother and genuinely hoped that something could be done for Christopher.

He and Josie later returned to a more radical view of faith and theology. John and his family moved to Brisbane where John worked as a youth worker in the Uniting Church and after a year he decided to train for ordination into the ministry of the Uniting Church. As we were training for ordination at the same time, we had some good comparing of notes along the way and we were ordained in the same week at the end of 1982. He and his family were then sent to north-western Tasmania, Hobart, Nhill and Launceston. He is now the minister at Mount Eliza, south-east of Melbourne, and is chairperson of the local presbytery there. He remains gentle and kindly, engrossed in music and quietly thinking things through. There is a lot of our father in John and their strong pastoral ministries are not unalike. When we hear each other preach, we agree that there are many similarities.

David spent some years at home with our parents after the rest of us had left. After doing extremely well at school, despite being something of a rebel, he then also went to Queen's College in Melbourne University and completed an Arts Degree and Diploma of Education.

After a brief stint in rural Victoria as a teacher, he married Myrna Walter who was also a high school teacher, and they moved back to Melbourne. At their wedding, which was daringly (for those days) conducted in their home rather than in a church, we were served jasmine tea. Many of the guests, including us, tactfully poured it onto the garden because we thought the taste was so strange. David and Myrna have two daughters—Jessica and Mitzi.

David later became a lecturer in education and spent some time with the Victorian Secondary Teachers Association. These days he is a consultant in education and mainly works for the federal government in program design, delivery and evaluation. He has reviewed the Disadvantaged Schools Program and is now working mostly in the field of Aboriginal education.

I have seen more of David over the years than the others because my life and work has often carried me back to Melbourne. He is still an irreverent, fun person. He rapidly fills any room with his largeness, loudness and energy. Unlike the rest of us, he has no links with the institutional church although he is devoted to living an ethical, just and spiritual life.

Unlike our parents who, apart from Dad's time in the army, never moved outside Australia, all of us have travelled widely. Even though we only intermittently communicate with each other, we are still very close. When I ended my marriage and wrote and told them about my sexuality— news which came out of the blue for them—they all simply asked me to tell them about it. Their support was unconditional and immediate. I feel so fortunate to have these fine human beings as my family. I would trust them with anything. They are good and loving people and I am proud to be their sister.

# 30  Our Children

Christopher was moved from Marsden Hospital into Marsden Rehabilitation Centre (euphemistically named) and then to a smaller facility, Wenona, back on the campus of his original hospital at Westmead. We are now anxiously facing his being moved into a community house due to the NSW Department of Ageing, Disability and Home Care deciding that 'devolution into the community' is good for all and sundry. Quite frankly, we feel this is pretty ridiculous for people like Christopher. There he was with about a dozen friends, most of whom have been his companions for the last 25 years, happily housed and cared for in a facility which was recently adapted for them. Now mostly in their forties, they are people who have little chance of really relating to the community because of their level of disability. Those like Christopher will certainly be very disturbed if they are shifted again into a smaller group with new and untrained carers instead of the wonderful psych nurses who have been their surrogate parents for many years.

At this point I make my confession that I have done almost no parenting of Christopher over the last 20 years. When I do pick him up to bring him home for a day, I almost always weep as I spend time with him, knowing how lacking in faithfulness I have been. Barrie has done better and I am grateful for that. He has had Christopher to his home far more frequently than I have, has attended more parents' meetings and has generally watched over Christopher's welfare. I really don't know who I am for Chris. He probably remembers that he comes to my house and likes the trip in the car and any cooking I might do for him. I have

Christopher on an outing to Canberra

no sense that he knows I am his mother or anyone special to him, other than a provider of food. When I take him back to Wenona, he leaps out of the car and runs eagerly ahead as though he is relieved to be home and I am deeply grateful for that. As I tearily returned him after his last visit, the staff member in charge said to me, 'Dorothy, you are forgiven', implying that I had offered care to others while he and his staff were caring for Christopher. I accept his absolution and cry with gratitude as I write this. However, even when you forgive yourself or receive absolution from others, you sometimes still grieve that you have not done better.


Robert is now known as Bertie which fits the quirky, fun person he is and his love of working with music and children. (Although I still find myself calling him Robert!) After a stint in the wardrobe department of the ABC, he moved around in drama circles for a while, helping to create sets and becoming involved with the folk music world.

At one point in his life, I asked Robert whether he wanted to tell me that he was gay. He was moving among some gay friends and seemed to be very gentle. He looked at me quizzically, and said, 'No, Mum. I am not gay. I thought you brought me up to feel free to enjoy my feminine side!'

After a while, Robert decided to complete a degree in Fine Arts at Wollongong University which he did in style, specialising in screen-printing and all sorts of artistic constructions. Having done all that, he then gravitated back to the music scene and began to develop skills working with children and people with disabilities. He is still a rather reserved sort of person, but he comes alive when he is Bertie the Frog or Bertie the Clown.

A couple of years ago he and Tess Malady, and her daughter Jessica, decided to share their lives together. In my view it was a wonderful day when Tess became Robert's partner—I guess every parent hopes that their children will find the right person with whom to share their life, and I am no different.

Their new daughter, Grania Shea McMahon Malady, arrived in November 2002 and I believe that she has transformed life for Robert. I watch his absolute pride and joy as he looks at his daughter. Grania is a truly interesting character. Melissa thinks she has eyes like two little sunrises and she looks at you assessingly with her bright eyes and decides whether she will, in her own good time, bestow a smile on you.

Bertie will never be rich, I suspect, but he will have given beautiful gifts to the world on the way through and held true to his calling as

With Ali and my son Robert and daughters and their families

a multi-skilled artist. I am proud to have a son who is not afraid to be true to himself and who models manhood in ways which challenge stereotypes.

After graduating with an honours degree in psychology and becoming a psychologist, Lindy worked for some years for the Salvation Army Crisis Centre and then for the Community Aid Centre at Blacktown in western Sydney as a case and community worker.

Lindy married Scott McDonald not long after she graduated. Scotty is a strong and gentle man, and absolutely committed to mutuality in relationships and the sharing of parenting. He and Lindy share a commitment to living simply. They don't have a car—they hire one for holidays—and they live and teach their children to live with as little participation in consumerism as possible. Having said that, they are sensitive to the need for their children to be part of their peer group.

Their first child, Brook, was born in 1996. She came into the world looking around carefully—just as Lindy did—and liking things to be orderly and well prepared. She has the same strong spirit as Lindy and has always had a very clear sense that girls should be recognised. When she was not quite three years old, I was looking at a picture book with her and said, 'Look at that little lamb, Brook, he's having a drink out of a bottle.' She said sternly, 'It might be a girl lamb, Grandma.' A year later, we were driving home and I observed that the driver in front was going slowly. I said, 'He might be looking for the right place to turn.' Brook replied, 'Did you check whether it was a woman driver or not, Grandma?' She once asked me if Ali and I were married or living together. I said that we would like to be married, but just now we couldn't do that. She said, 'Well, I asked my mum if I could marry Alana when I grow up and she said that, if I still wanted to do that by the time I grow up, I might be able to.' Thank you, Lindy!

Xander came along in 2001. He looks very like Lindy and often reminds me of Christopher at the same age. He is a clever and solemn little boy who carefully checks how everything works, where it should be, and why things are as they are. At two years old he could easily advise about how to insert and eject videos, turn things on and off and organise all things technical. He is fond of our cat, but has strong feelings about what cats do and where they should be. When our cat sat on the dining table, as is her habit, Xander suggested that this was no place for a cat and asked me to take her off. When I didn't do it immediately, he asked, 'Do you eat cats, Grandma?' He is also very polite. When I asked him whether his bread and Vegemite was okay recently, he said, 'It's simply delicious, Grandma!'

Lindy tells me what sort of mother I am, with deeper understanding since she became a mother herself. I was very glad when she told me I am an okay sort of mum!

After spending eight months by herself in Europe, mainly in Paris, the year after she completed her schooling, Melissa came back to Sydney and completed an arts degree at Sydney University—studying French, linguistics, philosophy and literature. Then she returned to Paris to study philosophy at the University of Paris. When she came back to Australia she went to live in Melbourne where she studied at Monash University and completed a master of arts degree. After this, she began her doctorate on the subject of Deleuze and Kant's critical philosophy at Sydney University. All this sounds very academic and so it is—Melissa is a person of great academic talent.

There have also been all sorts of adventures overseas and good friends all over the world. At nine years old, when I asked Melissa what she wanted for her birthday cake, she asked for a chocolate-hazelnut torte. When I said that I couldn't make such a cake, she was astonished that I wouldn't just find a recipe and make it! From then on, she developed excellent cooking skills which have far outstripped her mother's.

On the day I wrote this, she submitted her doctoral thesis and, by the time this book is published, I have no doubt that she will be Dr Melissa McMahon. I wait with interest to see what is next in her life and work.

Melissa, too, is my friend and mentor. She also lets me know what sort of mother I have been and how this has impacted on her life. I am always grateful for this—when I have recovered from hearing it!


I feel the most fortunate mother in the world. I regret my failings as a parent, but accept that I did my best at each stage and that my children have forgiven me. I grieve for Christopher, of course, but will leave that to the mysteries of the universe for now. I believe that the other three are adults of maturity and grace and I will always be proud of them as people who have faced tough things in their family life with honesty and courage.

# 31    Until Death do us Part

I first met Ali (Alison) at a party of mutual friends when I was still with Jen. I sat and talked with her for most of the afternoon and our paths briefly crossed at intervals in similar situations over the next few years. It was not until my relationship with Jen had ended that I really 'met' her. It was not long after the ending of that relationship, although I had been long enough on my own to realise that I could live with myself if necessary—something I had not really done before. When Ali and I recognised that we were attracted to each other, I warned her that I might still be in the dangerous rebound phase and I wanted time to decide about things. I went overseas on a planned trip to Bali with a friend and, as soon as I did that, I wondered if I had put at risk my life with Ali—would someone else claim her before I got back? I wrote to her and told her to wait for me and that I thought I loved her.

That was back in 1992 and I would say that our relationship is as alive today as it was then and certainly deeper because we know each other so well. When we decided to live together I made all sorts of plans so that if anything happened to our relationship, I would still be in a position to set up a home for myself. I stored lots of things just in case I needed them and couldn't afford to replace them. Those provisions are now all gone. I have not the slightest doubt that we are in a life-long relationship.

Ali is from Christchurch and I love all her family—her parents, her two sisters and two brothers, most of whom still live there. All of them have been most accepting and including of me in family life. Ali's childhood has had a significant impact on her life. When she was three years old she began to be an uncharacteristically whinging little girl, seeming to indicate that she was in pain. Her parents took her to doctors who mainly suggested that she had growing pains. Finally one doctor ordered an X-ray and it was discovered that she had tuberculosis of the hip and had indeed been in serious pain all the time.

She then spent virtually the next five years—a period of three years, and then two one-year stays—in hospital at a time when parents were only allowed to see their children once a month and her siblings could only view their sister from a distance. Nurses were supposed to be stern with the children and to discourage emotion in case it got out of hand. She was not supposed to cry when her parents visited in case it upset her mum. I can hardly bear to think of the three-year-old Ali being taken to hospital and left there alone and in pain for what must have seemed like forever. It wasn't simply the terrible and frightening separation from family, but all the consequences which followed for schooling and relationships. When I told my then seven-year-old grandchild, Brook, about Ali's time in hospital she said very perceptively, 'But that would be awful. You wouldn't be able to choose your own friends and if you did choose someone they would go away quickly.'

Ali had to do some very serious therapy later in her life to work through some of the trauma of her childhood and adolescent years. However, what really formed her and defined her childhood experiences was her own brave spirit, which still prevails. I love some of the stories of her time in the hospital ward. There was the time when she realised that, if she didn't like some of the food she could poke it down under her full-body plaster cast for concealment. Of course, finally it fermented and the smell emanating from her revealed all and she had to have the whole cast cut off and replaced.

Then there is the one of the grand escape. By this time, Ali was easily the longest resident in the ward and thus a leader. She and several others decided that the time had come for an escape from the hospital. They plotted and planned together for the day. They made little bundles on sticks containing what they thought would be necessities for the adventure. Then, one night when the coast was clear, a little bunch of them made their move. Of course, Ali had to crawl in her plaster cast but they managed to get out of the ward without being seen. They made their way down the corridor and towards a ramp outside the hospital. Then they all looked at each other in dismay. First of all they had no money and secondly they weren't sure where they could go if they caught a bus. By this time all the alarms were sounding and they were caught and dragged back to the ward. I love that story—it mirrors Ali's determined cheek, although she is a better planner than that now!

When she was finally released from hospital, she went home on crutches. She had already had some surgery but her hip area was so damaged that she still needed major surgery to get her on her feet, although this could not take place until later. She went to school for the first time at nine years old. Not only had she had little basic education, but she had no experience of real school and was significantly marginalised as a child with a disability. Like most children who are a little different, there were cruel experiences in the playground.

However, even though this was very tough, members of her family tell of how she gained a reputation for being a little girl whom you did not lightly cross. They remember a disgruntled woman from down the street coming to their mother and complaining that Ali had been attacking her son. This local bully boy had been harassing Ali and so she hit him with a crutch, climbed a tree and hauled his bike up into the tree beyond his reach with her crutch! She remembers standing by her mother looking innocent and vulnerable as the boy's mum made her complaint!

I also love the story from her childhood which gives a picture of the sort of children that she and her siblings were. At this time, their father was a road contractor and they had a large area at the back of their house for his trucks and equipment. Ali and her brothers and some friends decided to build an underground room for themselves beneath the large area where the trucks entered and turned. The slaved away, doing an immense amount of digging to construct an underground room and some little side passages. To cover their handiwork when they'd finished, they would put a piece of galvanised iron over it and cover that with earth. Goodness knows how they were not detected. They also felt it appropriate, as good little Catholics, to install a small shrine within it, so they duly placed there a small statue of the Virgin Mary with a candle beside it. Maybe thanks to the intervention of Mary, or to good luck, they were not in their underground chamber when a huge truck drove over it and sank to the axles in the hole they had created. All was discovered and they were significantly punished. None of that stopped them being a very cheeky and determined lot!

The final major operation for Ali meant that her hip was pinned in a manner which cannot be undone and corrected today because a significant ligament was removed. One leg ended up about five centimetres shorter than the other and because of the way the operation was done, she could not have an adequate lift put on her shoe to correct the imbalance. This has had significant consequences for her body as time has gone on. Ali was taught by her father to believe that she could do anything and not to see herself as a person with a disability. Often this was very tough as she tried to keep up, but it certainly meant that she does not relate to others as one who lives with a disability.

She was educated in a Catholic school at a time when the teachers were nuns and were being trained to teach as they went along. She recalls being the sort of child who liked to ask questions, especially about the religious side of things, and was rewarded by many whacks over the knuckles. She also recalls being taken to a service at the local Catholic church where there was a visiting priest who was carrying relics of some saint around the world and claiming that they had the power to heal people. Her father took her along on her crutches in hope, but it didn't work. Like many such scenes in the church, people were not helped to cope with their raised and dashed hopes—such a significant thing for a child and her hopeful father. Ali does not have good recollections of her schooldays nor the Catholic Church.

When she ended her fairly brief schooling Ali trained as a nurse— obviously her long years in the hospital environment were not a deterrent. I suspect that she saw what the best of nurses could be like and had also learned to be comfortable with all sorts of sights and procedures which might shock other people—including me, who can't even bear to watch a needle go in! When she was 21, she boarded a boat to England by herself and lived in London for seven years. It was at this stage in her life that she claimed her sexuality and when she returned to Christchurch she brought back with her a female partner—Tina, with whom she spent the next 13 years. They felt that Christchurch was not for them and migrated to Sydney. Tina is now one of our best friends and is like family to Ali.

In the period of time in London, Ali developed her skills further and became a clinical nurse specialist in renal nursing. At one stage she also worked in management for a Swedish-based medical supplies company. A few years ago she qualified for a degree in social sciences, majoring in sociology and politics.

As my daughter Melissa says, Ali is the one with taste. Our house shows Ali's excellent eye for art and her good collection of original works. She is a fine photographer and when I suggest such things as taking a photo of the spiderweb by the birdbath, she tells me not to be so clichéd—rightly! Her other key interest is gardens and she plans to come back in the next life as a gardener with a stronger body than she has now. We do our best with our own little garden and visit and admire famous gardens both here and around the world when we travel.

We do many things together but are also free to develop our own interests. We have had marvelous travelling holidays and have each visited more than 30 countries. We love best going to various parts of the UK and to Paris, provincial France and northern Italy, but have explored many other parts of the world, especially when I was working twice a year in Geneva. We enjoy classical concerts and movie-going or just exploring Sydney and other parts of Australia and New Zealand. In all this, we share a common interest in life which is wider than ourselves. We take part in various efforts for change and discuss politics together. Ali reads more significant books on social and political comment than I do and tells me all about them when I am lazily reading crime stories. I tell her she is my researcher!

With Ali on a South Coast beach

We are very different people in many ways, but these differences enhance our life together and invite a healthy critique and good changes in each other. Because of the deep love which is at the heart of our relationship, we are not afraid of these encounters—in fact they energise and stimulate us. Our values about life and relationships we hold in common. We hold similar views on political issues and the state of the world in general and support each other in any actions we may take in response to that. I love Ali dearly because she is a beautiful human being in every sense. She is a person of depth and spirituality, even though she is not part of the institutional church. In some ways I find that helpful because it gives me a greater awareness of when I am being pious and stops me from being caught up in religiosity. It is with her that I grow in life because she challenges me to be more fully alive. It is she who teaches me that it is safe to be human because she loves me as I am. She is not afraid of my strength or my vulnerability and I think I could say that I am not afraid of either in her.

I love her authentic response to people and events. I say to her, 'So what offended you about that person/situation?' and she answers, 'How did you know I was offended?' My stock response to that is to say, 'I could see the steam issuing from your ears!' Ali is a person who finds it almost impossible not to be honest and direct and that is very special. She asks me to be more honest with myself than I have ever been and to stay with the more negative side of my life to find that I will not be destroyed by it. She challenges my tendency to generalise and to be casual about facts and figures. In fact she stops me being slack generally and from bluffing my way through things instead of doing the work. She helps me to say no to too many requests for my time and energy. She is my very best critic as well as my deepest support. I like to think I offer her my eternal optimism and somewhat ridiculous qualities.

Ali is my reference point for truth about myself and the one who gives me courage to believe that liberation is our calling. It is she who so enhances my life that we both can look at the world and believe that transformation of all things is possible and that we can be part of it in our own humble ways. She makes life a place of laughter; the laughter of delight and the laughter at the absurd in ourselves. I introduce her to my friends, my children and grandchildren with pride and joy. There was a time when I had almost consciously decided that I would die at 70 years old, like my mother. Now I walk and exercise and take my body seriously so I can spend more years with Ali, having extra adventures and exciting growings. I am the most fortunate of women.

When I debate the issues around homosexuality with my opponents in the church, I sometimes remind them that they are fixated on the sexual aspects of homosexual relationships instead of their holistic nature. It is about loving someone body, mind, heart and soul and, as far as I am concerned with Ali and myself, until death do us part.

# 32 Who I am Now

My recent seventieth birthday celebrations went on for some time, and in some ways symbolised the different facets of my life. On the Sunday before, the celebrations began with the people of South Sydney Uniting Church giving me a cake at morning tea after our service. While we were doing our usual laughing and talking, I mentioned that my funeral would be at Pitt Street Church and they enthusiastically said that they would all come!

On my actual birthday, I climbed the Harbour Bridge with Robert, Lindy and Melissa. We had a great time and I was pleased to find that I found the cimb no more difficult than five years before.

On Easter Sunday about 30 friends from different parts of my life visited our house for an afternoon tea prepared by my daughter Melissa with her sister Lindy as support server and washer-up.

Then the following week, my three younger children travelled with their children to Woodend in Victoria for a lunch gathering with my siblings, apart from John who was working in Scotland. At night, some of my nephews and nieces and their families came from various parts of Victoria and we had a noisy and lively gathering. Since I didn't want any speeches, the family had made a beautiful book for me with the things they wanted to say to me, or about me. David did a whole analysis of the ways in which I am like our mother. Given my struggles with Mother, I was a bit taken aback. Then I looked at it carefully and decided it was all true!

The birthday ended a few days later when our hosts from Woodend, Tina and Moira, shouted me to *The Pearl Fishers* in Melbourne, not knowing that the main aria from this opera, 'In the Depths of the Temple', was on the first record I ever bought—around 45 years before! It was a grand ending to a wonderful birthday which brought together many things which are important to my life—church, music, friends, childlike loves, climbing high to look wider, and my family.

I have now lived for most of my life in Sydney and I love it with a passion. Over the years I guess I have taken on the somewhat irreverent spirit of the city and have fallen in love with its landscape and its bridges. Not long ago, I walked down Pitt Street Mall in the middle of the city fairly early in the morning. As I did so, I became aware that there was a man in a three-piece suit walking through the mall singing an operatic aria quiet loudly. People in the mall were sniggering with mirth as they watched. When I came to the lights at King Street, the man drew level with me and I said to him, 'I really enjoy your singing!' He went quiet and looked at me sideways as though I might be a bit odd, then crossed the road hastily to get away and resumed his singing as he strode up the street. Only in Sydney!

At this moment in my life I know that what I ultimately aspire to be is a truly human being. That might sound very ordinary, but in my view it is not—I believe that to dare to be human is, in itself, a religious act. As a truly human being, I know that I am not, and never will be, God. This is a critical safeguard in my life. It means that I must offer my idea of truth and listen to those offered by others with openness and humility, and see myself in perspective.

As a human being, I try to act like a little child who, in spite of tough experiences, trusts every relationship and is optimistic about what might be. When we lose that capacity, I believe we descend into cynicism and hopelessness. I believe in the paradigm lived out in Jesus that new and stronger life is discovered on the other side of tough, vulnerable and passionate journeys into the deathly parts of human life.

I aspire to hold onto all that was within me in my creation—the feelings of compassion, the awareness of pain in my own life and in others', so that I can sustain the longing to respond to injustice, oppression and needs. If I lose my indignation about what I see as small and large injustices, I will know that I have begun to die. I take great pleasure in being involved in small battles for change and achieving my aims. I am told that I can invoke fear in others when I make my move and I confess that I feel an unholy sense of glee in moments like these!

As a human being, I have also learned to live with not seeing the changes I desire take place—just leaving them to the future, knowing I have done my best. I have learned to stand back more wisely and use less energy in attacking people who attack me—deciding which problems belong to them and which to me. I know that I will make many mistakes in the future and that I need to face who I am, forgive myself and accept the grace of God and others in relation to this. I am grieved that I have wounded so many people as I have thrashed around in my life, but I can live with the fact that I am no more or less human than anyone else.

As a small speck in the universe, I laugh daily at the absurdity of life and myself. I am sure that God has a sense of humour too, and would love my wind-up Jesus that glides across the floor lifting its arms up and down in blessing! I rest and play, write poetry and listen to music because I know that life is far more than I will ever know and can only be glimpsed in the mystery and the magic of different art forms.

There may have been times in my life when I thought that to be human was not nearly grand enough, but I have changed my mind.